BRAIN, MIND, AND HUMAN BEHAVIOR IN CONTEMPORARY COGNITIVE SCIENCE

BRAIN, MIND, AND HUMAN BEHAVIOR IN CONTEMPORARY COGNITIVE SCIENCE

Critical Assessments of the Philosophy of Psychology

Jeff Coulter
and
Wes Sharrock

With a Foreword by
P. M. S. Hacker

The Edwin Mellen Press
Lewiston•Queenston•Lampeter

Library of Congress Cataloging-in-Publication Data

Coulter, Jeff.
Brain, mind, and human behavior in contemporary cognitive science : critical assessments
of the philosophy of psychology / Jeff Coulter and Wes Sharrock ; with a foreword by
P. M. S. Hacker.
    p. cm.
  Includes bibliographical references and index.
  ISBN-13: 978-0-7734-5315-9
  ISBN-10: 0-7734-5315-6
1. Psychology--Philosophy. 2. Cognitive science. 3. Neurosciences. 4. Philosophy of
mind. I. Sharrock, W. W. (Wes W.) II. Title.
  BF38.C759 2007
  153.01--dc22

                                                    2007029273

hors série.

A CIP catalog record for this book is available from the British Library.

The Edwin Mellen Press   The Edwin Mellen Press
        Box 450   Box 67
  Lewiston, New York   Queenston, Ontario
  USA 14092-0450   CANADA L0S 1L0

              The Edwin Mellen Press, Ltd.
              Lampeter, Ceredigion, Wales
              UNITED KINGDOM SA48 8LT

          Printed in the United States of America

TABLE OF CONTENTS

i

ACKNOWLEDGEMENTS

The authors wish to acknowledge the editors and publishers of the journals SOCIAL RESEARCH and VISUAL STUDIES for their kind permission to reproduce materials from previously published papers: Jeff Coulter, "Materialist Conceptions of Mind: A Reappraisal", *Social Research* 60:1, Spring 1993, 117-142, and Wes Sharrock & Jeff Coulter, "Dissolving the 'Projection Problem'", *Visual Studies* 18:1, 2003, 74-82. The authors also thank Ahmad Bleik and Wassim Bleik for their assistance in the technical preparation of this work for publication. Amal helped as well.

FOREWORD

From the point of view of human advances in knowledge, the twentieth century was the century of physics. The new millennium opened with the promise of a century of progress in the sciences of life, and especially in neuroscience. Within neuroscience, the endeavours to understand the neural basis of human cognitive abilities has attracted a great deal of public attention and academic speculation. For it seemed that the discoveries, or anticipated discoveries, of neuroscience would shed light on a multitude of problems that have preoccupied human beings for millennia – problems such as: What is the mind? How is it related to the brain? Is thinking a process in the brain? Do human beings have a free will? What is consciousness? Are our memories stored in our brains? These kinds of question have been discussed by philosophers. But they have produced no scientifically reputable theories to resolve them. To some neuroscientists it seems that it is time for philosophy to step aside and make room for proper scientific investigations.

It was perhaps an accident that the early advances in cognitive neuroscience coincided with the invention of the digital computer, that the invention of the computer coincided with the demise of behaviourism and the beginnings of the cognitive (or, more properly, *computationalist*) revolution in psychology, and that this in turn coincided with the rise of Chomsky's generative linguistics. Any one of these intellectual earthquakes would have sufficed to keep reflective minds occupied for some decades, exploring the ramifications of these discoveries, inventions and theories. The conjunction of all four proved a heady draft, which led to the emergence of so-called *cognitive science*. This was supposed to be a synthesis of cognitive neuroscience, computational psychology, artificial intelligence, theoretical linguistics, and philosophy. It aimed to produce scientific theories about the nature of the mind, of consciousness and self-consciousness, of the self, of thought and imagination, of knowledge and memory, and of freedom of the will. With such high ambitions, and with the impressive discoveries of neuroscience in the twentieth century, it is small wonder that this new 'science' intoxicated the media and swept a large number of scientists and intellectuals off their feet.

Cognitive science rightly rejected the traditional dualist conception of the relationship between mind and body. It correctly denied that the mind is a spiritual substance. But instead of trying to elucidate the concept of mind afresh, it replaced the mind by the brain, or reduced the mental to the functional correlation of inputs and outputs with some neural 'realization'. So too, it replaced the dualist conception of the operations of the mind by the allegedly computational operations of the brain. This left intact the *logical structure* of the classical dualist conception (merely allocating to the brain the roles previously allocated to the mind). Moreover, guided by AI on the one hand, and Chomskian linguistics on the other, it both mechanized and intellectualized (computationalized) the psychological powers of mankind and their exercise. The promises were enticing, and the support of leading intellectuals of the day encouraged many to join the (well-funded) bandwagon.

More angelic thinkers feared to join, preferring not to rush in, but to pause and think. Can empirical discoveries really shed light on such questions as 'What is the mind?'? Is such a question really like 'What is cancer?' Or is it more like 'What is knowledge?' or 'What is a number?'? Before equating the mind with the brain, or comparing the mind to the software of the supposed computer-like brain, or holding mental states to be identical to states of the brain, should one not be clearer what one is talking about? The *concept* of the mind calls out for clarification, the *concept* of a mental state demands elucidation, as indeed does that of a *brain state* (has anyone ever proposed a criterion of identity for such a thing?). Conceptual clarification may enable one to see whether it even makes sense for the mind to be identical with the brain, or for a mental state to be identical with a brain state. And if it does not even make sense, then the question of whether it is true or false cannot even arise. But to determine whether it makes sense requires scrutiny of the concepts in question – a clarification of the concepts of mind, mental state and brain state, and so too of knowledge and memory, of perception and imagination, and so forth. But concepts cannot be clarified by scientific experiments, the logical connections constitutive of concepts cannot be elucidated by scientific investigations. On the contrary, scientific investigations and experiments *presuppose* those concepts and their web of logico-grammatical connections. Conceptual elucidation is the province of philosophy.

In this book, Jeff Coulter and Wes Sharrock have undertaken a series of conceptual investigations into some of the more dramatic claims made by contemporary cognitive neuroscientists, cognitive scientists, and theoretical linguists. It takes courage to resist the current, and skill to master it. Coulter and Sharrock have both. They challenge some of the deepest presuppositions of the cognitive scientific enterprise, and show, from case to case, on what quicksands they are founded. They disclose the flaws in the dogmatic materialist conception of the mental without falling back into the errors of dualism, arguing that *both* materialism and dualism need to be rejected. The errors they identify are purely conceptual – for it cannot be the business of philosophical criticism to assess the truth or falsity of a scientific theory. What they convincingly show is how deep conceptual confusions run and how damaging they are in cognitive neuroscience, psychology and theoretical linguistics.

How can philosophy take upon itself the burden of demonstrating that the latest scientific theories are conceptually confused? Is science not the 'measure of all things'? It is doubtful whether it *is*. But be that as it may, it certainly is not the measure of what does and does not make sense. To be sure, philosophy does not *determine* the bounds of sense either – but part of its task is to show, by *argument*, when they have been transgressed. This Coulter and Sharrock do with exemplary finesse. They effectively dismantle the claims of neuroscience to shed light on the problems of freedom of the will. They show how the current debate about the nature of consciousness rests on wholly confused presuppositions about what consciousness is and about what the qualitative character of experience might be. They disclose muddles about the concept of memory that inform Kandel's inferences from his brilliant experimental investigations into the reflex actions of the sea-slug. And they probe the influential but deeply confused conception of syntax that lies at the heart of Chomsky's theoretical linguistics. And so on.

This is a controversial book. It will annoy those who have nailed their flag to the mast of cognitive science. It will rock the boat of intellectual complacency in sciences and putative sciences that are well known and very well advertised, yet anything but well-established. But its arguments must be confronted, and the case they make cannot be evaded. If Coulter and Sharrock are right, as I believe they are, then extensive rethinking is needed.

Dr. P. M. S. Hacker
St. John's College, Oxford

INTRODUCTION

In the ensuing discussion, we want to make one major point which will pervade the treatment we accord to almost all of our adversaries in this book. It is this. Our main disagreement with them all is that, notwithstanding their claims to scientific status, they are not talking about brains, or minds, or about the nature of both, appearances notwithstanding. We are talking about language, and this is true for those who oppose us as well. There are no empirical data which confound any of the arguments which we espouse here, nor that occasion or require the doctrines that our opponents recommend.

Academic disputes can sometimes degenerate into propaganda warfare. In this book, we aim to reverse the academic barrage which is put out by the dominant position in contemporary philosophy of mind. We are not dealing here with a matter that is discussed solely within the confines of academic exchange, but with one that is very prominently presented in the public media, even though the coverage is massively dominated by one point of view.

That dominant point of view tends to present itself as though it were virtually unopposed, an unchallengeable orthodoxy, and any serious argument over it is thought by many to proceed only within its established terms. Its proponents present themselves as if they were virtually scientists, or as standing up for science, as if they were setting out a position that is justified by and ultimately dependent upon the most up-to-date and secure scientific findings. They often also present themselves as though they were philosophers who are merely drawing upon the most recent developments of the natural sciences. Opposition to such an orthodoxy is easily defeated (rhetorically) by accusing opponents to it of being unscientific or, even, *anti*-science.

The dominant orthodoxy to which we refer is the philosophical school sometimes termed 'naturalism'. Our own difficulty in developing an oppositional line of argument against this trend is this: our line is apt to be regarded as already well known and *démodé*, as already refuted and bankrupt as a line of thought. We, however, seek here to show, by argument and example, that this is far from the case. In fact, the point of our book is to seek to demonstrate just how far from logical constraints our opposition has ventured. We think that now is the time to pull them back to the ordinary language case and to what this has to show. Conceptual propriety has taken something of a back-seat in recent logical and philosophical treatments of the mind/body/conduct nexus: what we shall show in this work is that such considerations are still alive, and can also be used to point out exactly where and how current work has lost its way.

The fact that tracts of physical (predominantly brain) science are presented in the course of a philosophical argument does not signify that the scientific work itself plays any great role or very active part in the argument. There is scant *integration* of the scientific and philosophical elements. Indeed, much of the literature involves claims that such integration is *on the way*, is the inevitable, only-to-be-expected, result of work currently underway. Hence, what is offered by most of these texts is a philosophical version of what the science signifies and what, therefore, the forthcoming results of neuroscience must mean. But the 'unification' of science and philosophy is not yet with us: nor is it the case that the neuroscientific work itself indispensably depends upon the philosophical presuppositions to which it is purportedly wedded. Indeed, much of the work that goes on in so-called neurophilosophy has nothing to do with understanding either the brain or the organization of conduct but is, rather, a matter of spin. Attempts are made to set out the philosophical issues and the empirical researches in ways that reinforce the plausibility of the dominant approach. The name 'neurophilosophy' itself, and the hyphenated expression 'mind/brain', are both part of the propaganda, intended to suggest the closest, intimate connection between neuroscience and philosophy. We shall show that neurophilosophy is no closer to science than any other philosophy, and that it has only an incidental rather than an intrinsic connection to genuine brain science. Rather than the findings of neuroscience being brought to bear upon, and providing solutions to, philosophical problems, the simple truth is that the main work of neurophilosophy consists in the application of only contestable *philosophical* suppositions to the construal of the results and (especially) the prospects of neural researches. It is not the physiology which drives this philosophical orthodoxy, but metaphysics, the idea that the findings of the sciences are now providing answers to the questions raised by metaphysics, providing a definitive statement as to what there really (ultimately) is. Our assiduous and thoroughgoing opposition to neurophilosophy stems from opposition to that assumption.

Opposition to the idea that science can be the fulfillment of metaphysics does not involve in any way opposition to science. If the objectives of metaphysics are spurious, then they cannot be fulfilled by science any more than they can be by metaphysics. The error which promotes the orthodoxy is, in an important respect, very simple and basic: it is to suppose that 'what anything is' is *identical* (in the very strongest sense) with 'what it is made of'. This elementary and elemental error generates more complex and sophisticated issues, but so much depends upon its initial, tacit and unreflective acceptance. The importance of this assumption here is that it leads to concluding that minds must be brains (or brains and parts of the central nervous system) because minds – if they exist – must be made of something (and what else is there but brain-matter for them to be made of?), and that when we understand how brains work we will, for the first time, understand how minds work because minds *are* brains, whence the hybrid expression mentioned above, the 'mind/brain'.

The problematics of 'identity' involved in characterizing the relationship between our 'mental lives' and our neurophysiology can perhaps be illuminated by an example from the writings of Steven Pinker. In his influential study, *How the Mind Works*[1], Pinker discusses what is involved in watching TV. He aspires to tell us what we really see on the television screen, with the idea that there is some *one* way of formulating what we see when we are watching television. The need for the word '*really*' here – we are really seeing a flat, illuminated surface with 'nothing' behind it, etc. – is an acknowledgement that there are other ways of saying what we see on television screens, ones that require us to be sensitive to *the sense* of what we are 'claiming' when we report that we saw something on television. When we watch TV, we sometimes talk among ourselves about what we are seeing on the screen. If we start by thinking of those things we say as hypotheses about what is on the screen, then clearly there will be a need to distinguish between 'what we claim to see on television' and what is really there to be seen. Thus, we will, according to such a conception, need to determine what is actually on the television screen in order to evaluate our 'folk' claims about what is on the television screen. Pinker believes that this can be accomplished by reference to 'the operation of our visual brain'. He writes:

> "When we watch TV, we stare at a shimmering piece of glass, but our surface- perception module tells the rest of our brain (sic) that we are seeing real people and places. The module has been unmasked; it does not apprehend the nature of things but relies on a cheat-sheet. That cheat-sheet is so deeply embedded in the operation of our visual brain that we cannot erase the assumptions written on it. Even in a lifelong couch potato, the visual system never 'learns' that television is a pane of glowing phosphor dots, and the person never loses the illusion that there is a world behind the pane."[2]

The supposedly 'scientific' account tells us that what we see is a flat glass surface constituted of glowing phosphor dots: that is all that there is for us to really see. Hence the idea that Pinker has that there must be some kind of 'illusion' involved in our vernacular claims about what we see on TV. It is

---

[1] Steven Pinker, *How the Mind Works* (N. Y. : W. W. Norton, 1997).
[2] *Ibid.*, p. 29.

certainly true that, as lay television commentators, we are not claiming to see scanned, glowing phosphor dots, but are talking rather about events in stories, performances by actors, interviews with politicians, theses being advanced in documentary programs, etc. But surely it is a peculiar kind of position to have gotten oneself into to suppose that these kinds of claims (about what we can see on TV) are *at odds with* those made by an electronics engineer describing how television sets work. After all, if we think of the production side of television, then viewers are ordinarily fully aware of the engineering account of television: they are, commonly, under no illusion that there is 'more' on the television screen than the glowing phosphor dots and that there is 'nothing' behind the screen other than the cathode ray tube and its associated electronics in the television box.– they are certainly not going to start opening up the casing of the television in the hope of seeing the little people inside. They are aware that there is 'nothing more than' the glowing phosphor dots on the screen from an engineering point of view. They are also equally aware that, and in no doubt that, from the point of view of television programming and viewing, there is 'much more than' just the phosphor dots on the screen. There is obviously much more to the work of television engineering than providing illuminated displays on screens by way of scanning phosphor dots, as if such engineering were an end in itself: the engineering involved is wholly in the service of broadcasting programs, of transmitting documentaries, dramas, comedy shows, the news, commercials, and so forth. And where are these TV programs if they are not on the screen? Well, now we are in danger of the screen's becoming over-crowded for whilst there is nothing but the phosphor dots it nonetheless appears that there is something other, something *more*, than these – there is the entire broadcasting content of television.

The materialist and/or reductionist is now in a puzzling situation, because, from his point of view, the engineer and the broadcaster and viewers are in conflict, although they themselves do not seem to think so. But in what is the 'conflict' supposed to consist? Is it that the engineers' claim that there are only glowing phosphor dots on the screen is *contradicted* by the broadcasters' and viewers' claim to be able to show, e.g., the President being interviewed? Is it that the broadcasters and viewers are thereby denying the truth of the engineering claim that there are glowing phosphor dots on the screen? Do the former suppose that the television screen involves something else instead of phosphor dots? Do they imagine that there are little people there, for instance? A claim about what is to be seen on a television screen is not to be understood as a claim about what a television screen is made of or about how a television screen works. That a television screen works in an engineering sense is something that is taken for granted in talking about the content of television broadcasting; it does not hinge upon the nature of the television screen at all. We are required, of course, to understand that the television screen is displaying broadcast images – if we are under some sort of illusion that there are people inside the television set then we are suffering from a major delusion, but this is not what most of us intend when we talk about seeing people on television, even if such idioms might, to the grossly uninformed, give the (false) impression that we do. However, we can (clearly) watch television in complete ignorance of the mechanics of television engineering and broadcasting work. So long as we understand that television delivers broadcast images then we are in no difficulty, although we may well be clueless as to what delivering broadcast images amounts to in engineering terms. Thus, our claims about 'what we see on TV' are characteristically about the broadcast content and can correctly be made quite independently of any basic understanding of the mechanics of broadcasting procedures and operations. Of course, there are occasions when the mechanics will intrude into our viewing – when, e.g., we can see that there is something mechanically or electronically wrong and that features of what is being shown are due to engineering malfunctions rather than being any authentic part of the broadcast content. In a similar sense, we can routinely make out what people in our everyday lives are doing and saying, and why they are doing and saying what they are, irrespective of any knowledge of their neurophysiology, although in cases of bizarre, unaccountable conduct we may have recourse to lay neurological speculations which might subsequently be confirmed or denied by a professional neurological examination. To resume the television case: understanding how the television works electronically will not lead us radically to revise our view of what we have all along been seeing on the screen, as though, e.g., we thought we were seeing the Beatles performing but we were only seeing some glowing phosphor dots. In the same way, better understanding the brain will not lead us to say, e.g., we thought we had been watching a game of baseball, but all we were really watching were a variety of neurally-produced bodily movements involving bats and balls.

'Seeing' just like 'more' has different kinds of uses and it is the failure to just acknowledge these that can lead us into conflicts and apparent 'mysteries' with their pseudo-solutions in the form of dualism, reductionism, and their kin. Recall: we noted at the outset that we are all, *au fond*, dealing here with language, with issues of conceptualization, although many of our opponents believe otherwise. So, first let us consider 'seeing'. Someone says: "I saw Tom Cruise on television last night". Suppose we explained in some detail the working of television sets to him. What should he then say? "My God! What a fool I have been. I thought I'd been watching Tom Cruise in person, and all along I was only seeing glowing phosphor dots! So my claim to have seen Tom Cruise on television was false." But there is no reason for him to retract his claim in this way. Any TV-wise viewer understands that the claim to have "seen Tom Cruise on television" is not a claim to have seen the named individual in person. To the contrary. After all, if they were deluded that they had seen Tom Cruise 'in person' why would they say "I saw Tom Cruise on television"? – the latter two words would be otiose, or would only be a locational expression (like: "I saw Tom Cruise in his neighborhood grocery last night"). Yet seeing Tom Cruise on television and seeing Tom Cruise in his neighborhood grocery would not be in conflict if scenes in which Tom Cruise appeared on television showed him in his neighborhood grocery. The risk that we are trying to forestall here is that of supposing that one must decide that there is one right way of formulating claims about having seen Tom Cruise, such that one might (erroneously) want to say: people claim to have seen Tom Cruise, but they (for the most part) have only seen *an image* of him and so must withdraw their claims to have seen him at all. This is not correct: note that "I saw Tom Cruise" when he was seen on TV is only to rephrase what is well understood by: "I saw Tom Cruise on television last night". It would be stupid to ask: "Did you get a chance to speak to him?" in relation to that in a way it would not if someone said: "I saw Tom Cruise at a party last night". Further, it is not as if because one saw an image of Tom Cruise one has necessarily seen Tom Cruise. One has not seen Tom Cruise, only an image of him, if he was seen on television. These matters are decided *not* by virtue of the word 'see(n)', but by the role of qualifiers such as "live", "on television", "at a party", etc. in *giving sense to* the claim "I saw" in the discursive context in which it is made.

It is the same with the use of 'more' in 'one sees nothing more than glowing phosphor dots when one watches television'. Equivalence does not entail substitutability. That is, although in the engineering sense there is nothing but the glowing dots, no other entities different from, or in addition to, more than, the dots, nonetheless whilst there are indeed only the dots these are not what viewers of TV programs typically see, unless they use a microscope. The array of phosphor dots, however, does *depict* what a viewer can see when, e.g., he sees Tom Cruise on television. However, what conceivable use would it be to a viewer who wanted to relay the content of a television program to an interested party to describe the patterned array of illuminated dots on the screen? Further, the depiction of Tom Cruise by the exact description of an array of phosphor dots on the screen does not guarantee that Tom Cruise can be identified thereby by a viewer - to be entitled to claim to have seen *Tom Cruise* on television is licensed not by the engineering depiction but by knowing in advance what he looks like (from his movies, or even from having met him in person), or by having read the program credits, by having heard his name announced or by having heard him introduced by a host, etc. None of this is part of an engineer's knowledge *qua* engineer, just as the exact pattern of the phosphor dot arrays is no part of an ordinary TV viewer's knowledge. Thus, you cannot just adopt the engineering description, even though it is equivalent to the vernacular, because what you need for the correctness of the vernacular description you cannot get from the engineering.

Although we certainly do not want to press any deep analogy between questions about how television works and questions about how persons work, nonetheless we can develop the following points a bit further. First, the claim that things are identical with what they are made of is no result of science, but an idea inherited from metaphysics and used in the interpretation of some of the achievements of some sciences. If things are exactly, only, and entirely, what they are made of, and if (some of) the sciences tell us what things are made of, and what laws govern their behavior, then it can seem as though science can tell us everything there is to know about anything and everything. But then we would have to accept – and why should we? – that we do not, cannot, know anything unless and until the sciences come along and tell us. Yet just as it is no part of engineering to explain how television programs are created, how they are scheduled, how decisions about their content are made, etc., it is no part of neurophysiology to inform us about people's intentions, motives, conventional ways of doing things, the grammar of their languages, their attitudes to things, etc. Secondly, science can be fallible, and sometimes progresses by rejecting its prior deliverances. Thirdly, saying that no science can tell us anything (informative) about the identification of last year's leading pitcher or whom we should date or what the capital city of Scotland is hardly slights the sciences, does not diminish them in *any* way.

When all is said and done, and however reasonable this and our subsequent arguments might seem, we need to anticipate some dissatisfactions that some readers might expect on the basis that they already know that the kind of arguments we are making here go wrong. Were they to accept our case, it would seem, they would be accepting a picture of themselves of the kind that we paint, one that would leave them with a considerably diminished image of humanity in general. One of the things they 'know' about our approach is that it is basically, really, a behaviorist one. The mentalists talk about the necessity to postulate a rich inner structure which converts raw external stimuli into complex behavioral outputs. Part of our argument, however, is that there is a need to set the record straight in relation to the interpretations that dominant positions in contemporary philosophy make of the philosophical legacy of Ludwig Wittgenstein and Gilbert Ryle. A reader persuaded that the charge of behaviorism is valid can point to the fact that Wittgenstein's argument against the possibility of a private language leads him to talk about pain behavior, which surely suggests that he is replacing the idea that pain is a sensation with the idea that pain is a pattern of behavior, and what could be more behaviorist than that? Furthermore, Ryle does make those contemptuous remarks about the itchings and irritations that are to be found by introspection, and is widely taken as construing mind as being – essentially – a collection of dispositions to behavior. The itchings and scratchings etc. seem a poor substitute for what people would like to think of as an inner life, and the dispositional emphasis therefore eliminates all but this minimal residuum of trivial sensations. It follows that a defense of Ryle and Wittgenstein against the charge of behaviorism has to consist in two parts: the rejection of any reductively behaviorist construal of 'behavior' and also the rejection of the displacement of 'the outer' by 'the inner'. The strategy is to reject dualism both with respect to body and mind *and* with respect to 'outer' and 'inner'.

Ryle's disparagement of 'the inner' is a dismissal of the Cartesian inner theater, a privatized auditorium within which a rich panoply of intellectual events are – must be – taking place. But introspection, whilst it might not be a method suitable for founding a psychological science, is up to the task of showing that nothing of this sort is to be detected. For Ryle, the fact that introspection does not give us a seat in this wonderful auditorium is reason to reconsider the basis on which we have been led to expect such a thing, to re-examine the ways in which Cartesianism initially sets up its dualism of mind and body, its sharp disparity between inner and outer. However, for our opponents, the non-appearance of the expected inner theater of mental states and processes is no reason to step back and reconsider, but to press deeper into this garden of forking paths. One way to go is to maintain that these inner processes must be taking place but in a location that is inaccessible to our conscious perception. Such a move is no kind of discovery and involves no empirical – and certainly no scientific – findings. Introspection yields nothing worth having here, certainly nothing about the brain, which is a busy, electricity-consuming, organ. Nonetheless, one may preserve the idea that there is after all truly an inner auditorium, the one in which we view the contents of our consciousness. This is a matter of making our experience of the world ('the world outside' in these terms) an *indirect* affair, involving an inner display of all the appearances that our contact with the outer world induces in us – meaning that we never really see the house across the street, only the house across the street as it appears in our consciousness. Ryle's dismissal of the Cartesian 'inner' does not differ all that much from that of Cartesianism's materialist continuers, for both are agreed that there is no inner theater in the original sense. But Ryle does not lead us into a position in which we find that the only way to preserve a use for anything like the Cartesian conception of the inner is at the cost of depriving ourselves of the 'outer', a situation in which we make no perceptual contact with the world out there but have *only* unconsciously operating causal connections to it.

Are we now in a dilemma: we can have the outer, but must give up on the inner, or we can preserve the inner, but by reducing our connection to the outer world to an indirect one? This is not the choice that Ryle offers us. He does not invite us to give up on anything except the Cartesian inspired conceptions of 'inner' and 'outer'. If we do give up on these, then we shall have lost nothing and gained only clarity with respect to the muddles of philosophy arising from the differences that our language does indeed mark. Wittgenstein is translated as writing of 'pain behavior' and this might seem *prima facie* confirmation of his behaviorism, taking the view that 'pain' is simply the bodily movements (note the ambiguity that attaches to 'move' in 'movements') of, e.g., gasping, rolling around on the floor, shouting 'I have an awful pain in my leg' in appropriate circumstances, but where these movements and words are unaccompanied by any sensations. This interpretive travesty, however, locates Wittgenstein as occupying the very position that his private language arguments are constructed to subvert, and is built upon the very conception of 'privacy' that he sought to uproot entirely. His 'beetle in a box' argument is, after all, a *reductio*.

Imagine a community in which everyone owns a box, the contents of which are private. They are private in the strict sense that only the person who owns a particular box has access to it, can look inside it and view its contents. Each owner has immediate and direct access to the contents of his box and is therefore quite certain of what is inside it. Recall that this provision is required by the Cartesian conception of privacy, which demands that no-one else can truly know what is in any given box (mind) – only its owner can be certain of this in his own case. In this imagined community the word 'beetle' is used solely to refer to the contents of one's box, thus the word is not being used in the same way as in our community where it is the name of a certain determinable creature. The participants in this imagined community can only learn the meaning of the word 'beetle' from looking into their own personal box since the word refers to the things in the boxes and not to anything that can be pointed to in the external world (for that would not fit the theory of meaning that goes along with this conception of the inner). Consequently, the word 'beetle' cannot, in this community, mean anything other than 'whatever is in the box' since all that anyone knows is what is in his or her box, and there can be no assurance that what is in anyone else's box is the same as is in one's own. Note that 'whatever' can as readily encompass 'nothing' as it can any one of an indeterminately large and varied ranges of possible 'somethings' in people's boxes, so 'beetle' might apply to something or nothing. It is another upshot of the terms of the 'privacy' conception that the contents of the box cannot feature in the *public* use of the word 'beetle' since if the use of the word betrayed the properties of the box's contents, to identify some kind of determinate kind of presence, then it would be apparent to the members of the community whether there was or was not the same thing in anyone else's box as there is in one's own. But for this to be the case would infringe the stipulations of the argument. Therefore, if the word 'pain' is construed after the fashion of 'beetle' and according to this model of privacy, then it simply would not matter from the point of view of users of the word 'pain' in our language whether or not people claiming to feel pains feel anything or nothing. This notion – that people in pain feel nothing – is not, we emphasize, Wittgenstein's position but is rather the inevitable – and absurd – conclusion of applying the concept of 'the inner' that he is opposing. In Wittgenstein's view, there is no question that people who complain of pains do (usually) feel something and, indeed, that they do feel pains, and we are, as speakers of the language, just as confident of this as we are of the fact that a wailing baby who has no language is experiencing pain or some other discomfort. Pain behavior is not, after all, a matter of bodily movements that include, e.g., rolling around, yelling out, etc., which might be logically disconnected from a set of inner feeling states. Pain behavior is a form of human reaction in which certain (natural) movements and feelings are organically connected. Gasping, crying out, etc., are things that go along with the feelings, so pain behavior in Wittgenstein's understanding includes what is felt along with the way in which, in a natural, even animal, conjunction one vents what one feels with a cry, a moan, doubling over, and so on. But this is to say that the (our) use of the word 'pain' *does* depend upon 'what is in the box' and that it is therefore possible for members of the language community in which that word is confidently used to make determinations as to whether what is in the box is the same in one case as in another.

Wittgenstein presents his opponents with a dilemma. Either the use of the word 'pain' depends upon features of 'the inner' or it does not. In the first case, it infringes the requirement of privacy, whereas in the second case it satisfies the requirement of privacy but only because the use of the word in no way requires that there be anything 'inner' for it to encompass. The opponents may want to have this cake and to have eaten it too, but Wittgenstein's dilemma does not eliminate 'the inner' in the sense that we do feel pains and have other sensations, but only aims to rid us of the Cartesian conception of 'the inner' since that is just incoherent. Giving up 'the inner' is a matter of giving up, at the same time, 'the outer' as a companion, contrastive, concept, conceived in Cartesian terms, and pain behavior, a natural conjunction of feelings and bodily reactions, quite clearly transgresses the Cartesian dichotomy, and must not be construed as an attempt to occupy one side of it.

In the chapters to follow, we shall be pursuing many inter-related arguments in which various attempts are made to unify neo-Cartesian conceptions of 'mentality' with the neural sciences. The coining of the hybrid notion of the 'mind/brain' is a central feature of, and plays a major role in, many contemporary efforts to link mentalistic conceptions to neurobiology. We shall find, time and again, that a deep philosophical adherence to Cartesian conceptions, especially of 'the inner' and 'the outer', animates even the most stalwart materialists involved in these efforts. It is now time to take up these themes in detail...

CHAPTER ONE

NEURAL METAPHYSICS

In this chapter, we identify some major sources of confusion and error within contemporary philosophy of mind and philosophy of psychology. We are especially concerned to mount a sustained critique of the sort of philosophizing which has become popular in recent years, viz., 'scientistic' philosophy. By this expression, we mean to disparage, explicitly and self-consciously, the kind of work in the field which portrays itself as applying findings from neuroscience to problems in the philosophy of mind and human conduct. In mounting this challenge we risk the charge that we are either at odds with, or ignorant of, contemporary advances and discoveries in the neurosciences pertinent to the solution of long-standing problems in the philosophy of mind. As we hope to show, such a charge is without merit. Indeed, and to the contrary, we believe that our work shows more clearly, and in detail, exactly where and how the practice of the neuroscientist can enlighten us and the logical limitations on what his or her work can aspire to contribute to the understanding of human life and individual conduct.

Technical and Ordinary Language

The title of this chapter alludes to the contribution of Patricia Churchland, especially in her book *Neurophilosophy*.[1] Many of her arguments about the 'mind/brain/behavior' nexus are very influential. She advances the thesis that her 'scientific' (to us, 'scientistic') approach is a significant improvement on the sort of work she disparages as 'linguistic analysis'. She writes: "What had instead

---

[1] Patricia S. Churchland, *Neurophilosophy: Toward a Unified Science of the Mind/Brain* (Cambridge, Mass.: Bradford Books, M.I.T. Press, 1989).

begun to seem promising was the new wave in philosophical method which ceased pandering to 'ordinary language' and which began in earnest to reverse the anti-scientific bias typical of 'linguistic analysis'".[2] Exhibiting a comparable contempt for conceptual investigations, and along similar lines, Francis Crick, the molecular biologist whose interests have recently turned to neuroscience, wrote: "Philosophers have had such a poor record over the last two thousand years that they would do better to show a certain modesty rather than the lofty superiority that they usually display".[3] In a footnote, Crick adds: "It has been unkindly said that a philosopher is too often a person who prefers imaginary experiments to real experiments and thinks that an explanation of a phenomenon in everyday words is all that is needed."[4] Do such pejorative comments really bite? Is it true that appeals to the logic of our concepts is a manifestation of an anti-scientific attitude to inquiry? We think not, for the fact that one does not pretend to be some kind of para-scientist does not entail that one lines up against it, any more than lining oneself up with science entails that one is thereby successfully in tune with scientific understanding and developments in a given discipline. Much of this work will be concerned to demonstrate that discerning the empirical truth of a proposition presupposes that its *intelligibility* has been or can be established. And considerations of 'sense', which are inescapably prior to considerations of truth, are a matter of *conceptual* elucidation. Churchland appears to us to conflate these separate enterprises when she comments negatively on one particular 'appeal to ordinary language':

> "A common philosophical tactic for criticizing neurobiological hypotheses concerning the identification of mental processes with brain processes used to be to brand these hypotheses as 'incoherent' or to cite them,

---

[2] *Ibid.*, p. ix.

[3] Francis Crick, *The Astonishing Hypothesis: The Scientific Search for the Soul* (N.Y.: Charles Scribner's Sons, 1994), p. 258.

[4] *Ibid.* In the light of such a stricture, it is worth pondering whether a closer attention to the logic of our concepts on Crick's own part might have inhibited him from producing such rather obvious reifications as the following: "Where, I wondered, might Free Will be located in the brain? (...) Free Will is located in or near the anterior cingulated sulcus." (*Ibid.*, pp. 267-68).

pityingly, as having tripped up on a 'category error'.... But one person's category error is another person's deep theory about the nature of the universe.... The important thing for getting at the truth about brains is not whether in customary usage ordinary humans-in-the-street do say that persons remember but do not say that brains remember: rather, it is whether we ought to say that brains remember – whether, given the empirical facts, it is a reasonable hypothesis that brains remember. Customary usage is perhaps of anthropological interest, but it will not determine much about the nature of reality."[5]

The last point can readily be conceded, but it is wholly beside the point. Conceptual ('grammatical') investigations into the logic of the use of our words (such as the word 'remember') are inquiries into what it makes sense to say, not into 'the nature of reality'. However, any responsible inquiry into empirical matters (such as the properties and functions of brains and their parts) is answerable to canons of intelligibility. We agree with Feyerabend's point (which Churchland quotes) about "the inadequacy of appealing to the common idiom as a source of truth",[6] but, again, grammar does not settle any matters of empirical truth, only matters of sense. So, is Churchland's linguistic proposal, that we can speak intelligibly about a brain's remembering something, defensible? An initial problem is this: does Churchland intend that we (lay, ordinary users of the language) should now say that brains remember *as well as* that people remember? Or is she advocating that we should say only the former and cease to say the latter? Is this a recommendation that, for example, we should ask Jack: 'Does your brain remember...?' Or should we ask Jack's brain if *it* remembers? And how could we do that except by asking Jack? So, we might as well stick with just asking Jack! The other view, that asking Jack if he remembers is really asking Jack's brain since it is Jack's brain that will remember, falls foul of the point that we cannot ask Jack's brain except by asking Jack, instead of Phil or Bill. There is no sense whatsoever to the claim that one could ask Jack's brain *rather than*, or *instead of*, asking Jack. Even if one insists, as Churchland wants to, that it is

---

[5] Patricia Churchland, *Neurophilosophy...*, pp. 273-74.
[6] *Ibid.*, p. 273.

Jack's brain that remembers, unavoidably one will only be in a position to assert that one has spoken to Jack's brain if one has spoken to Jack: the question, 'Do you remember... ?' will be put to Jack. This highlights the sheer obscurity of Churchland's reductionist position pertaining to the relation between the concept of 'a person' and the concept of 'a person's brain', since the former concept is indispensable to the latter.[7]

One objection can be anticipated: it has been advanced often enough before. We may say that we are not attempting to interfere in any way with serious empirical investigation, but, no matter what we say, the logic of our argument surely involves the attempt to regulate the use of technical terms by empirical investigators in the name of 'ordinary language'. The objection is misguided. The opposition of 'technical' and 'ordinary' use of language is their – our opponents' – opposition, not ours. Our opposition is to the philosophical abuse of expressions. Both 'ordinary language' and 'technical terms' can, therefore, have an ordinary use, a grammar of development in those environments in which they 'go to work', and both kinds of terms can also be subject to involvement in philosophical confusions where, having been taken 'on holiday' from their working lives, they lack the genuine application that the setting of their ordinary use affords them.

The impression that our opposition is of 'ordinary' to 'technical' may seem to have some substance since many of the problems involved attend not distinctively technical terms – ganglion, neuron, etc. – but ones which are

---

[7] A further point: why is Churchland's example: 'brains remember' rather than, say, 'brains geflunkt'? The answer is because the word 'remember' is a word from the ordinary language. Churchland is illicitly trading upon the fact that, in many specialized sciences, what such specialists say amongst themselves may be all of their's and no-one else's business – outsiders may well have no idea at all about what they mean by what they say. In order to understand various portions of specialized discourse, people interested in pursuing them may well have to study the science involved in some considerable detail before they can actually get a grip on the sense of what is being said. In this case, however, no such thing is involved. There is no specialized use of 'remember' being deployed in what she is talking about: just the ordinary one.

recognizably ordinary ones: mind, thought, intention, information, remembering, and, as we will eventually argue, even 'in', and ' part'. But the objection may continue, surely there is a difference between such expressions in their ordinary use and in their technical, 'scientific' application. If we object to neuroscientists saying that it is the brain that remembers on the grounds that, in ordinary use, it is the individual person who remembers or fails to do so, surely we are trying to impose an *a priori* restriction on what those scientists might legitimately want to say in light of their empirical researches, assuming for ourselves not only the authority to overrule the civil rights of scientists to a specialist jargon but also an amazing capacity to anticipate the results of empirical investigations in neuroscience, as is manifest in our attempt to rule out in advance the necessity to say certain kinds of things.

Again, the objection is misguided, and the error originates in our opponents' ambiguity about or inconsistency over the status of many of the expressions that they use. Our argument is not that scientists should have no right to give previously ordinary words a new use, a new role as a distinctively technical expression in some branch of inquiry. Doing this, however, means that there is a discontinuity between ordinary and technical discourse, that when one is talking about 'remembering' or 'information' one is no longer talking about the same thing as when one makes ordinary use of those expressions and claims about the capacity of brains to remember do not, could not, stand in contradiction to, nor carry implications for, our ordinary assertions that it is persons (not their brains, arms or bottoms) who remember things. One can indeed say that fluids and metals remember their prior forms, but this means only that they can revert to their prior forms under certain conditions, not that they have memories in any literal sense.

We have no reason to believe that the terminological innovations that neurophilosophers introduce are motivated by the pressing needs of articulating new empirical findings, nor are they required by the need to state the empirical features to which they seek to draw our attention. Rather, it is our contention that all such linguistic innovations are inspired by (and justified by) *a priori* metaphysical requirements.

The idea that an appeal to ordinary language-use in conceptual inquiries amounts to an appeal to what lay speakers *believe* is a fundamental mistake, and one which nurtures the equally mistaken claim that conceptual analytic arguments are in some sense or another 'anti-scientific'. Moreover, Churchland's position, which she shares with many other philosophers in the thrall of Quine's 'naturalism', construes philosophy as a kind of 'super-science', one which seeks to develop massively general and abstract conclusions from considerations of theories and findings in specialized natural-scientific pursuits. Our arguments in this book will (in large part) be designed to show how 'scientistic' claims in the philosophy of mind, claims to be able to explain 'the human mind' and its workings by making highly abstract inferences from work in neuroscience, lead not to advances in our knowledge but rather to confusion and incoherence. One way in which we aim to demonstrate that this is the case is by revealing the degree to which various theoretical formulations (especially those of a programmatic character) made by some neuroscientists (and *especially* those of a programmatic character) themselves embody essentially metaphysical speculations. In this way, we can begin to see how one mode of metaphysics trades off other modes of metaphysics, and not off any genuinely scientific discoveries.

The fundamental purpose of this book is to advance a range of inter-related conceptions about the analysis of human mentality and conduct which are logically sound and scientifically uncontentious. In the pursuit of such an objective, we must attempt to clear away a multitude of misconceptions which, we believe, have dominated much discourse on these matters for a long time. In the course of our inquiries, we shall develop lines of criticism of a predominantly conceptual and methodological kind, many of which originate within the later writings of Wittgenstein.

The major sources of inspiration for the scientistic strain in philosophy have been some highly contentious dogmas, such as the claim that no clear distinctions can be made between *a priori* and empirical assertions; the view that our 'ordinary' language (especially our ordinary language of the 'mental' and 'experiential') embodies one or more 'lay' or 'commonsensical' or 'folk' *theories* (e.g., a 'folk-psychological' theory) which are *in toto* susceptible to 'correction' or even abolition in the light of scientific work[8]; the notion that 'technical' concepts, being extraordinary in some sense, immunize their users to conceptual errors of the sort typically diagnosed by logical-grammatical investigations, and the position that philosophers should aspire to generate scientific explanations of their own but at a much higher level of generality and abstraction than characterizes those of the specialized sciences upon which they depend for their data, evidence and theoretical argumentation.

---

[8] John Cook has commented on the idea that our uses of (certain) words are "in jeopardy from the advancement of science" in his paper "The Fate of Ordinary Language Philosophy", *Philosophical Investigations*, 3 (2) 1980: pp. 1-72. (quote from p. 57). His point does not pertain to the fact that some words become obsolete (e.g., 'phlogiston' in the face of the modern theory of combustion) but rather to the idea that many of our ordinary words have been misconstrued as referential and that their meanings can be changed by changed conceptions of their putative referents. He wrote: "... philosophers, and even scientists themselves, have misconstrued the bearing of scientific discoveries on ordinary language, and ... one of the reasons for this is that they have first read into our ordinary words various philosophical pictures of their own. For example, psychologists as well as philosophers have long been in the habit of assuming that our ordinary use of 'mentalistic' words involves a dualistic conception of human beings. And Sherrington ... was clearly assuming that our everyday uses of the words 'life', 'living' and 'alive' embody a commitment to vitalism. Still other philosopher-scientists have attributed to the plain man's words a metaphysical theory of time. Now this repeated tendency to read metaphysics into our workaday words is not merely a series of unrelated misconceptions about these various words. It is traceable to the very general idea that words ought to, are intended to, point to something in the world..." (pp. 57-8). Using ordinary words like 'belief', 'thought', 'understanding' and even 'mind' itself does not *eo ipso* commit the user to any theory whatsoever, although lay people can certainly advocate any of a range of substantive psychological theories. However, their advocacy is as much susceptible to conceptual clarification and possible critique as is any professional advocacy of such theories. Sometimes, it will be found that their substantive claims are *confounded* by the grammar of their non-theoretical uses of various key words.

We shall begin our discussion with a detailed scrutiny of what two recent scientific texts have to tell us about some topics pertinent to our study. Our intent is logical: we have neither the expertise nor the ambition to query any (confirmed) neuroscientific findings *per se*. However, we do not accept that the kinds of things that some philosophers (Dennett, the Churchlands, and many others) have to tell us about what these findings actually amount to constitute the last word on the philosophical significance (if any) which they may have. Indeed, a good deal of our effort may be characterized as one of disentangling the metaphysics from the physiology.

The Cartesian Heritage and Neuroscience

In order to give the reader a flavor of the arguments we wish to make, namely that some neuroscientific sources have themselves been significantly affected by metaphysical proclivities, we shall take up some passages from a widely used and respected technical work, Kandel, Schwartz and Jessell (eds.), *Principles of Neural Science* (3rd edition)[9]. We select this modern classic because it remains a canonical text. We shall also consider, again schematically, some sections from the September 1992 special issue of *Scientific American* ('Mind and Brain') in which less rarified and more 'popularized' versions of several relevant issues are presented by highly competent professional investigators. First, to reiterate a caveat: we make no effort to question any of the reported neurophysiological data and can claim no technical expertise in the conduct of empirical, neurophysiological inquiries (any more than can our philosophical adversaries). Our solution to the problem of interdisciplinary competence, then, is a simple one: for our purposes, we shall assume the truth of every purely empirical claim under discussion: that is, since our interests are reflective and conceptual, we can best proceed by taking for granted each and every empirical

---

[9] Eric R. Kandel, James H. Schwartz & Thomas M. Jessell (eds.), *Principles of Neural Science* (Third Edition: N.J., Englewood Cliffs, Prentice-Hall International, 1991).

claim embodied in the strictly technical works under review. It is up to other physiologists to correct, enlarge upon or even refute outright whatever 'factual' materials are contained in these reports if and when that is required. We are not interested in any way in mounting a challenge to the *science* involved: far from it. Our aim is solely to examine various issues of conceptualization which arise and which, in our view, cause problems for philosophers and lay readers alike. The neurosciences are, of course, technically specialized fields, but their successes are not unique to their propounders: insofar as we can *all* derive knowledge from them, such knowledge is a gift to mankind. It is, after all, not just true *for neuroscientists* that electrochemical discharges from certain neurons travel at certain speeds and have certain effects. It is, if true, true in general and a possible component of anyone's knowledge. We thereby trade upon the *universality* of the achievements in this domain in undertaking the kind of critical inquiry we argue is required.

We will begin our preliminary review, then, with the usual way in which the problem-space has been set up: the contrast between Cartesian dualism and scientific materialism. We shall explore this contrast in greater detail in a subsequent chapter. For the moment, we wish to note that this contrast-class is widely construed as exhaustive of the intellectual options for conceiving of human mentality, and we shall later challenge this assumption in detail. Cartesian dualism is, of course, the foil: it is the traditional point of departure and the major basis for the disparagement of the contributions of 'philosophy' (cf. Crick above) to thinking about mentality. However, in many discussions, the version of Cartesianism which is disputed is actually quite a restricted one: it is thought that the central dogma which postulates a 'mind' as an immaterial, non-corporeal, phenomenon of some kind is the essence of the Cartesian picture. By transposing various of the attributes, properties and functions which Descartes assigned to the metaphysical mind (the 'res cogitans') to the (obviously material and corporeal) human central nervous system, especially to the brain, it is often believed that the threat of dualism is vanquished and that all vestiges of Cartesian thinking are thereby eradicated. Only the scientific details remain to be worked out. Descartes is depicted primarily as the victim of ignorance of relevant empirical information in the period when he first formulated his dualist philosophy of mind and body. For example, Fischbach remarks:

> "Three centuries ago he [Descartes] described the mind as an extracorporeal entity that was expressed through the pineal gland. Descartes was wrong about the pineal, but the debate he stimulated regarding the relation between mind and brain rages on. How does the non-material mind influence the brain and vice versa? In addressing this issue, Descartes was at a disadvantage. He did not realize the human brain was the most complex structure in the known universe, complex enough to coordinate the fingers of a concert pianist or to create a three-dimensional landscape from light that falls on a two-dimensional retina ... If Descartes had known these things, he might have wondered, along with modern neurobiologists, whether the brain is complex enough to account for the mystery of human imagination, of memory and mood. Philosophical inquiry must be supplemented by experiments... "[10]

Fischbach goes on to suggest that we "agree to think of the mind as a collection of mental processes rather than as a substance"[11], asserting that only such a shift can facilitate empirical studies into their nature. The Cartesian notion that, e.g., our thinking, understanding, reasoning, imagining and remembering are to be construed as 'mental processes' remains intact, as does the idea that the 'retinal image' (as distinct from the physical fact of the irradiation of our photoreceptor cells) plays some role in the causal explanation of our visual capacities and their exercise.[12] We would add at this juncture that we also find no

---

[10] Gerald D. Fischbach, "Mind and Brain", *Scientific American*, Vol. 267, No. 3, September 1992, p. 48.
[11] *Ibid.*
[12] For a conceptual examination of the fallacy of imputing any causal role at all to the 'image' formed on our retinae (an epiphenomenal function of its convexity, detectable only by special instrumentation!), see John Hyman, "Introduction" to his edited anthology, *Investigating Psychology* (London & Boston: Routledge, 1991), and his fuller discussion of this issue in his *The Imitation of Nature* (Oxford: Basil Blackwell, 1989), p. 49 et seq. Cf. James J. Gibson's arguments in his *The Ecological Approach to Visual Perception* (Boston: Houghton Mifflin, 1979), esp. p. 147.

compelling reason for the celebrated anti-Cartesian philosopher, Gilbert Ryle, to continue to promulgate the notion that such predicates (thinking, perceiving, etc.) require the epithet 'mental' as a component of their logical elucidation, as when he speaks of, for example, 'mental conduct concepts' in his classic work, *The Concept of Mind*[13]. Expurgating the non-corporeality of the 'mind' does not liberate one from the inter-related panoply of problems bequeathed to us by the Cartesian legacy. On the contrary: we can begin to discern the successor to Cartesian-inspired speculations about brains in the emergence of what we call "neural Cartesianism"[14]. It is a major feature of neural-Cartesian reasoning that person-level[15] predicates such as thinking, understanding, remembering, perceiving, etc., are ascribed (at the level of theory-construction) to the cortex or regions thereof rather than to the erstwhile stuff of the metaphysical 'mind'; they are still construed as 'mental', only now, under the auspices of the materialist transformation of the frame of reference, the 'mental' has become 'neuralized', and the proper subject for their predication is held to be the hybrid phenomenon, prominently referred to in Patricia Churchland's sub-title (as elsewhere in the literature), of the 'mind/brain'.

---

[13] Gilbert Ryle, *The Concept of Mind* (Harmondsworth, Middlesex, England: Penguin University Books, 1973: originally Hutchinson, 1949), p. 9, pp. 16-17, p. 20, pp. 26-27 & p. 61. On this point, see Elmer Sprague, *Persons and their Minds: A Philosophical Investigation* (Boulder, Colorado: Westview Press, 1999).

[14] One of us, Jeff Coulter, coined this term and discussed some of the issues raised by its critical use in: "Neural Cartesianism: Comments on the Epistemology of the Cognitive Sciences" in David M. Johnson & Christina E. Erneling (eds.), *The Future of the Cognitive Revolution* (Oxford: Oxford University Press, 1997), pp. 293-301.

[15] In emphasizing this, we do not wish to be taken as affirming a Strawsonian descriptive-metaphysical argument for the putative 'primitiveness' of the concept of a person. (See P. F. Strawson, *Individuals*, London: Methuen, 1959). Rather, we are insisting upon the point made some time ago by A. J. P. Kenny in his paper, "The Homunculus Fallacy" (in his *The Legacy of Wittgenstein*, Oxford: Basil Blackwell, 1984) concerning the loci of proper (i.e., criterially satisfying) ascriptions of such predicates. A failure to recognize the relevant conceptual constraints here results in what Bennett and Hacker discuss under the rubric of 'the mereological fallacy' (the fallacy of attributing to parts of living creatures what can only rationally be ascribed to the whole living creature) in their *Philosophical Foundations of Neuroscience* (Oxford: Blackwell Publishing, 2003), Chapter Three.

Churchland's (and others') claims about the nature of the 'mind/brain' derive their inspiration, if not the precise form, from philosophical arguments first advanced more than thirty years' ago by U. T. Place, J. J. C. Smart and David Armstrong. Their 'mind-brain identity' thesis eventually became a fundamental assumption of much neuroscientific theorizing as well as in the philosophy of mind. Paul Livingston has nicely documented its source in a systematic misreading of Ryle's position on sensations (a misreading which Livingston argues, correctly in our view, was partly attributable to Ryle's own misleading way of making his argument)[16]. However, denying that sensations (and experiences more generally) consist solely in 'dispositions to behave' in certain ways – as Place and Armstrong imagined Ryle was arguing - does not itself license the 'identity' thesis. In what did this thesis consist? Essentially, 'consciousness' and related 'mental' predicates (especially those of sensation) were to be thought of as reducible to neural events and processes yet to be empirically discovered. The argument that such a 'reduction' can make sense was analogical: reductive identities variously proposed as a justification for mind-to-brain reduction(s) included several drawn from empirical sciences: lightning is electrical discharge, clouds are dense constellations of water droplets, water is H2O, heat is mean kinetic energy, and so forth. Some of these putative 'identities' were with clearly compositional (usually physical, usually microstructural) properties of the 'reduced' terms: phenomena were being identified with *what they are composed of.* This move, however, ignored the fact that the rules of use for the concepts of such phenomena are not exhausted by statements about their compositional properties. Sometimes, only synechdochal versions of their grammars could be thus formulated, and often the complexity of the concepts involved simply defied any such simple 'identity' claims. In the mind-to-brain case, the prior reification and stipulative homogenization of the so-called 'mental'

---

[16] Paul M. Livingston, "Ryle on Sensation and the Origin of the Identity Theory" in his *Philosophical History and the Problem of Consciousness* (Cambridge, England: Cambridge University Press, 2004), Chapter Four.

concepts (consciousness, thought, memory, etc.) were requirements for efforts to identify 'it' or 'them' with the brain or brain events. Along with a battery of other arguments, many philosophers (notably Norman Malcolm in some much-neglected writings on this subject[17]) did indeed question the very coherence of advancing such 'identity' claims as genuine scientific hypotheses susceptible to empirical adjudication of any kind. Despite Ryle's tendency to over-use his famous notion of a 'category mistake', this idea did enable him to identify a major source of ramifying confusions: the propensity to misassimilate concepts belonging to different logical-grammatical domains. He showed very clearly how some concepts which may appear to behave like 'episodic' ones (e.g., understanding, recognizing) and which thus might qualify for some sort of compositional analysis, are, in fact, 'achievement' types. Insofar as he succeeded in exposing such misassimilations and their consequences, he elucidated not, as Churchland would have it, "one person's category error" (as if, were it truly a hitherto undiagnosed species of logical error, it might be that of just 'one person'!), but a source of *systematic* confusions at the very core of the philosophy of mind.

Another source of confusion has been what we can call the premature 'phenomenalization' of a range of concepts defined within the Cartesian tradition as 'mental', and their 'globalization'. Consider the typical rubrics under which are subsumed various arguments and theoretical considerations: we read about 'Perception', 'Recognition', 'Memory', 'Thought' and, Crick's favorite, 'Consciousness', as if capitalizing such words turned them into 'phenomena' amenable to reductive scrutiny. Globalizing such notions has pernicious effects, for this practice seeks to depict the problems of the philosophy of mind as *ab initio* empirical ones, where the concepts in question are simply assumed to be

---

[17] Norman Malcolm, "Rejoinder to Mr. Sosa" in C. V. Borst (ed.), *The Mind/Brain Identity Theory* (N. Y. : Macmillan, 1970) and his "Mind and Brain" in *Nothing is Hidden: Wittgenstein's Criticism of his Early Thought* (Oxford: Basil Blackwell, 1986), Chapter Ten.

substantives, names or labels for elusive objects or mysterious albeit discrete domains of investigable phenomena. The polymorphous nature of some of these concepts, the 'intentionality' of others (after Brentano and Husserl), and the diverse logical-grammatical features of the rest, once carefully inspected, are irreconcilable with such theoretical treatment. Consider, for example, the (Brentano-)'intentionality' of thought. The word 'thought' is an ordinary, not a technical, one. It is a *relational* (that is, not a free-standing) term, not detachable from complementisers and object-complements, in contrast to, say, a word like 'cup'. I can have a cup filled with coffee (i.e., a cup of coffee), empty the coffee, and still have the cup ('freely standing', so to speak). However, I cannot have a thought of something, delete the 'of something', and be left with the 'thought' *simpliciter*. The word 'thought' is not free-standing, not detachable from what it is of or about. It is true that one need not in every case *mention* what one's thought is of or about, but a 'thought' which is not of, about or that something (is such-and-such), is no thought at all. One can think that, of, about, up, over and through but one cannot simply 'think'. Note that there cannot (logically, conceptually) be, e.g., neuronal firings of or about anything, so no simple reductive move can be made in this case. No identity, nor even isomorphism, with neural phenomena can be aspired to here. (We shall consider various other related reductive strategies later on).

Problems with 'Information'

A central concept in neurophilosophical speculation has been that of 'information'. The brain (and CNS) is depicted as receiving, processing, storing, transforming, encoding, decoding, retrieving, etc., 'information' from the 'external world'. According to Eric Kandel: "Information coming from the peripheral receptors that sense the environment is analyzed by the brain into components that give rise to perceptions, some of which are stored in memory"[18]. This assertion may appear simply to be a statement of established neuroscientific fact. But appearances here are deceptive, for the observation is wholly contentious. Discerning what the facts actually are can be troublesome, as it is in this passage where a heavily 'theory-laden' portrayal is presented. We wish to note that, for us, 'theory-ladenness' is not to be construed (as it has been in much of the work of Hanson, Feyerabend, Kuhn and others in the philosophy of science) as an intrinsic and ineliminable property of *any* factual claim in the sciences. On occasion, a shareable, pre-theoretical depiction of a datum or finding can be the source for *later* theoretical conflict or competition: on other occasions, the very claimed identification of the datum is itself tied inextricably to a (perhaps contestable) theory. The only commonality of concern to us in respect of the depiction of empirical data is that all must be, in one form or another, *conceptualized* – and we wish to resist any attempt to conflate all discourse about concepts with discourse about theories. Not all concepts are theoretical concepts: theories comprise propositions, whilst concepts enable the sense of expressions: theories can be true or false, whereas concepts have no truth-values and are only intelligible or unintelligible in their contexts of use. Kandel's observation, then, raises for us the following questions: What is meant by 'information'? What is meant by 'environment'? What is meant by 'analyzed'? What is meant by a 'component' of 'information'? What is meant by 'perceptions'? What is meant by 'stored' in relation to 'perceptions'? And what is meant by the phrase 'stored in memory'? For each of these terms and expressions may be taken as problematic in ways we shall discuss.

Starting with 'information', we can note that this term has varied uses, some 'technical', others not. There is also more than one 'technical' meaning. In computational terms, 'information' can signify the binary-digitized form of alphanumerical input into a device facilitating its transformation, storage,

---

[18] Eric Kandel, in Kandel et al. (eds.), *Principles of Neural Science*, op. cit., p. 18.

retrieval, etc. It is this usage which has dominated the 'information-processing' paradigm in cognitive psychology and cognitive neuropsychology, drawing upon the computer analogy. Although those inspired by the work of J. J. Gibson have traditionally taken the notion of 'information extraction' to be non-computational, Marr has argued that Gibson's was, in fact, a theoretical precursor to the full-blown information-processing approach to the explanation of visual perception: Gibson, Marr claimed, had simply failed to appreciate the complexity of the 'neural computations' required to 'extract information' from ambient light[19]. Another 'technical' use is to be found in Shannon and Weaver's mathematical theory of communication, where the 'information' conveyed by a signal is specified in terms of the reduction in uncertainty or the elimination of possibilities represented by the event or state-of-affairs at the source of the signal[20]. Dretske's attempt to develop a 'semantic theory of information' on the basis of the Shannon-Weaver framework constitutes yet another technical variant[21]. G. P. Moore cogently reminds us that: "Much that has been said on the subject of information processing by the nervous system is either misinformed, incorrect or only metaphorical. The simple statement 'neurons process information' poses profound philosophical problems and consists of three words whose meaning is unclear – in contrast, say, with the statement 'neurons transmit impulses', which has an unambiguous meaning under properly defined circumstances"[22]. Hilary Putnam, once a champion of the Turing-machine functionalist conception of the

---

[19] David Marr, *Vision: A Computational Investigation into the Human Representation and Processing of Visual Information* (San Fransisco: Freeman, 1982), pp. 29-30 & p. 212. For some discussion of Gibson's proximity to the tradition he ostensibly opposed, see Wes Sharrock & Jeff Coulter, "On What We Can See", *Theory and Psychology*, Vol. 8, No. 2, 1998, pp. 147-64.

[20] Claude Shannon and Warren Weaver, *The Mathematical Theory of Communication* (Illinois: University of Illinois Press, 1949).

[21] Fred I. Dretske, *Knowledge and the Flow of Information* (Cambridge, Mass.: M.I.T. Press/Bradford Books, 1981). For a critical discussion of Dretske's and Gibson's thinking about 'information' in the behavioral sciences, see Jeff Coulter, "The Informed Neuron: Issues in the Use of Information Theory in the Behavioral Sciences", *Minds and Machines*, Vol. 5, No. 4, 1995, pp. 583-96.

[22] G. P. Moore, "Mathematical techniques for studying information processing by the nervous system" in H. M. Pinsker & W. D. Willis Jr. (eds.), *Information Processing in the Nervous System* (N. Y.: Raven Press, 1980).

mind-brain relationship, declares: "[T]he Turing machine model need not be taken seriously as a model of the functional organization of the brain. Of course, the brain has digital elements – the yes-no firing of the neurons – but whether the larger organization is correctly represented by something like a flow-chart for an algorithm *or by something quite different* we have no way of knowing right now"[23]. On a strictly physiological interpretation of the evidence, electrochemical impulses do certainly traverse nerves which "come from the peripheral receptors" after these have transduced the energy input from the physical environment into such (ionic) pulses, and one could if one wished simply *stipulate* that such a process shall be termed: "information flow". But nothing has been gained over and above the purely physiological description, and much confusion is risked, even encouraged, by the redescription. This is because Kandel seeks to exploit an equivocality in the expression: "Information... is analyzed by the brain" as between 'information' as just stipulated and 'information' in the ordinary sense - *knowledge*-of or –about something - in contrast to misinformation or disinformation. Only the latter is a logically appropriate candidate for 'analysis' into 'components' some of which might be 'stored in memory', but knowledge is scarcely the sort of commodity one might envisage flowing through the nervous system. At a minimum, and to exploit the computer analogy to the hilt, this would presuppose some symbolic (e.g., alphanumerical) medium of expression or representation, and Kandel gives us no argument (and certainly nothing like *evidence* of a neurophysiological sort) to justify this idea[24]. Nonetheless, and this is the central point, we shall show how Kandel tacitly exploits more than one, mutually inconsistent, meanings in developing his assertions, generating a neural-Cartesian picture of what brains are supposed to be doing.

---

[23] Hilary Putnam, "Reductionism and the Nature of Psychology" in John Haugeland (ed.), *Mind Design* (Vermont: Bradford Books, 1981), p. 216. (Emphasis added).
[24] This sort of speculation is probably most closely associated with Jerry Fodor. See, *inter alia*, his *The Language of Thought* (N. Y.: Thomas Crowell, 1975).

The Physical and the 'Symbolic' Environments

Let us turn now to the concept of an 'environment'. George Herbert Mead, the Chicago-based 'social behaviorist', argued cogently that human beings inhabit not one but *two* (sorts of) environments: the physical and the 'symbolic'. By the latter conception, Mead was drawing the attention of the behaviorists to the critical difference between an 'environment' described in terms of the bombardment of receptor organs of 'stimuli' (various energy quanta, such as acoustic wave-forms, photons, etc.) and an 'environment' *as intelligibly experienced* (such as: a classroom, an urban neighborhood, mountains, trees and rivers, and so on). From the perspective of a neuroscientist (who is, when immersed in his specialized work, like the television engineer who is interested only in the fact that the phosphor dots are being impeccably displayed, and who has no interest in what the television content is), the only environment that could engage his interests is the physical one (or, better, the *physically-describable* characteristics of an environment for human beings). What strike the receptor cells in my cochleae are acoustic wave-forms; what impinge upon my photoreceptor cells are photons, etc. In brief, we must characterize the relevant physical dimensions of an environment in terms of their diverse kinds of energy emissions, and only those energy quanta transducible by receptors can enter into the causal account being given. Environments construed as 'symbolic' (i.e., as conceptualized), such as, *inter alia*, one's apartment, the program on TV, the street, the church, the classroom, the restaurant, etc., *cannot enter into the causal story at all*: their conceptualization is simply at the wrong logical level even to qualify for introduction into the kind of explanation which a neuroscientist might aspire to adduce, an explanation in which, necessarily, he must be dealing (at least in the primary phase of his inquiries) with energy emissions and their reception by specialized receptors facilitating their transduction into electrochemical impulses within the nervous system. Even if it is discovered that impulses transmitted through the brain and CNS have a 'binary' character, it is still a very long way from being able to argue that such pulse-trains are in any rigorous sense 'computational'.

Furthermore, Kandel claims that our brains 'analyze' such transmissions into 'components', some of which eventuate (in our brains) as 'perceptions' and some of which are 'stored in memory'. Quite what it might mean to say that the brain (or parts thereof) are engaged in *analyzing* anything is problematic – but far more troublesome are the consequences of allowing such an assumption to rest unchallenged. What must first be noted is that the concept of a 'perception', in its visual application, is not a name for any object, entity or event, such that it might 'exist' or 'occur', but signifies 'that which is (has been) seen correctly'. Thus, what I perceive (note: not my *brain!*) consists in what is/was there to be seen by me. Since my perception consists in, e.g., 'the street outside my window', if and only if there is indeed a street outside my window to be seen, and which I am (was) in a position to (have) see(n), then ['the street outside my window'] is *not* something which could logically be an object, still less an event, *inside my brain*. Perceptions are necessarily of something, being non-detachable from an object-complement, and one does not 'perceive' impulses reaching one's striate visual cortex from one's photoreceptors. One could revert to what John Hunter once felicitously termed 'the plain neurological explanation'[25] and say that events in one's visual cortex (e.g., the firing of angle-detector neurons, etc.), consequent upon the impingement of impulses arriving via nerve fibers, facilitate one's being able correctly to claim that one's visual environment has such-and-such objects, features, properties, events, etc., but in such a version the idea of perceptions themselves as 'end-products' *within* the cortex evaporates. This is certainly to be preferred, since it avoids begging the question of who or what has access to such putatively 'inner' perceptions, since it is certainly not the person *qua* perceiver.

---

[25] J. F. M. Hunter, "On How We Talk" in his *Essays after Wittgenstein* (Toronto: University of Toronto Press, 1973), p. 168.

The Storage Conception of Memory

Finally, let us consider Kandel's claim that "some [perceptions] are stored in memory". We have said enough, we hope, to counter the assumption that a 'perception' could logically be a candidate for empirical investigation as any sort of 'phenomenon' or 'event' inside the cortex. What sense, then, could be made of the claim that a 'perception' (say, of someone's face) might be 'stored in memory'?

The notion of 'memory storage' is deeply pervasive in neural-Cartesian accounts, buttressed as it has undoubtedly been by appeals to mechanistically-operating devices like computers which possess 'buffers' (or 'memory chips'), for, indeed, alphanumerically-representable 'information' can be encoded in bits or bit-strings for later retrieval. From Aristotle, whose notion of memory was one of depicting experiences which literally change our form (thence, 'informare', the Latin root of 'information') to Karl Lashley whose search for the 'engram' – the hypothesized neural locus of a 'memory' – one or another conception of storage in relation to memory has appeared to many to be indispensable.

The triumph of neuralized thinking about memory-storage in the twentieth-century, along with the pervasive use of the concept of 'information', may partly be traced to a remarkable intellectual confluence, one which so impressed Turing and Shannon[26] that both men embraced the idea that the future of theoretical psychology and neurophysiology lay in the development of engineering sciences, a notion at the heart of AI theorizing by researchers such as

---

[26] Andrew Hodges wrote: "They [Turing and Shannon] also discussed the idea implicit in *Computable Numbers*, an idea of which they were independently convinced. Shannon had always been fascinated with the idea that a machine should be able to imitate the brain; he had studied neurology as well as mathematics and logic, and had seen his work on the differential analyzer as a first step toward a thinking machine. They found their outlook to be the same: there was nothing sacred about the brain, and that if a machine could do as well as a brain, then it would be thinking... This was a back-room Casablanca, planning an assault not on Europe, but on inner space." *Alan Turing: The Enigma* (N.Y.: Simon & Schuster, Touchstone Book, 1984), p. 251.

Minsky and Papert. One dimension of this confluence was the shared interest in the mathematical treatment of information: the other was the discovery by Ramon y Cajal of the neuron, and especially of its apparently binary feature – its ON/OFF firing pattern – and the interconnectedness of neurons by microscopic fibers which transmit minute electrical discharges. Newell and Simon were later to herald the new grand scheme in which the cortex is to be understood as a 'physical-symbol manipulating system'[27]. The plausibility of the entire scheme was enhanced by reference to the work of Penfield, who had found that 'memories' could be triggered by the electrical stimulation of certain regions of the temporal cortex.

Against such a background, then, Kandel would appear to be uttering only a truism: to recall someone's facial appearance just must be a matter of retrieving a prior impression or 'perception' from the memory store. The neuroscientist's task is to specify in what mode of neural 'encoding' are perceptual memories stored in brains and by what mechanism(s) are they retrieved. We shall restrict our discussion at this point to a consideration of the most elementary example of 'remembering someone's face'. This is because (i) work using inverse inferences from brain lesions in the case of the disorder of 'facial agnosia' has been very extensive and (ii) the example is clearly less troublesome for storage theorists than that of, say, 'remembering what one intended to do', 'remembering that, in English spelling, 'i' comes before 'e' except after 'c'', 'remembering wishing that something would happen', and so on. Faces are, clearly, more 'discrete', less amenable to multiple formulations or depictions, less abstract, less troubled by individuation problems, less 'proposition-like', and in various other ways devoid of many of the problems confounding efforts at much greater explanatory generality. (We shall return to discuss these issues in more detail in a later chapter). However, an initial observation might serve to show that all is not as straightforward as it may appear in establishing the exact nature of the

---

[27] Alan Newell and H. A. Simon, *Human Problem Solving* (N.J.: Prentice-Hall, 1972).

explanandum – viz., remembering someone's face. Setting aside for the moment any theoretically-driven preconceptions, in what might this apparently elementary accomplishment ordinarily consist?

Note that we say 'accomplishment' here, for, despite the '-ing' suffix, which can give the (false) impression of the verb's grammatical category as a present-continuous-tense type, remembering is not a temporally extended process or activity (whether in or of the person or his or her brain). We logically can contrast 'trying to remember', which may take some time and may have many diverse manifestations, with 'actually remembering', and the latter with 'thinking (incorrectly) that one remembers'. Playing is a process, winning is not: traveling is a process, arriving is not: seeking is an activity, finding is not: trying takes time, succeeding does not. To remember something is an achievement, not an act, activity or process. To remember her face is to be *correct* about her features (or enough of them). One can misremember, seem to have remembered, etc., but to have remembered is to be (broadly or precisely) right, just as one cannot 'discover' something and be mistaken about it. These are, again, grammatical and not empirical remarks. But what about *sudden* recollections? Surely here we make a temporal reference in relation to remembering. Suppose that I suddenly visualize a face and take it to be the face of someone I know or knew. What tells me that *that* face is *her* face? I may visualize the face with the instantaneous conviction that it is her face, but being convinced of something, feeling certain about it, does not, in itself, establish that I am correct. What makes the visualization a case of a *memory*-image is that it correctly/accurately (within certain tolerable limits) portrays the one whose face it is, or was, which I have seen before. As Wittgenstein reminded us: "… no image, not even an image which presents scenes with hallucinatory clarity, can carry a stamp of the past on its face. It takes memory to tell us that what is thus presented is a representation of the past.[28]"

---

[28] Cited in P. M. S. Hacker, *Wittgenstein: Mind and Will (Vol. 4 of An Analytical Commentary on the 'Philosophical Investigations')*, Oxford: Basil Blackwell, 1996, p. 490.

A sudden recollection of someone's face, then, cannot be analyzed simply into a sudden visualization of a face. Such an instance of occurrent recollection may be facilitated by visualizing, but the recollection has properties which are not intrinsic purely to the image itself. The image must be one which correctly portrays someone I have seen before. If I am right about whom my visual image of a face portrays, then it may be said of my sudden recollection that it consisted in the sudden acquisition of an ability or range of abilities which may or may not actually be manifested in words and/or deeds: the ability to reproduce pictorially the image, to be able to give a correct description of it, or to react appropriately to a picture, photograph, description or 'live' exhibition of, the face of the person whom I have seen before. Abilities are not themselves candidates for *any* mode of storage.

Notice in all of this, as well, a subtle shift from 'perceptions' (misconstrued by Kandel as what could be 'stored') to 'visualizing' – the occurrent production of an image. What was my original perception? It was a perception of her face. I cannot literally store someone's face: and, as we have already seen, it makes no sense to say that I can 'store' a 'perception' either, since a 'perception' is neither an object nor an event but instantiates a relational concept as well as an achievement. Perceiving is an achievement, contrastable to misperceiving, whereas visualizing is an activity. My visualizing may enable me to recollect her facial features, but my recollection cannot consist in my visualizing: one cannot analyze an achievement into an activity, nor vice-versa, any more than one can analyze finding into seeking, looking for into finding, or arriving into traveling.

None of this is designed to undermine in any way what Hunter called 'the plain neurological explanation', only to undermine the neural-Cartesian, hence metaphysical, work-up of the neurological account. The critique of the neural-Cartesian facets of Kandel's text does not gainsay the obvious fact that neural events and processes, describable in the language of anatomy, biochemistry, electro-physiology, etc., co-constitute our capacities to see, to recollect, to visualize, and many other things as well.

'Neuraliizing' Voluntariness

We turn our attention here to another contribution to the same anthology, taking up for discussion the chapter by Claude Ghez who seeks to explain 'voluntary movements' in wholly neuroscientific terms:

> "The neural events leading even to a simple voluntary movement, such as reaching for a glass of water, involve three complex processes. First, the glass is identified and its position located in space. Second, a plan of action is selected that will bring the glass to the mouth. To specify which body parts are needed and in what direction they are to be moved, the location of the glass must be assessed in relation to the position of the hand and body. This information allows the motor systems to determine the hand's trajectory. Finally, the response is executed. Commands are conveyed by the cortical and brainstem descending pathways to the final common pathway, the motor neurons. These commands specify the temporal sequence of muscle activation, the forces to be developed, and the changes in joint angles. In addition, while reaching, the hand and fingers are adjusted to fit the contours of the glass, coordinating movements of the shoulder and arm with those at the wrist and digits so that the glass will be grasped on contact without delay."[29]

We shall have a lot to say further on about the inadequacy of treating all human conduct in a simple, bi-polar fashion as comprising things done 'voluntarily' and things done 'involuntarily'. At this juncture, we would note that, since it makes no sense to describe someone as 'reaching for a glass of water involuntarily', it makes no sense to describe all cases of 'reaching for a glass of water' as belonging to a class of 'voluntary' movements. Just consider one scenario: two men have been stranded in the desert without water for days. They come across an encampment in which they spot a table with a jug and a full glass

---

[29] Claude Ghez, "Voluntary Movement" in Kandel et al. (eds.),, *op. cit.*, pp. 609-10.

of water on it. One of the men is armed, the other is not, and the armed man orders the unarmed one to reach for the glass of water and to give it to him. The unarmed man responds to the order, backed by the threat of harm, with extreme reluctance. Has he 'reached for the glass voluntarily'? Not every characterization of an action in its context is, as J. L. Austin noted, 'adverb-hungry', and not every action which is *not* voluntarily done is a case of something done 'involuntarily'.

The neuroscientific concern for this distinction is motivated by seeking to establish a contrast between 'simple' and 'complex' actions. Beginning with the classical conception of the reflex arc, it is clear that more elaborate theories would be required to deal with conduct of some complexity such as, e.g., tying one's shoelaces (to say nothing of, e.g., composing a concerto). However, fermenting within such reasoning were the germs of some serious misconceptions, among them the idea that human conduct exhibits an empirically-analyzeable continuum from the simplest 'involuntary' response or movement to the full-fledged 'voluntary' cases of activity. The 'voluntariness' involved in the ways in which people behave, it was thought, was tantamount to their greater complexity. However, what makes an action a case of a 'voluntary' one (however momentary or however momentous) has little or nothing to do with its componential complexity and everything to do with the circumstances within which it is performed. It is, for example, the circumstances of there being an official draft into the armed forces into an unpopular war along with one's family's conviction that one should not fight are ones which make of one's 'signing one's name' on an official form a case of 'voluntarily enlisting' as distinct from simply 'accepting to be drafted' into the army. The actual 'behavioral events' involved may be quite elementary (e.g., 'signing one's name'), but the voluntariness or otherwise of the action ('joining the army) is not a facet of the action which could logically be illuminated, much less explained, by neuroscientific investigations.

'Complexity', as one may recall from the troubled history of behaviorism, appeared to be the central challenge and, as we can see in Ghez's discussion above, this idea still animates the *form* of the explanatory framework being appealed to. According to Ghez, an ordinarily simple activity such as 'reaching for a glass of water' now seems to take on extraordinary dimensions. For example, note what we might describe as the 'componentializing idealization' in his characterization of what is involved in such an action, and note as well the invocation of the idea of 'complexity' in the specification of the three 'processes'. First, a glass of water is 'identified': let us assume that this means, simply, seen or noticed, spotted or espied. Noticing the glass of water presupposes seeing where it is located. Fine, so far. However, the second phase is asserted to involve the selection of a 'plan of action' (shades of Galanter, Miller and Pribram?) which, if implemented correctly, will succeed in delivering the glass to the mouth without spillage or other misstep. The question now looms (but is not faced): who or what is 'selecting' this 'plan' and in what could it consist? Given the obvious experiential fact that, special circumstances aside, one does not ordinarily conjure up anything that could plausibly qualify as a 'plan of action' when reaching for a glass of water, the presumed answer to such a question is: one's brain or specific parts thereof. And now we again embark upon another neural-Cartesian crusade in which brain functions are depicted (although not elucidated) in a wholly personified manner in order to accommodate to a prior stipulation about the properties of the *explanandum*.

We read on: "To specify which body parts are needed and in what direction they are to be moved, the location of the glass must be assessed in relation to the position of the hand and body" (Ghez, above). Again, given the context of these assertions, we can only assume that it is (regions of) the brain that are implicated in such 'specifying' and 'assessing'. The subsequent invocation of that ubiquitous but unclarified concept of 'information' compounds the problem: in this case, the relevant 'information' must be information about the relative location of glass to hand and body, presumably formulable discursively in terms of some mathematically-given set of spatial co-ordinates, since it is (allegedly) this information which "allows the motor systems to determine the hand's trajectory" (Ghez, above). We shall read 'determine' here as in the causal rather than the 'discovery' sense of the word, but, even so, the missing clarification pertains to the actual role of 'information' in the account, especially since the only sense it can make is 'information-*about*' (the location of the glass, etc.). We have already noted that this concept of 'information' is predicable only of *persons*, not of their bodies or parts thereof. In these, and similar formulations, cognitive neuroscientists appear to personify the brain.

'Commands' has become something of a staple concept within much of neuroscience, command neurons being technically postulated as neuronal master-sources of relatively unimpeded electrochemical discharges to muscular activating centers. Nonetheless, the notion that 'commands' in such a restricted, technical sense, can be understood to 'specify' the temporal sequence of muscle activation such that one succeeds in grasping the glass of water begs several questions. A typical problem here is that movements which may be formally describable in terms of accord with some Gaussian function are being depicted as though they were the outcome of an interior computation of such a mathematical function. Here again we discern a neural-Cartesian gloss overlaid upon what are, otherwise, physiologically-describable phenomena, but note that no description of the physiological events involved uniquely captures the activity, for the same bodily movements depicted in the analysis of what it is to 'reach for a glass of water' can be applied to many *diverse* action scenarios. Just as the physics of falling bodies is logically silent as to the ways in which, e.g., human bodies can fall – by being pushed (homicide), tripping (accident) or jumping (suicide), so too must neuroscience remain silent about what the vast range of movements might instantiate at the level of human *actions*.

Polanyi discussed the example of cornering on a bicycle. He noted that, ergonomically-speaking, a cyclist must, in order to maintain his balance while cornering, keep his balance by adjusting the curvature of his forward path in proportion to the ratio of his unbalance over the square of his speed[30]. However, Polanyi refrained from projecting such a principle to the brains of competent cyclists. He understood, as did Wittgenstein, the crucial difference between conduct-following-a-rule and conduct-describable-as-in-accord-with-a-rule, no matter how 'simple' of how 'complex' the rule or principle. Many cognitive neuroscientists have lost sight of this distinction.

Seeing Colors

As a final example in our introductory chapter, we will take up for critical examination another mode of neural-Cartesianism within contemporary neuroscientific theorizing: the issue of color vision. Peter Gouras's chapter in the anthology on which we have been commenting will comprise our source.

> "Color is a property of an object. However, the wave-length composition of the light reflected from the object is determined not only by its reflectance, but also by the wave-length composition of the light illuminating it. Since the composition of incident light varies, color vision compensates for this variation so that the object's color appears roughly the same. A lemon, for example, appears yellow whether seen in sunlight (which is whitish), under the light of a tungsten filament bulb (which is reddish) or by fluorescent (bluish) light. This property of color vision is known as color constancy. Color constancy is not entirely foolproof, however, as anyone can testify who has bought paint or a dress in artificial light and later was startled to see it appear as a different shade in daylight... Color vision does not, therefore, simply record the physical parameters of the light reflected from the object's surface. Rather, it is a sophisticated abstracting process. But what sort of abstraction is being

---

[30] Michael Polanyi, *Personal Knowledge* (Illinois: University of Chicago Press, 1958), Chapter Four.

performed? Clearly, the brain must somehow analyze the object in relation to its background..."[31]

Our major point of contention in relation to such claims is, again, conceptual and not empirical. We are not prepared to accept as coherent any account of what it is to see the color of an object that it portray such an achievement in terms of an 'abstracting process'. As explained before, an achievement cannot be decomposed into any sort of 'process'. When we see what color something is, it is rarely a case of trying to see what color it is and succeeding: if this were the ubiquitous or paradigm case of 'seeing what color something is', then some process-version might be workable. But this is manifestly not the case. Secondly, the idea that 'seeing what color something is' must be construed as an 'abstraction' is redolent of the ancient primary/secondary qualities distinction bequeathed to us by Galileo and Descartes.

Let us entertain for a moment (but only for a moment) the plausibility of the contention that the color which an object has is solely a matter of its being a 'cerebral' or 'neuronal' abstraction of some sort. The issue then arises: how is the neuronally abstracted 'color' combined with the object whose color it is? Where is the 'abstraction' re-inscribed into the object? In what does this 'abstraction' consist? And, most significantly, what assures us that the *right* color is inscribed neuronally into the relevant objects? If these are postulated to be merely contingent, causal processes, then, presumably, the chances are not nil that the wrong color will be combined with the object seen. If this is the case, then how can be sure that *any* object has the color that it has?

The primary distinction upon which we insist is that between 'what color something *appears to be*' and 'what color something *is*'. We object to any effort to analyze the latter into the former. On what grounds? Are we here essentially

---

[31] Peter Gouras, "Color Vision" in Kandel et al. (eds.), *Principles of Neural Science*, op. cit., pp. 467-68.

insisting upon a purely 'linguistic' stipulation about which the neuroscientific evidence might be conclusively skeptical, requiring a radical revision of the ways in which we ordinarily speak of such matters as the ordinary identification of colors? Is it conceivably the case that the color which an object has (as distinct from the color which it may appear to have) is a function of the brain's 'analysis' [sic] of the object in relation to its background? We think not. In arguing this, we do not contravene the neurophysiology of color vision in any way: rather, what we contravene is a misconceived gloss overlaid upon the basic neurophysiological facts.

We immediately and readily acknowledge that the ways in which things are visually presented to any observer, the colors which objects possess, are complex functions of the presentational formats and circumstances, along with the ways in which the person (and, indeed, his/her CNS) relates to any such formats and circumstances. So far, there is no dispute. However, the key issue here is this: if the neuroscientist wishes to argue that the colors which objects actually are or have (as distinct from the variable ways in which they may differentially appear) are *themselves* wholly to be analyzed into functions of a relativistic kind (e.g., to the variable, circumstance-specific, environmentally-relative, operations of the CNS) then we part company. First and foremost, before a colored object can *appear* to be such-and-such, something must be determinable as counting as its actually *being* such-and-such. Before I can pretend to V, there must be a case of one's *actually* V-ing. One cannot pretend to V unless there is an already established practice of V-ing *simpliciter*[32]. The same is true for the so-called 'secondary qualities': unless there are cases in which something is red *simpliciter*, there logically cannot be cases in which something might merely 'look' or 'appear to be' red. So, what makes something actually (and not just apparently) red? Is

---

[32] A caveat, derived from a critical remark by Steven Woolgar: of course, the *Star Trek* actors may indeed, in their fictional series, say such things as: 'Beam me up, Scotty!' and there is no real-worldly analogue of any such practice. But, then, this is *not* a case of 'pretending to beam someone up': it is just a wholly fictitious scenario.

this also just a matter of there being a certain impact of milimicrons of wavelengths of light upon the cones of the retinae and their subsequent transduction into our CNS, contingent upon the circumstances of an environment? Does the neurophysiological account explain what it is to be able to see that something *is* 'red'?

Yes and No. Yes, in the sense that, for anyone to be able to see what color something is, there must be normal/normative conditions under which our neurophysiological activity is such that the impact of the milimicrons of wavelengths of light upon our retinal photoreceptors and their subsequent transduction is such as to enable us to see that an object actually *is* red. No, in the sense that unless we have mastered the concept of 'red' (i.e., we have mastered the rules of use, in our language, of the word, which in English is, 'red'), then, no matter how hard we look, we cannot see something which we can tell is red. In other words, unless we know how to use the word 'red' (or whatever other linguistic item expresses what this word expresses in English) then no matter how normally our visual system is operating, we still cannot know what color the object actually is. We certainly cannot 'see that it is red'. As Wittgenstein reminds us:

> "Do not believe that you have the concept of color within you because you look at a colored object – however you look. (Any more than you possess the concept of a negative number by having debts)."[33]

Naturally, the capacity one has to distinguish between e.g., 'red' and 'green' (or between 'red' and any other color) is partly explicable in neuroscientific terms: i.e., our cones and optical nerve are intact, normally functioning, etc., and the object we are looking at is, in fact, properly to be called 'red'. But this is far from being the terminus of the story. Indeed, just as a pre-

---

[33] Ludwig Wittgenstein, *Zettel* (eds.: G. E. M. Anscombe & G. H. von Wright: trans.: G. E. M. Anscombe), Oxford: Basil Blackwell, 1967, para. 332.

linguistic infant can experience what we (concept-users) would call a 'pain' without its being able to tell that what it feels is a 'pain', so also must we say that one might see (what to a concept-user is) something which is 'red' (or 'rouge', 'rojo', 'ahmar', etc.) without being able to tell (to say) that it is 'red' (a 'red object') that one has seen. Hacker remarks:

> "It is only in the context of fairly stable sunlight, fairly constants surface structures, that we introduce our color vocabulary and typically use it. (And were this background wildly unstable, our color grammar would be as useless as tennis equipment on the moon). Once introduced, the concept of normal observational conditions can then be explained as those conditions under which things which are red (sweet, fragrant, etc.) are visibly (perceptibly) red (sweet, fragrant): i.e., those conditions under which the actual perceptual quality of something can be discerned by looking (tasting, smelling, etc.)."[34]

The stable background, in addition to normal neurological processes, enable us to develop our conceptual resources for identifying, naming and telling what colors objects are actually *are*, and not solely what colors some of them may appear to be. There is, thus, no requirement to insist that colors are merely 'mental', 'subjective' or neurophysiological *addenda* to the *other* properties of objects.

In this chapter, we have addressed a sample of problems arising from a certain way of thinking about the role of the brain in relation to our conduct and experience. We shall return to develop further some of the critical arguments we have raised here. One prominent theme has been the issue of materialist reductionism which we have been treating as a source of philosophical – logical, conceptual – confusion. Indeed, we have argued that many of the issues raised are not themselves genuinely scientific ones but are, rather, artifacts of a commitment to a 'materialist metaphysics'. We now turn to discuss this argument in detail.

---

[34] P. M. S. Hacker, *Appearance and Reality* (N. Y.: Basil Blackwell, 1987), p. 128.

CHAPTER TWO

MATERIALIST CONCEPTIONS OF MIND: A REAPPRAISAL

So entrenched are doctrinal contrasts in philosophy and the human sciences that it is assumed that anyone purporting to advance a critique of materialism must be some sort of idealist or Cartesian dualist. The adherence to oversimplified dichotomies is clearly at work in the widespread, but utterly false, characterization of Wittgenstein, who sought to undermine Cartesian mentalism, as "one of the most influential philosophers in the *behaviorist* tradition"[35], to quote a recent source. It is also at work in the claims of some of the defenders of one or another form of mind-brain identity thesis or 'reductive materialism' who miscast their opponents as necessarily embracing dualist assumptions[36]. In this chapter, we shall present a case against various theses in the contemporary philosophy of mind that have been called 'materialist' in inspiration and form. One point which will emerge is that, in fact, dualism and monism in thinking about 'the human mind' are only two faces of the same defective logical coin.

The Origins of Materialism in the Philosophy of Mind

Descartes' 'mind-body dualism' may be summarized as the position according to which a human being comprises two essentially distinct 'substances': the body, a physical, biological – material – entity (the *'res extensa'*) conjoined to a non-corporeal, non-physical, non-biological - immaterial – entity: the mind (the *'res cogitans'*). One of Descartes' earliest and most stringent critics was Julien

---

[35] Paul Churchland, *Matter and Consciousness* (Cambridge, MA: MIT Press, 1984), p. 54, emphasis added.
[36] Paul Churchland clearly makes this assumption in his *Scientific Realism and the Plasticity of Mind* (N.Y.: Cambridge University Press, 1979), p. 110, and in his *Matter and Consciousness*, p. 21 *et seq.*

Offray de la Mettrie. In his book, *L'Homme Machine* (Man, the Machine) published in 1747, La Mettrie, who was a physician and physiologist, sought to argue that all that Descartes had called our 'mental' activities, states, and processes arise from the organization of our physical constitution and involve no inmaterial substance or 'mind-stuff'. A formative influence on the mechanistic materialism of Ludwig Feuerbach, Marx's Young Hegelian precursor in German materialist thought[37], La Mettrie cited evidence to show that physical substances affected thinking (for Descartes, the essence of mentality): fatigue, drugs, diet, pregnancy, diseases of various sorts were all discussed in relation to their effects on thinking[38]. While Descartes had allowed for a mind-body interaction mediated by the pineal gland, La Mettrie proposed that all human mental life could, in principle, be explained in terms of physical states and processes. Since Descartes' position could have no substantive empirical *evidence* to support it, La Mettrie

---

[37] When Feuerbach wrote that he sought to unite the "sanguine principle of French sense-perception and materialism" with the "phlegm of German metaphysics" (*Samtliche Werke*, 2:591, cited in David McLellan, *The Young Hegelians and Karl Marx* (London, 1969), p. 105), it was undoubtedly to La Mettrie's work, among others, that he was referring. Feuerbach's materialism had a considerable impact on the formation of Marx's thought, which, for all of its 'dialectical' subtleties, nonetheless remained fundamentally materialist in its anti-Hegelian (and anti-Cartesian) assumptions about the operation of the human 'mind': "To Hegel," Marx wrote, "*the life-process of the human brain, i.e., the process of thinking*, which, under the name of 'the Idea', he even transforms into an independent subject, is the demiurgos of the real world, and the real world is only the external, phenomenal form of 'the Idea'. With me, on the contrary, the ideal is nothing else than the materials world *reflected by the human mind*, and translated into forms of thought." (*Capital*, vol. 1 [Moscow: Foreign Languages Publishing House, 1954], p. 20: emphasis added. Although here Marx is not reducing thought processes *purely* into brain processes (by analogy to the way in which "bile is secreted by the liver or urine by the kidneys", cf. Franz Mehring, *Karl Marx* [Ann Arbor: University of Michigan Press, 1962], p. 280), allowing a crucial role for "the external world" in the generation of thought, he is clearly under the spell of La Mettrian materialism in identifying the "process of thinking" with "the life-process of the human brain". It is instructive to note in this connection that La Mettrie's enemies among the ecclesiastical authorities "hounded him first out of Paris and then the Netherlands" before he was accepted by the philosophers "at the court of Frederick the Great in Berlin". (Pamela McCorduck, "Artificial Intelligence: An Apercu", *Daedalus*, Winter 1988, issued as vol. 117, no. 1 of the *Proceedings of the American Academy of Arts and Sciences*, 'Artificial Intelligence', p. 71). Although McCorduck claims that after La Mettrie's death in Berlin, these philosophers "discarded his ideas and refused even to mention his name" (*ibid.*), his ideas had an historical impact upon some of the members of the Young Hegelian movement, especially Feuerbach and, through him, on Marx. For an illuminating account of 'scientific materialism' in Germany from Feuerbach to Vogt and Buchner, see Frederick Gregory, *Scientific Materialism in Nineteenth Century Germany* (Boston: D. Reidel, 1977). Cf. Marx Wartofsky, *Feuerbach* (Cambridge: Cambridge University Press, 1977), p. 397.

[38] See P. McCorduck, "Artificial Intelligence", *op. cit.*

insisted that it must remain a purely speculative conjecture whereas his mechanistic approach could, at least, be developed and checked by more and more detailed physiological investigations of the structure and functioning of the human body. Vaucanson's lifelike duck (whose internal mechanisms enabled it to display drinking, eating, quacking, and splashing in water) was a contemporary engineering achievement which figured significantly in the debate inspired by La Mettrie about mechanistic materialism in the eighteenth century.

In the twentieth century, we encounter a similar, albeit more technically advanced, debate between Cartesian dualism (of the kind represented by Sir John Eccles in neurophysiology[39]) and mechanistic materialism (of which there is now a variety of versions[40]). Have the much more substantial neurophysiological data accumulated since Descartes' day, and the displacement of Vaucanson's duck as a materialist icon by the general, multipurpose digital computer (or the parallel-distributed processing system), significantly affected the fundamental terms of the dispute?

We do not think that any of the various contemporary materialist positions are adequate as frameworks for analyzing the mind and the mental. They are, in our view, no more satisfactory than the leading alternative to Cartesianism in the early twentieth century, psychological behaviorism, turned out to be: indeed, in

---

[39] For a recent statement of his position before his death, see Sir John Eccles, "Brain and Mind, Two or One?" in Colin Blakemore and Susan Greenfield (eds.), *Mindwaves: Thoughts on Intelligence, Identity and Consciousness* (Oxford: Basil Blackwell, 1987), pp. 293-304.

[40] Among these are: *central-state materialism* or the mind-brain 'identity' thesis (associated with Ullin Place, J.J.C. Smart, David Armstrong and Herbert Feigl and, in a distinctive 'token-token' form, Donald Davidson); *'emergentist' materialism* (associated with Mario Bunge: see especially his "Emergence and the Mind", *Neuroscience*, 2 [1977], pp. 501-09 and *The Mind-Body Problem* (Oxford: Pergamon, 1980)); *functionalism* (associated with Hilary Putnam, Jerry A. Fodor and Daniel Dennett, though all have since changed their positions in ways which are not fully reconcilable with the original 'Turing-machine functionalist' thesis, especially Putnam, its originator: see his "Reductionism and the Nature of Psychology" in John Haugeland (ed.), *Mind Design* [Vermont: Bradford Books, 1981] and his *Representation and Reality* [Cambridge, MA.: MIT Press, 1988]); and *'eliminative' materialism* (associated with Richard Rorty and Paul and Patricia Churchland).

some respects, they constitute a regression to late-eighteenth- and nineteenth-century mechanistic forms of thought. Their proponents, however, appear to believe that if no form of materialist conceptualization of the mental attributes of mankind can be rendered demonstrable or defensible, then there exists *no* conceivable or, minimally, 'plausible' solution to the mind-body problem. The 'problem', of course, is only recognized as such in virtue of the radical transformation of our thinking about the human *body*, a transformation ushered in by Charles Darwin and his successors in the biological sciences. Dualism and Darwinism clashed, and a solution had to be found which sustained the achievements of Darwinism but which acknowledged the unresolved problem about the nature of 'mind' given our new knowledge about the nature of the human organism. Certainly, no widespread resuscitation of Cartesian dualism appeared likely or desirable (notwithstanding the serious efforts of Eccles, Popper and Beloff, among the few remaining Cartesian dualists in the post-Darwin intellectual period)[41]. Churchland, for example, has argued for a parallel between the solution to the 'vitalist/mechanist' debate about life in the nineteenth century and the current prospects for a resolution in favor of materialism of the mind-body problem:

> "Many thought that living tissue contained or instanced a 'vital principle' that was entirely distinct from anything that mere matter could display, however organized it might be in its merely physical respects... The strength of the suggestion, of course, was inversely proportional to one's familiarity with the great complexity of actual and possible chemical phenomena, and with the explanatory potential of a dynamical and structural chemistry as it was taking shape in the last century... Chemical theory already contained both the conceptual and the technical resources for a systematic attack on the problem of living tissue, construing it as a question of the chemical/structural/dynamical organization of matter... Returning now to the sentient/intelligent behavior of humans, the

---

[41] This is surely to be explained by the predominance of a *philosophical worldview* shaped in large measure by evolutionary biology, engineering and computer sciences, and positivist and realist preconceptions about the nature of 'explanation' in general, as well as by the failure of Cartesians to make their position fully intelligible or generative of empirical research. Churchland makes this point forcefully in what follows.

prospects for a materialist account must be reckoned in much the same fashion. The background weight of a materialist ontology is orders of magnitude greater now than ever before."[42]

Churchland remarks that the potential for explaining "the behavioral properties of humans in terms of the material organization of the nervous system is enormous, immediately available, and partially realized already"[43]. By contrast, 'dualism' in the human sciences, like 'vitalism' in the life sciences, fails to provide any comparable conceptual resources: it also contributes to the neglect of evolutionary continuities in nature. Indeed, "the gulf that appeared to divide the living from the non-living finds no parallel in the case of purposive or intelligent behavior ... [and] we must not forget our own evolutionary history, and its wholly material beginnings."[44]

Problems of the Materialist Theory of Mind

The general intellectual impetus toward the formulation of coherent materialist accounts of the mental properties of human beings is both cogent and persuasive, and it is shared by every contemporary thinker who has attempted to counter the Cartesian dualist story. No modern intellectual can tolerate the idea that our 'minds' set us aside from the rest of nature and create a permanent barrier to scientific (or some other form of nonmystical) explanation. Ryle, for example, spoke of traditional Cartesianism "with deliberate abusiveness, as 'the dogma of

---

[42] Paul Churchland, *Scientific Realism and the Plasticity of Mind, op. cit.*, p. 110. Churchland neglects to mention in this connection the role of Du Bois-Reymond, who, with Brucke, Helmholtz and Ludwig, had signed in 1845 an anti-vitalist oath "to put into power the truth: no other forces than the common physico-chemical ones are active within the organism" but who, in 1872, abandoned reductive materialism in the domain of the mind-body problem and criticized Vogt, a 'scientific materialist', for creating the false impression that "the soul's activity is in its own nature as intelligible from the structure of the brain, as is the secretion from the structure of a gland", adding that the issue of how the brain gives rise to thought is one about which science must confess: *ignoramibus*! (see Stuart G. Shanker, "Review of *Mindwaves*", *Human Studies* 13 [October 1990]).
[43] Churchland, *Scientific Realism.*
[44] *Ibid.*

the Ghost in the Machine'", seeking to prove not only its falsity in detail but its falsity in principle.[45] (However, it should be remembered that Ryle was *also* concerned to show that 'mechanism' is as much of an intellectual bogy as Descartes' 'myth'[46]). Wittgenstein, whose *Blue Book* and *Brown Book* comprised a main source of inspiration for Ryle's and others' efforts to undermine Cartesianism in philosophy, attacked the idea that "the mental world in fact is liable to be imagined as gaseous, or rather, aethereal" and sought to "dissolve" the "problem of the two materials, *mind* and *matter*".[47] Insofar as both thinkers rejected completely the conceptualization of the human mind as constituted by something immaterial ('mind-stuff', 'aethereal' stuff, etc.), then *to this extent* both shared a centrally important point of view with materialists of all stripes.

What is insufficiently recognized – indeed, persistently neglected – by most proponents of anti-Cartesian materialism is that neither Ryle nor Wittgenstein embraced anything we could intelligibly refer to as a 'materialist' conception of mind, and had excellent reasons for rejecting *any* such assimilation of their respective positions, whatever the form of materialism offered for their possible 'incorporation'. Materialism today comprises the identity thesis (the theoretical reduction of 'mind' to [neural] 'matter'), functionalism (the theoretical reduction of 'mind' to a certain functional organization of sensory inputs, internal states and processes, and motor outputs, whatever the physical 'instantiation' of such properties), or eliminativism ('mind' as explainable by reference to biological structures and functions, but denying the possibility of reducing our pretheoretical ('ordinary-language') mental predicates to neurophysiological ones in a one-to-one mapping). The fundamentally *nonmaterial* aspects of the analyses of both Ryle and Wittgenstein, if considered seriously at all as such, are usually dismissed as (1) the products of the precomputer age (although Wittgenstein knew

---

[45] Gilbert Ryle, *The Concept of Mind* (Harmondsworth: Penguin, 1973), p. 17.

[46] *Ibid.*, pp. 74-80.

[47] Ludwig Wittgenstein, 'The Blue Book' in *The Blue and Brown Books* (N.Y.: Harper & Row, 1965), p. 47.

Turing and argued against a Turing-machine model of mentality[48]), (2) functions of a lack of knowledge of – or respect for – the neurosciences and experimental psychology (although Wittgenstein actually did some experimental-psychological work on musical perception), and/or (3) the results of a basically flawed methodology.

Since no materialist critic of Wittgenstein or Ryle has succeeded in undermining or refuting a single conceptual/grammatical point advanced in their respective analyses of the mental *solely* by invoking some specific empirical error, by introducing overlooked empirical information then available, or even by appealing to scientific and/or technical advances made since the time they were writing, it is not necessary to consider objections of types (1) and (2). Where the work of these thinkers has been corrected, the error has not been due to any identifiable *empirical* lacuna but rather to a mistake in what both referred to as 'logical grammar'. Thus a more useful pursuit is to consider objection (3) pertaining to the methodology of this form of inquiry.

Churchland has explicitly attacked the idea that there could be such a thing as a 'conceptual truth', and has argued that "these are not prosperous times for the notion of *a priori* knowledge, in any of its presumed guises, and any philosophical methodology that rests on it must be regarded with suspicion".[49] Claiming that

---

[48] See Stuart G. Shanker, "Wittgenstein versus Turing on the Nature of Church's Thesis", *Notre Dame Journal of Formal Logic*, 23: 4 (1987); Wittgenstein also discussed with Turing the issue of 'learning to count' in his *Lectures on the Foundations of Mathematics* (Chicago: University of Chicago Press, 1976), pp. 31-2, anticipating (and refuting) a Chomsky-type account according to which 'learning to count' is equivalent to 'mastering *No* numerals' (cf. Chomsky's view that 'learning to speak' amounts to 'mastering *No* sentences" in a language). For a more general discussion of Wittgenstein's arguments with Turing on topics in the philosophy of mathematics, see Ray Monk, *Ludwig Wittgenstein: The Duty of Genius* (Harmondsworth: Penguin, 1990), pp. 417-422.

[49] Paul Churchland, "The Continuity of Philosophy and the Sciences", *Mind and Language*, 1 (Spring 1986), pp. 5-6. For a contrasting conception of 'logical truth' deriving from Wittgenstein, see Ilham Dilman's critique of Quine's arguments against what Quine called 'two dogmas of empiricism' in: "Are There Logical Truths?", Dilman, *Quine on Ontology, Necessity, and*

"language, perception, and consciousness" are "such patently *empirical* subjects", he notes that the presumption that such topics might yield to *a priori* considerations should be treated with skepticism.[50]

> "... we might well ask in which books the apodictic fruits of so much *a priori* labor have been written down. There is no such accumulated compendium of important *a priori* truths on any of these topics... But if it is just plain silly to expect this for planets, matter, and life, why should it be sound philosophy to expect it for language, mind, and perception?"[51]

There are several problems raised by these comments. The first concerns the blanket skepticism advocated for conceptual analysis and its results in the absence of any adequate formulation of specific or representative examples of it. Leaving aside the interesting but secondary question of whether logico-grammatical analyses can yield *a priori* knowledge in the strictly Kantian sense, it could certainly be claimed that there exist *many* monographs and compendia in which the fruits of conceptual analysis (*especially* in the philosophy of mind) are available for scrutiny.[52] Granted, the best of such work is comparatively recent in the history of philosophy itself, but then presumably Churchland would acknowledge that the best *science* in the field is comparatively recent also. It is not only scientists who stand on the shoulders of giants, and perhaps sometimes modern philosophers have seen further – and differently – than their forebears. More telling, however, is the explicit assumption that 'language', 'perception', 'mind' and 'consciousness' are somehow purely *empirical* topics, and should be regarded as investigable phenomena just as we regard the structure of physical

---

Experience: A Philosophical Critique (Albany: State University of New York Press, 1984), pp. 72-105.

[50] Churchland, "Continuity", p. 6: emphasis added.

[51] *Ibid.*, p. 8.

[52] Conceptual analysis certainly does not claim a priori knowledge of empirical fact, maintaining that philosophical reflection encompasses rule-like understandings, and that any 'a priori knowledge' it might have consists in an understanding of rules, not in any amazing but implausible advance grasp on what empirical investigations will reveal. Churchland rides roughshod over the difference between a rule and an empirical proposition, between the requirements for the intelligible use of an expression and the means of determining the truth of an intelligible proposition.

objects, planets, life (an earlier list contains: "light, matter... fire, cosmology... weather, medicine"[53]). This surely begs the major questions at issue: *in what sense* are 'language', 'mind', 'consciousness', 'perception', *empirical phenomena*, if at all, and, if it is conceded that *some* dimensions of their study are genuinely empirical (and not just metaphysics masquerading as empirical science), does this mean that *every* aspect of their study must or should be 'empirical'? What are the limits of *empiricism* here? Would a conceptual inquiry employing empirical examples or instances be 'empirical' or '*a priori*'?

Consider, first, 'language' as a topic for analytical investigation. Is 'language' an empirical phenomenon? Chomsky argued that a language can be adequately analyzed only by the use of mathematical techniques (especially the use of recursive-function theory) and he disavowed *any* appeal to actual instances of 'usage' or 'talk' as his 'data', arguing for a priority for the linguist's own 'intuitions', proclaiming the 'pragmatics' of languages to be degenerate in contrast to the *real* subject-matter: linguistic competence construed in Cartesian-mentalistic terms. The products of the grammarian's intuitive reflection (the grammarian's 'hypothetical sentences') scarcely amount to empirically-collected data in the usual scientific sense, and indeed there is no good reason to suppose that sentences which professional linguists make up are 'data' in any real sense. Would the Chomskian corpus qualify as 'empirical' inquiry, or is it, being *essentially* mathematical, *a priori*? Some linguists (e.g., Katz[54]) consider language in Platonist terms to be an 'abstract object' (and the Platonist philosophy here, of course, is closely tied to its deployment in the philosophy of *mathematics*). Other investigators argue that language cannot directly be apprehended as such (i.e., as an 'object' of study, comparable to plants or planets), and that only human *discourse*, oral and textual, qualifies as an empirical (observable, recordable,

---

[53] *Ibid.*, p. 7.
[54] J. J. Katz, *Language and Other Abstract Objects* (Totowa, N.J: Rowman & Littlefield, 1981).

reproducible) object of study. (We have in mind the conversation, discourse, textual, sociolinguistic and pragmatics analysts, among others).

More pointedly, perhaps, one can raise the question of the exact extent to which human behavior itself is an *empirical* phenomenon. Before considering the putatively empirical status of mind and consciousness, it is as well to ask ourselves how human conduct can be identified, individuated, observed, etc., in accord with the tenets of *any* acceptable form of empiricism. This issue is especially pertinent for Churchland's materialist arguments, given his stated view that a materialist ontology provides the potential for "explaining the behavioral properties of humans in terms of the material organization of the nervous system".[55] This all depends upon what exactly we are prepared to identify as the *explananda*. Undoubtedly, there are many movements which human beings make which are facilitated by (chains of) events occurring in their CNSs, and some of these (various involuntary ones) are no doubt *caused* by such events such that their causes completely explain their occurrence. Yet within the domain of the 'philosophy of action', conceptual analysts in the post-Wittgensteinian tradition such as Hamlyn, Hart, White, Ebersole, Harrison and Pitkin, to name but a few, have demonstrated the critical distinctions which obtain between descriptions of a (human) body's *movements*, descriptions of a *person* moving (parts of) his body, and descriptions of what a person is doing, of what *activity* he is engaged in. It is not only against behavioristic efforts to reduce human conduct to (sequences of) 'colorless bodily movements', 'organismic responses' and the like that such distinctions have been registered; they are constraints against *all* forms of comprehensive biological reductionism in the domain of human action. There are several levels to these arguments.

The first pertains to the difference between saying of a person's *body* that *it* moved and saying of a *person* that *he/she* moved. These characterizations are

---

[55] Churchland, *Scientific Realism and the Plasticity of Mind, op. cit.*, p. 110.

not interchangeable: the former is not a more exact or 'scientific' description of the latter, but a description of a wholly different state of affairs, one typically involving contexts of *involuntariness*.[56] It will not suffice to posit a reduction of an action to its component biological or organic features, since any single description of the latter is compatible with a wide array of different actions: there is no one-to-one correspondence between a description of the bodily components of an activity and a description of the activity being engaged in. Consider the flexing of one's right index finger. This may be fully characterized in terms of neuronal firings, muscle movements, etc., as Carlson has elegantly shown:

"The entry of Ca++ into the cytoplasm of a single muscle fiber triggers a series of events that results in movement of the myosin cross bridges. These protrusions alternately attach to the actin strands, bend in one direction, detach themselves, bend back, reattach to the actin, etc. The cross bridges thus 'row' along the actin filaments... A single impulse of a motor neuron will produce a single twitch of a muscle fiber".[57]

Nothing here has informed us about what *conduct* one is engaged in. One may, alternatively, be simply flexing one's (cramped) forefinger, beckoning someone, pulling the trigger of a gun one is holding, killing someone, murdering someone, giving an example of a simple human action in front of a class, gesturing in code, et., etc. By holding my arm upward and moving my outstretched palm subtending an arc of 30 degrees from left to right, one may,

---

[56] In this connection, it is worth noting that the correct reply to Wittgenstein's question, "what is left over if I subtract the fact that my arm goes up from the fact that I raise my arm?" (*Philosophical Investigations*, trans. G. E. M. Anscombe [N.Y.: Macmillan, 1968], para. 621) does not require reference to differential neural events/processes any more than it requires reference to an 'act of will'. The point is to deny that the former description is logically applicable to the latter. That is to say, when 'I raise my arm', this is an irreducibly distinct state of affairs from that in which 'my arm goes up'. The latter describes an occasion in which, e.g., "I place myself sideways close to a wall, my wall-side arm hanging down outstretched, the back of the hand touching the wall, and if now keeping the arm rigid I press the back of the hand hard against the wall, doing it all by means of the deltoid muscle, if then I quickly step away from the wall, letting my arm hang down loosely, my arm without any action of mine, of its own accord begins to rise..." (Wittgenstein, *The Blue and Brown Books*, *op. cit.*, p. 151). When I raise my arm, *my arm* does not *raise*: *I raise* it!

[57] N. R. Carlson, *Physiology of Behavior* (Boston: Allyn & Bacon, 1981), pp. 288-89.

alternatively, be greeting someone, bidding farewell, hailing a cab, trying to attract someone's attention, simulating any of these things in a theatrical setting, etc. By flexing one's circumoral muscles one may be smiling at someone, sneering at someone, commencing to laugh, etc. Note that the non-isomorphism of movements and actions involves the converse: one may greet someone (a simple action) by, *inter alia*, winking at them, saying 'Hi', nodding to them, grasping their hand, etc., each of which comprises a wholly different configuration of my body. And many activities can be performed without observably or relevantly altering one's bodily comportment at all, as when one 'refuses to answer a question', 'withholds vital information', 'snubs' someone, etc., by not making any physical movement through some specific interactional moment. Explanations of the physical components of someone's behavior, then, in probably the vast majority of cases (especially when we broaden the domain of actions to encompass speech acts) are not even at the right conceptual level to qualify as relevant to the explanation of one's conduct.

In addition, we confront the vexed questions of the *socially-organized, context-dependent* character of human actions, the problematics of action-*individuation*, and the *ethical* issues involved in ascribing actions of a wide range of types, topics familiar in the conceptual analysis of conduct, but overlooked entirely by programs such as Churchland's. Feinberg illuminated the 'individuation' issue nicely in the following:

> "... an act, like the folding of a musical instrument [an accordion], can be squeezed down to a minimum or else stretched out. He turned the key, he opened the door, he startled Smith, he killed Smith – all of these are things we might say that Jones *did* with one identical set of bodily movements. Because of the accordion effect we can usually replace any ascription to a person of causal responsibility by an ascription of agency or authorship. We can, if we wish, puff out an action to include an effect, and more often than not our language obliges us by providing a relatively complex action word for the purpose. Instead of saying Smith did A (a relatively simple act) and thereby caused X in Y, we might say something of the form

'Smith X-ed Y': instead of 'Smith opened the door causing Jones to be startled', 'Smith startled Jones'".[58]

The neurobiological account of those human muscular operations involved in key-turning (and, obviously, in other forms of conduct), however sophisticated and informative in itself, cannot be explanatorily informative with respect to either the turning of the key, the opening of the door, the startling of Smith or his being killed. Nor should anyone expect otherwise. Moreover, these descriptions of the action[59] in question are clearly differentially intelligible and relevant in different contexts. There is no logical space for a context-neutral specification of a human action. Solutions to theoretical problems involved in explaining sensorimotor coordination by employing a model of state-space point representation and coordinate transformation in the brain[60] cannot constitute explanations of human *actions*.

How can we be so sure about all this? After all, don't we have to agree with the materialists that human actions are exclusively the productions of human *bodies*? And aren't human bodies biological phenomena through and through? There are significant distinctions to be respected, on pain of incoherence, between the concept of a 'human being' (a 'person') and of a 'human body', and these have nothing to do with the existence of any sort of mysterious addendum which converts human bodies into people.[61] Rather, the differences are grammatical, and

[58] Joel Feinberg, "Action and Responsibility" in Alan R. White (ed.), *The Philosophy of Action* (Oxford: Oxford University Press, 1968), pp. 106-07.
[59] In speaking here of 'the action', it is being assumed that issues of individuation of act from consequence can be settled unambiguously and indefeasibly in this or *any* case, which is a strong assumption to make...
[60] For an account of this approach, see Paul Churchland, "Cognitive Neurobiology: A Computational Hypothesis for Laminar Cortex", *Biology and Philosophy*, 1:1 (1986).
[61] A 'person' exists in the space created by his or her life, cumulative experience, enculturation, and relationships, and on the same logical level as these, realized through placements, configurations and trajectories of the whole body, which placements, configurations and trajectories are not reducible, either, to physiological properties of persons' bodies. A related point is to be wary of the concertina-like expansion and contraction of the expression 'biological' – everyone agrees that language is related to biological nature (humans have it, lice do not), but this does not mean that the understanding of linguistic phenomena has to fall under the disciplinary

they establish logical constraints upon the applicability of predicates and schemes of explanation which might otherwise mistakenly be thought to apply, across the board, to both bodies and persons. We do not, when we look at someone's face, see only anatomical details (unless we have a very special reason for looking at it in that way) such that we must always *add* something (by inference, presumably) before we can see his or her sadness, joy, concentration, interest, recognition, etc. Wittgenstein gave a particularly helpful example in this connection:

> "'I see that the child wants to touch the dog, but doesn't dare.' How can I see that? – Is this description of what is seen on the same level as a description of moving shapes and colors? Is an interpretation in question? Well, remember that you may also mimic a human being who would like to touch something, but doesn't dare. And what you mimic is after all a piece of behavior. But you will perhaps be able to give a *characteristic* imitation of this behavior only in a wider context... "[62]

It is true that some predicates true of human bodies are *eo ipso* true of persons, but there are many important cases in which this interchangeability does not hold. Hacker furnishes several examples in the context of his discussion of Wittgenstein's reflections.[63] If my body weighs 170 pounds, then I weigh 170 pounds; if my body is out of condition, then I am out of condition: but I may be ashamed of myself without being ashamed of my body, and I might be proud of myself without being proud of my body. I will cease to exist before my body ceases to exist, for when I die I leave my remains behind. You may like some person without liking his or her body, and *vice versa*. A person is not identical with his or her body: a person has a body – does a body have a body? No eliminativist, reductionist or other program of ontological materialism can be fully reconciled with these distinctions in logical grammar. And, if these distinctions

---

provenance of biology, nor does it *require* the postulation (however speculative) of specific formations of neural circuitry.

[62] Ludwig Wittgenstein, *Remarks on the Philosophy of Psychology, Vol. 1*, ed. G. E. M. Anscombe & G. H. von Wright (Oxford: Basil Blackwell, 1980), para. 1066.

[63] P. M. S. Hacker, *Wittgenstein: Meaning and Mind, op. cit.*, pp. 247-49. Hacker also discusses Wittgenstein's analysis of the concept of 'I' in related terms. See pp. 483-93.

are simply ignored (e.g., 'for the purposes of theorizing') the phenomena (of human conduct, of corporeality and of personhood) to be explained have merely been stipulatively and generically *redescribed* to fit the arbitrary requirements of a preexisting commitment, or distorted to suit its needs. A good example of this latter proclivity can be found in an early programmatic assertion by Jerry Fodor:

> "There is, obviously, a horribly difficult problem about what determines what a person (as distinct from his body, or parts of his body) did.... But whatever relevance the distinction [has]... there is no particular reason to suppose that it is relevant to the purposes of cognitive psychology."[64]

So much the worse for 'cognitive psychology', then! If there are logical barriers to the explanatory programs of materialist (neurobiological) reductionism in the domain of concrete human actions, the situation is even more precarious in the domain of the *mental*, and this is not because the mental predicates are concepts of immaterial phenomena. Although Descartes clearly believed that the *res cogitans* is responsible for those mental activities which he considered unattributable to bodies, we do not have to follow him in this: mental predicates are attributable to *persons*. People are not dichotomously analyzeable into bodies with mental addenda. More importantly, the idea that our 'mental' predicates are names of *activities* (events or processes) going on in some immaterial zone, invisible to all but their agents, is a tissue of confusion against which Ryle and Wittgenstein leveled some of their most powerfully effective counterarguments. 'Understanding', 'remembering', 'recognizing', 'seeing', 'perceiving', 'realizing', 'knowing' and a host of related predicates are *not* concepts of activities or processes at all, *a fortiori* not concepts of mental activities or processes. They are (defeasible) achievement verbs, 'result' or 'success' verbs, akin to ability or capacity concepts. 'Believing' and 'thinking' are likewise, although for very different logicogrammatical reasons, not activity or process verbs. Neither are they simply dispositional verbs. Their logical grammars are more complex and

---

[64] Jerry A. Fodor, *The Language of Thought* (N.Y.: Thomas Y. Crowell Company, 1975), p. 52.

variegated than that. Instead of confronting these complexities squarely, materialists of all stripes tend to homogenize their classifications; some have even treated these (and other) 'mental' predicates as 'natural-kind' designators, ripe for simple reduction to or identification with neural phenomena, while others (the eliminativists), seeing the futility of such efforts, seek to dispense with the mental predicates altogether while still, *mirabile dictu*, aspiring to address themselves to the investigation of the human mind.

Some, like Rorty, concede "a whole raft of mental states to Ryle" but still remain hesitant about the ontological status of "pains, mental images, and occurrent thoughts – short-term mental states which look, so to speak, event-like rather than disposition-like".[65] From such qualms, the issue of their possibly nonphysical status arises. Note, however, that we are not given a clear analysis of the concept of the physical at all in this connection, aside from a reference to spatiotemporal location as a supposedly essential, constitutive property[66] – but then one wonders what to make of such perfectly intelligible expressions as: 'physical illness', 'physical needs', 'physical capacities', 'physical beauty', etc. Why classify pains as mental, especially when we speak routinely of *physical* pain, and distinguish this from, e.g., *mental anguish*. Why should we allow thoughts to be construed as states (especially after Brentano and Husserl demonstrated via their Intentionality thesis that thoughts cannot be separated from their object-complements)? Why should mental images themselves be construed as events, rather than, say, the having of them?

---

[65] Richard Rorty, *Philosophy and the Mirror of Nature* (Princeton: Princeton University Press, 1979), pp. 18-19.
[66] Rorty claims that "… it is hard to see more in the notion of being 'physical' than being 'material' or 'spatio-temporal'". (*Ibid.*, p. 20). We shall return to this theme more systematically when we discuss the 'problem of consciousness'.

Rorty expresses a sentiment quite widely shared among materialists:

"What more could a defender of mind-body identity ask for than the admission that talk of how one *feels* is just an alternative way of reporting on how suitable portions of one's anatomy (presumably neurons) *are*?"[67]

Disregarding for a moment the major issue begged by this quoted fragment, viz., the notion that the concept of 'mind' is best construed as the concept of some kind of phenomenon which might be theoretically reduced to another phenomenon (e.g., a body or its parts), notice how Rorty assumes that talk of how one 'feels' might be construed generically as a sort of 'report'. It is as if Austin had never written anything about the 'descriptive fallacy' and Wittgenstein had never articulated the analysis of a first-person avowal of sensation as (a component aspect of its) *expression* in contrast to its being a 'description' or 'report'. But in addition to this, consider the strangeness of being told to imagine that one's first-person expressions of, e.g., pain, are merely "alternative ways of reporting on how suitable portions of one's anatomy... *are*". It is radically unclear what this passage could possibly mean, let alone how one might aspire to adjudicate its truth. If one complains about a pain in one's leg, is one doing something that could be paraphrased without residue into, or conceived as an equivalent to, asserting something in physiological terms about how a part of one's anatomy *is*, that, for example, one's left leg is penetrated by a sharp projectile? Surely that would, at best, be to assert a *cause of* one's pain. And what are we to make of the suggestion that the genuine (real, authentic, scientific) 'alternative' account would consist in a report on the state of one's neurons? The 'suitable portion' of one's anatomy here is surely one's *leg*, not one's neurons! Even though C-fiber firings may enable one to experience *the pain in one's leg*, why on earth should the avowal of the pain in one's *leg* be treated as an 'alternative description' to a report on something going on in one's *brain*? After all, one did not 'feel' anything in one's brain! And this is where Rorty began –

---

[67] *Ibid.*, p. 19.

with the claim that "talk of how one *feels* is just an alternative way of reporting on how... [neurons] *are*". When someone talks about how he feels, he is not remotely interested in, let alone offering a substitutable description of, his neurons. This would be tantamount to proposing that whenever someone cries out, he does so out of ignorance of the description of the causal condition of his anatomy which precipitated the cry. It will not suffice to argue that we might one day be in a position to substitute detailed and correct descriptions of our neuronal states and events here, for one cannot conceptualize an account of the causal conditions or enablements of something as the same thing for which the causal condition or enablement can be specified. The dilemma for the materialist, then, is this: either the statements in neurological terms are translations of what we ordinarily say, in which case there is no reason to substitute them for after all 'there's a pain in my leg' just means whatever the neurological description says, or they do not mean the same, in which case one cannot substitute one for the other without loss.

Churchland begs even stranger questions in his discourse about 'sensations-of-red'.[68] For one does not actually (in normal circumstances, at least) ever have a 'sensation' of red: one may spot something which is red, gaze at it, look at it, stare at it, notice it, etc., all of which, incidentally, comprise quite diverse perceptual circumstances or states of affairs. But what could it mean to 'have a sensation' of 'red'? One might have a sensation such as being momentarily blinded by the glare of a red object, but if one simply sees something which is red, that does not license any talk of 'sensation'. In attempting to argue for a reductionist claim, Churchland conflates perception with sensation. He wants to propose that "the qualitative character of my sensation-of-red is really a spiking frequency of 90 hertz in a certain neural pathway".[69] But seeing something red is not to have any discernible sensation at all. Note as well that 'seeing' is an

---

[68] Paul Churchland, *Matter and Consciousness, op. cit.*, p. 40.
[69] *Ibid.*

achievement-verb, and that even genuine sensation words like 'pain' cannot be adequately analyzed without residue into the phenomena causally related to them.

Invoking the standard analogy with the relationship between the temperature of a gas and the mean kinetic energy of the molecules of the gas, Churchland countenances a reduction such as the following: "... joy-in-a-human = resonances in the lateral hypothalamus".[70] How restrictive an analysis of the concept of 'joy' this is, even granting the involvement of events in the lateral hypothalamus. Joy is, after all, a complex concept whose elucidation requires reference to specifications of forms of human activity, situations and objects, natural reactions, sensations, propensities and so forth of quite variable combination and manifestation in a human being. None of this is to deny for one moment that something correlative may be taking place in a human brain, but not even the most impoverished characterization of the multiplicity of the forms of joy could succumb to such a meager and homogenizing semantics as the claim that all it consists in is a specific and unitary phenomenon such as a 'resonance' in a part of the brain. This is a neuroscientific 'identity' conceit taken too far. Wittgenstein, for example, remarked that one can see 'consciousness', and a "particular *shade* of consciousness", in another's *face*: "You see on it, in it, joy, indifference, interest, excitement, torpor and so on... "[71] Would an expression of joy have to be construed as an ignorant substitute for a description couched in neurophysiological terms? And why should anyone even be interested in neurophysiology in this way in the rounds of their actual daily affairs? Some may be, but would this make their spontaneous emotional expressions the equivalent of vulgar approximations to theoretical assertions in science? Eliminativist approaches to problems of mind and experience are surely among the least promising candidates for their elucidation.

---

[70] *Ibid.*, p. 42.
[71] Ludwig Wittgenstein, *Zettel*, eds. G. E. M. Anscombe and G. H. von Wright (Oxford: Basil Blackwell, 1967), para. 220.

The 'Mental' and the 'Physical'

Rorty's passing comment that "the opposite of 'mental' is 'physical'"[72] betrays a common oversimplification of our conceptual resources. Such an oversimplification has been the historical hallmark of most discussions of Descartes' conception of human beings. After all, for Descartes himself this antinomy appeared compelling, just as for the behaviorists this fundamental ontological dichotomy is preserved in the distinction between 'observable, physical behavior' on the one hand and 'mental phenomena' on the other – tacitly acknowledging the Cartesian dualist conception, even if most behaviorists were (at least methodological) anti-mentalists. Dichotomies, however, sometimes prove to be impoverished as classification schemes, and in these domains the lesson to be learned is that such school-book-grammar 'opposites' often do more to obfuscate than to illuminate the available conceptual possibilities which language makes available to us. If we do explore these resources without theoretical preconceptions, we can fail to recognize their richness. To insist that, e.g., 'thinking' *must* be *either* 'mental' *or* 'physical' is to prejudge the analysis of the rules of use of the concept which grammar affords, and leads to theoretical wrangling where detailed, unprejudiced explication of uses-in-contexts would serve us better. It turns out that *neither* category ('mental' or 'physical') is helpful in the analysis of what thinking is (what count as cases of 'thinking') in the life world. Moreover, restrictions upon analysis which turn upon insisting upon the ubiquitous relevance of the 'mental/physical' dichotomy end up operating as blinkers: we have a propensity to conceive of the mental and the physical as necessarily comprising 'states', 'processes' 'events' or 'occurrences'. From there, as Wittgenstein observed:

---

[72] Rorty, *Philosophy and the Mirror of Nature*, *op. cit.*, p. 20.

"We talk of processes and states and leave their nature undecided. Sometime perhaps we shall know more about them – we think. But that is what commits us to a particular way of looking at the matter. (*The decisive movement in the conjuring trick has been made, and it was the very one we thought quite innocent*). – And now the analogy which was to make us understand our thoughts falls to pieces. So we have to deny the yet uncomprehended process in the yet unexplored medium. And now it looks as if we had denied mental processes. And naturally we don't want to deny them."[73]

The characterization of 'thinking' as a process 'in the mind' is radically misleading in that it encourages analogies with physical processes such as fermentation, digestion, or neuronal firing sequences, none of whose properties (except for temporal duration) are predicable of thinking. The basic issue is to note that 'thinking' is not by itself a sufficiently rich or full predicate for specifying what someone who is doing it is actually doing! After all, to say of someone *only* that he or she is 'thinking', when the context does not itself provide for a fuller specification, begs the question of 'what' the individual is thinking (of, about, etc.), as well as in what the 'thinking' actually consisted: was it, e.g., reflecting on the day's events? Trying to recollect where some object has been placed? Pondering the racing odds? Calculating a sum 'in one's head'? Trying to find the right translation for a sentence in a foreign language? And so on... Being told that someone is 'thinking' *simpliciter* is not yet to have been told what that person is doing, what activity (or 'process') he or she is engaged in.[74]

Rorty remarks:

"... why should we be troubled by Leibniz's point that if the brain were blown up to the size of a factory, so that we could stroll through it, we should not see thoughts? If we know enough neural correlations, we shall

---

[73] Ludwig Wittgenstein, *Philosophical Investigations, op. cit.*, para. 308: emphasis added.

[74] For a fuller discussion of the problems raised by equating 'thinking' with a putative 'process in the mind', see Hacker, *Wittgenstein: Meaning and Mind, op. cit.*, pp. 308-12.

indeed see thoughts – in the sense that our vision will reveal to us what thoughts the possessor of the brain is having."[75]

Addressing himself to a similar reflection, only this time in Cartesian terms, Wittgenstein noted that: "If God had looked into our minds he would not have been able to see there whom we were speaking of."[76] Substitute 'thinking of' for 'speaking of', and we have a flat contradiction of the idea that a god might, by having privileged access to our silent soliloquies, thereby know of what (of whom) we were thinking. The point is that no soliloquy, silent or spoken, in itself, independent of any contextual information whatsoever, can reveal to someone (even a god) of what or of whom we are 'thinking'. After all, any such locution can express very different thoughts depending upon the circumstances of its (silent) articulation. By parity of reasoning, the same argument can be leveled against Rorty's neurologistic *gedankenexperiment* concerning thinking. No matter what neurophysiological phenomena have been correlated with some silent soliloquy, one cannot read off what *thought* has been expressed by any such soliloquy without knowing in what circumstances and for what purpose(s) it has been produced. Leibniz's point is ultimately vindicated by a conceptual argument.

Our concepts of the 'mental' are explicable by reference to behavioral and circumstantial criteria. Some of these are indeed 'organic' in the extended sense in which Hunter speaks of the 'organic' nature of our 'form of life':

"We do not generally include in the biological what is overt, what is learned, what is done at will or what is intelligent, but only what goes on within us, unaware and without our direction. Yet we can move by easy stages from automatic, unwilled, non-conscious processes like nutrition, through reflex actions, many of which are learned or at least *acquired*, and which, though not done at will, can often be *resisted* at will; then through speaking and writing just insofar as it is forming the words with our mouths or drawing the characters on paper, where, though we may form a

---

[75] Rorty, *Philosophy and the Mirror of Nature*, op. cit., p. 26.
[76] Wittgenstein, *Philosophical Investigations*, p. 217e.

word at will, we do not (generally) will the physical manner of our forming it; to, finally, expressing ourselves *in a certain way*, where although it is generally done at will, we do not will the *willing* of it... "[77]

Wittgenstein viewed many of our practices as rooted in our natural forms of life: "Commanding, questioning, recounting, chatting, are as much part of our natural history as walking, eating, drinking, playing."[78] That we generally laugh when amused, cry out when in pain, look in the direction pointed toward, react effectively to training, follow rules 'blindly', utter the 'appropriate words' spontaneously, unreflectingly, without hesitation, all these are aspects of the natural history and form of life of living human beings, and comprise common behavioral phenomena and resources of the species within which are formed the socially-shared, rule-governed concepts we have, including our concepts of the 'mental'. Because the behaviorists had a propensity to regiment, formalize, decontextualize and operationalize these dimensions of our lives, we have, in response, tended to let our consideration of them wander in the opposite direction, toward the *over-intellectualization* of these primordially natural, human functions - and then we begin to lose our grip on their *naturalness* in favor of mentalistic stories involving cognitive 'structures', internal rule-systems, and the rest of the apparatus of the putatively 'hidden mechanisms of the mind' which will one day reduce to those of the brain.

An essential feature of the natural history of humanity is its *sociality*. If our natural, organically given human reactions and responses were not attuned to one another's, if there were no such thing as what Wittgenstein termed "agreement ... in form of life"[79], no common conceptualization could be established, no 'grammar' could work. If people varied randomly in the ways in which they naturally react to pain, for example, there would be no anchor for the

---

[77] J. F. M. Hunter, "'Forms of Life' in Wittgenstein's *Philosophical Investigations*" in E. D. Klemke (ed.), *Essays on Wittgenstein* (Urbana: University of Illinois Press, 1971), p. 278.
[78] Wittgenstein, *Philosophical* Investigations, para. 25.
[79] *Ibid*., para. 241.

concept of 'pain'. If no child ever laid claim to having (had) vivid experiences of all sorts on waking up from sleep, there would be no anchor for the concept of 'dream' to emerge in our lives. If our discriminatory capacities varied extremely widely, we could share no common perceptual vocabulary. There is no *a priori* guarantee in all of this: facts of natural history are *contingent* facts. However, the stability and permanence of so much of our endowment as a species enables us to make sense of each other: "The *common behavior of mankind* is the system of reference by which we interpret an *unknown* language."[80]

Stressing the "extremely general facts of nature"[81] and our "animality"[82] in connection with our conceptual capacities, as Wittgenstein did, is by no means an invitation to physicalistic or biological reductionism, nor is it a license for any generic materialist metaphysics. Taken in conjunction with his incessant emphasis upon the social character of our human nature, these remarks lead us toward a respecification of the dichotomy of the 'natural' and the 'cultural'. Speaking a language is a natural fact of human *praxis*, but languages are, *par excellence*, sociocultural phenomena.

---

[80] *Ibid.*, para. 206: emphasis added.

[81] *Ibid.*, p. 56e.

[82] Ludwig Wittgenstein, *On Certainty*, eds. G. E. M. Anscombe and G. H. von Wright (Oxford: Basil Blackwell, 1969), para. 359.

CHAPTER THREE

NEURAL CAUSATION AND FREEDOM OF ACTION

In our opening chapter we briefly discussed some observations of Claude Ghez pertaining to 'voluntary' movements. In contradistinction to the exclusive focus on motor functions, some contemporary researchers and theorists have sought to address the issue of 'voluntary' behavior in neuroscientific terms, and we seek to address this issue more fully in the ensuing discussion. Kosslyn and Koenig formulate the issue in a way which appears to displace the role of human agency by asking not: 'who' decides what to do next? – but rather: "*What* decides what to do next? We have inferred that there must be a 'decision subsystem' [in the brain] but have not said much about it."[83] Johnson-Laird also asserts that in efforts to explain human conduct in exclusively neuroscientific terms, theorists must confront what he calls "the problem of 'control'" of voluntary actions.[84] This 'problem' is construed as one of locating within the brain the center or centers of control over 'voluntary' actions, as distinct from those neurophysiological events and processes responsible for 'involuntary' movements. Thorp, for instance, argues that a mutually exclusive and exhaustive polarity in conceiving of human conduct comprises the distinction between the 'voluntary' and the 'involuntary' such that, pervasive in most anatomy and physiology texts, it is invoked to distinguish between cases in which some organ or muscle is 'subject to the will' or to 'conscious control' and cases where this is not so.[85] Thus: "The beating of the heart is not subject to the will, but the opening and closing of the epiglottis

---

[83] Stephen M. Kosslyn and Olivier Koenig, *Wet Mind: The New Cognitive Neuroscience* (N.Y.: Free Press, 1995), p. 401. Emphasis added.

[84] Philip Johnson-Laird, "How could consciousness arise from the computations of the brain?" in Colin Blakemore and Susan Greenfield (eds.), *Mindwaves: Thoughts on Intelligence, Identity and Consciousness* (Oxford: Basil Blackwell, 1987), p. 248.

[85] John Thorp, *Free Will: A Defence Against Neurophysiological Determinism* (London: Routledge & Kegan Paul, 1980).

is."[86] On the basis of applying this distinction, he observes, allusions are very often subsequently made to some 'higher' (or 'deeper') centers in the brain as the hypothetical locus for what is variously referred to as 'executive control' or 'higher-order decision-making' for those organs thought to be 'subject to the will'. Recent experiments on so-called 'bio-feedback' seem to show that even the rate of the human heart-beat can, within distinct limits, be subject to the exercise of 'will power'. This only deepens the sense of mystery with which we wish to deal.

The mystery is established as such by the strong conviction that human bodies, in every facet of their physical operations, are governed by lawful causal mechanisms, and the introduction of concepts like 'the will' or 'will power' *seems* to subvert that intuition. Thorp argues that anyone acknowledging the 'existence' of 'the will' is confronted with a conundrum, that of reconciling our essentially deterministic views about the operations of electro-chemical, biochemical and physiological phenomena involved in facilitating the movements of our bodies or parts thereof with the idea that we as persons ourselves can exert conscious control over (at least some of) our behaviors. Thus, we can, in some instances, refrain from doing something that we seem otherwise unable to avoid doing, and, in other instances, we can do something with considerable effort which otherwise we could not (normally) do. Some thinkers have sought to pacify this problem by postulating *in*determinism as a characteristic property of certain neural phenomena (by analogy with quantum phenomena), but this option does not help in settling the matter: bondage to deterministic processes is replaced with an hypothetical bondage to *randomness*, and neither of these forms of bondage seems to be compatible with our ordinary, everyday notions of self-control, of free decision-making, of personal responsibility and so on.

---

[86] *Ibid.*, p. 127.

The Problem of Determinism

Determinism has, of course, been classically counterposed to freedom of will. We may think that we are free to do what we want to do or decide to do, that it is entirely up to each one of us what our own next action will be. We do not *have* to do any specific next thing, but can do whatever we might like to do. But then when we think 'scientifically' about ourselves, this intuition is at odds with the view that events in the world – including our individual actions – are subject to lawful regulation and the laws that regulate us state causal connections between events and their successors. To hold to the view that we are free to do whatever we would like surely places us in a contradiction with what, *faute de mieux*, we believe because we accept science. If what neuroscience, for example, tells us is true, then we appear to be driven to the conclusion that our next doing, like every other event in the universe, must be subject to the laws of the universe and the causal compulsions that these laws enumerate. Whatever we do next will be explained, will it not, by these laws, through the identification of initial conditions and the deduction of effects. What we do *must* be determined in both senses of the word: (a) *if* we knew enough laws, and *if* we knew enough about initial conditions, then we could figure out, could *determine*, each individual's next action in advance of their supposedly deciding 'what to do' and (b) whatever people believe about their freedom to act, what they do is not down to them but is compelled by, determined by, nature's laws (here as instantiated in the laws discovered by neuroscience).

Descartes, Kant and others in the modern philosophical pantheon, had a way to address this issue: determinism pertains to the body, but free will to the mind. The mind is a transcendentally rational seat of agency, controlling those actions we deem 'voluntary' and giving us our dual natures as both rational *and* law-governed beings. But as soon as the materialist turn is made, and the metaphysical *res cogitans* – the Cartesian 'mind' – is expelled from the world-picture, the Laplacean conception of material nature as wholly deterministic leaves us without any transcendental source of free agency such as the Cartesian picture offered. The problem is now acute, since, in a post-Cartesian frame of reference, it is admitted that nothing inside the human being is 'transcendental' in the required sense, i.e., exempt from the causal control of the essentially material, physical, phenomena of the brain and central nervous system (and other causal mechanisms as well). The classical (Cartesian) conception of the tripartite faculties of the *res cogitans*, the cognitive, emotional and *volitional*, translate into the vernacular trichotomy of thought, feeling and *will*. As Ryle remarked in his critical assessment of the Cartesian conceptualization of 'volition', the picture was one in which 'the mind' gets its ideas (or 'intentions') translated into action via the exercise of the 'volitional capacity', and this meant that to describe, say, someone as intentionally pulling the trigger was to state that a "mental thrust did cause the contraction of the muscles in his finger"[87], but such a 'cause' must be a 'special' sort of cause, one originating not within the mechanically physical functioning of the person's body (because that would make the movement an involuntary one) but originating rather from within the *meta*physical realm. *Para*-mechanical causality seemed to co-exist with mechanical causality in this account, even though the nature of this para-mechanical causality was left mysterious.

Under the materialist transformation of these theses, there is clearly no room for para-mechanism at all, but the essential conceptual structure of the earlier account was left largely intact, and, as we hope to show, it is *this* (move) which generates the illusion of a mystery, of the apparent incompatibility of rational and lawful explanation. Note that even Thorp's valiant defense of 'libertarianism', the notion that it *is* intelligible and often true to say of someone's having done something 'of his/her own free will', is organized exclusively around an effort to come to grips with the specter of neurophysiological determinism. For the contemporary neuroscientist, of course, there is obviously no place for 'mental

---

[87] Gilbert Ryle, *The Concept of Mind* (Harmondsworth: Penguin University Books, 1973), p. 62.

thrusts', only, if you will, electrochemical ones, and no-one can obey an order to 'fire such-and-such neurons' or fire them 'at will'. Thus, it appears, the impulses, the 'thrusts', that determine all of our muscle movements in the actions we perform are components in causal chains of operation which must, therefore, be outside of our 'conscious control' or 'voluntary decision-making capacity''. If all of our movements are thus 'naturally necessitated' (to use Thorp's terms), then it would seem that, although we may often have the strongest conviction that we could have done otherwise, and that it is we as agents who can (under normal circumstances) exercise control over what we do, nonetheless, everything we do (circumstances notwithstanding) is, in fact, the end-result of a chain of causally-describable processes inside our bodies. Apparently, the story goes, *we* are in control, but, in reality, it is our internal biochemistry and electrophysiology which are our true masters. Genuine personal responsibility is now portrayed as an illusion, a fictional entailment of a commitment to a (vulgar*) pre-scientific* conception of what we are: notions like 'free will' and 'will power' are now depicted as elements of an out-dated (still popular, but actually defunct) 'folk psychology', doomed to ultimate elimination by the eventually triumphant march of cognitive neuroscience.

Before we present a systematic response to these dilemmas and apparent contradictions, it is as well to consider in some detail the conventional interpretation of the Kornhuber-Libet experiments. These pertain to the case of the 'voluntary finger-flex'. We have encountered in the previous chapter the 'plain' biological account of the phenomenon of the finger-flex: what distinguishes the Kornhuber-Libet observations is their claim to have identified certain neurological precursors to this movement which are identified theoretically as neural correlates of 'acts of will'. The idea that 'volition' has a neural basis is clearly founded in the more general presupposition that what distinguishes a 'voluntary' bit of behavior from an 'involuntary' one is the prior occurrence of an 'act of will'. Since Cartesian dualism is now obsolete in neuroscience, the only way to make sense of the idea that it is something antecedent which constitutes an action as 'voluntary' is to locate that 'something' (e.g., an 'act of will' or 'willing') in the brain. This, according to many interpreters, is what Kornhuber and Libet have actually demonstrated in their empirical researches.

Reconceiving Kornhuber-Libet

In a series of well-know papers[88], Kornhuber and his colleagues reported the measurement of electrical potentials in the human cortex prior to the 'voluntary' flexing of their right index finger by experimental subjects. Subjects were asked (instructed is a better term) to initiate their finger-flexings 'at will' at irregular intervals of many seconds in controlled environmental conditions. Electrodes recorded cortical activity at various locations as well as the precise instant of finger-flexing. Two hundred and fifty records of the potentials evoked at each of the electrode sites were averaged, revealing a slowly rising negative potential which commenced 800 milliseconds before the onset of the muscle action potentials. The Kornhuber team referred to this as a 'readiness potential'. At only 90 milliseconds before the movement of the index finger, there were detectably sharper potentials, positive then negative, and at 50 milliseconds prior to the muscle response a sharp negativity developed over the area of the motor cortex localized to the left precentral hand area. Subsequently, Libet drew from these findings the following cognitivist conclusion: "... voluntary acts can be initiated by unconscious cerebral processes before conscious intention appears [sic] but... conscious control over the actual motor performance remains possible."[89] He added: "conscious volitional control may operate not to initiate the

---

[88] L. Deecke, P. Scheid & H. H. Kornhuber, *Experimental Brain Research*, Vol. 7, 1969: L. Deecke, B. Grotzinger & H. H. Kornhuber, *Biological Cybernetics*, Vol. 23, 1976, and H. H. Kornhuber, "Cerebral Cortex, Cerebellum and Basal Ganglia: An Introduction to their Motor Functions" in F. O. Schmitt & F. G. Worden (eds.), *The Neurosciences Third Study Program* (Cambridge, Mass.: M.I.T. Press, 1974).
[89] Benjamin Libet, "Unconscious Cerebral Initiative and the Role of Conscious Will in Voluntary Action", *The Behavioral and Brain Sciences*, Vol. 8, 1985, p. 529.

volitional process but to select and control it, either by permitting or triggering the final motor outcome of the unconsciously initiated process or by vetoing the progression to actual motor activation."[90] Eccles had earlier proffered his own uniquely Cartesian version of these results: for him, the 'readiness potential' can "be regarded as the neuronal counterpart of the voluntary command"[91] and, a year later in another publication, he added: "Apparently, at the stage of willing a movement, the influence of the voluntary command is widely distributed onto the patterns of neuronal operation".[92]

It is precisely at this juncture that we begin our response to all of the foregoing. 'Willing' and 'intending' are clearly depicted here as events or processes brought about by, or equivalent to, neural events that are themselves initiated 'out of the awareness' of the agent. Yet 'willing' is, in this context, itself an unexplicated theoretical term and not the ordinary one. In ordinary language, one can will one's property (will = bequeath) to one's offspring, hence 'willing' it to them, but this is obviously not the meaning intended here. However, without being informed about its meaning here, adjudicating the subsequent claims becomes an idle exercise. Of course, it is possible to define it in such a way that it dissolves into the very conception which is supposed to explain it (i.e., one could stipulate that 'willing' is the neural process as defined by Kornhuber and Libet), but this is an obviously circular and hence utterly uninformative move. Consider, further, the use of the word 'intend': in ordinary language, this word is conventionally used to signal a degree of commitment to an action or state of affairs, with a stronger commitment signaled by the verb 'to promise' and perhaps

---

[90] *Ibid.* For some discussion, see Stuart G. Shanker, "Wittgenstein versus James and Russell on the Nature of Willing" in J. V. Canfield & S. G. Shanker (eds.), *Wittgenstein's Intentions* (N.Y.: Garland Publishing Inc., 1993), pp. 230-37.

[91] J. C. Eccles, "Brain and Free Will" in Gordon G. Globus, Grover Maxwell & Irwin Sarodnik (eds.), *Consciousness and the Brain* (N.Y.: Plenum Press, 1976), p. 116.

[92] J. C. Eccles and Karl R. Popper, *The Self and Its Brain* [Part 2] (N.Y.: Springer International, 1977), p. 285. It is worth noting that in this work, the 'readiness potential' is to be regarded "as the neuronal consequence of the voluntary command" (*Ibid.*) and not as in the 1976 paper, its "counterpart". Whether this change signified a theoretical revision or was merely an error cannot be settled: regrettably, both authors are now deceased.

the strongest by the verb 'to swear'. No-one has proposed that 'promising' and 'swearing' have neural correlates, but 'intending' is often singled out for such a theoretical treatment. This is because of the persistence of a residual and unreflective allusion to a Cartesian notion – 'intending' was thought to be the name of a 'mental process'. Once the Cartesian misconception of the grammar of this word is removed, the theoretical gambit is revealed as incoherent. Wittgenstein warned against confusing stipulative (invented) uses with ordinary ones in the following:

> "How is 'will' actually used? In philosophy one is unaware of having invented a quite new use of the word, by assimilating its use to that of, e.g., the word 'wish'. It is interesting that one constructs certain uses of words specially for philosophy, wanting to claim a more elaborated use than they have, for words that seem important to us. 'Want' is sometimes used with the meaning 'try'. 'I wanted to get up, but was too weak'. On the other hand, one wants to say that wherever a voluntary movement is made, there is volition. Thus if I walk, speak, eat, etc., then I am supposed to will to do so. And here it can't mean trying. For when I walk, that doesn't mean that I try to walk and it succeeds. Rather, in the ordinary way I walk without trying to. Of course it can also be said 'I walk because I want to', if that distinguishes the ordinary case of walking from that in which I am shoved, or electric currents move my leg muscles."[93]

We may speak of 'exercising will power' in contexts such as trying and succeeding in giving up smoking, etc., and we may speak of 'doing something of one's own free will' when we mean that the actions were *not* coerced, unavoidable, obligated, required, reluctant, done under duress or threat, etc., were not undertaken *in*voluntarily, etc.[94], but we do *not* have a non-philosophical use for 'willing' as *a verb of action at all*, except in the case of bequeathing. Relatedly, constructions such as 'acts of will' or more ponderously 'acts of volition' have no counterparts in our ordinary language, and thus must be

---

[93] Ludwig Wittgenstein, *Remarks on the Philosophy of Psychology, Vol. 1* (eds. G. E. M. Anscombe & G. H. von Wright: trans. G. E. M. Anscombe): (Oxford: Basil Blackwell, 1980), para. 51.
[94] Here we can see that the criteria for an action's voluntariness are *negative*.

understood as either (a) arbitrary metaphysical postulates or (b) theoretical terms. If they are to be treated as the latter, then the following problem arises: how are cases of them to be identified, and by what criteria? The various commentators on the Kornhuber-Libet researches are silent on this point. Such silence raises the question of their nature as possible *explananda* in any empirical enterprise.

Let us, briefly, re-visit some of the details of the Kornhuber experiments themselves. The first point to note is that the experimental subjects were given an instruction as to what they were expected/supposed/required to do so as to make the experiment come to life. They were *told that* they should flex their fingers 'at will'. They were, thus, engaged in the production of 'instructed actions', although, of course, the periodicity of the flexes was left to their discretion (within distinct limits, however, since were a subject to construe his or her instructions broadly, he or she might have chosen to flex a finger once an hour, once a day, or once a week, thus frustrating the point and purpose of the experiment itself). The nature of whatever 'voluntariness' one chooses to ascribe to the subjects' actions in the experimental situation is thus highly circumscribed, *as distinct from* cases in which a person's discretionary latitudes are not so restricted. One can, after all, contrast cases where something is done on the basis of an instruction and cases where something is done 'freely', and one can also distinguish between cases where someone's doing something 'at will' is not restricted in temporal scope from cases in which it is. We note as well that a conceptual sleight of hand is at work in redescribing the injunction to do something 'at will' as an injunction to perform an 'act of will'. The former may be understood in complete independence of any reference to the latter (whatever it might be taken to mean).

On these grounds, we reject completely Eccles' gloss on the Kornhuber-Libet results as casting any light upon what could conceivably be involved in 'acts of will' or in 'willing'. However, we still need to address the question: in what could the voluntariness of any action (e.g., flexing one's finger) consist? Clearly, a Cartesian residue is at play in the available interpretations of these researches within cognitive neuroscience in which 'voluntariness' is a property of a class of actions in virtue of their being preceded by (or accompanied by) a mental event or process. We wish to propose that the voluntariness of an action has nothing to do with distinctive neural events or processes, but rather that (a) the voluntary character of an action is a complex contextual function of its performance and thus (b) there is no such thing as *a class* of 'voluntary actions' which might be listed or enumerated independently of contextual considerations of varying complexity. For example, one may join the army voluntarily as contrasted to having been drafted, but if there is no draft then the question: 'Did you join the army voluntarily?' might make no sense (unless the context featured such relevancies as: one's family was known to have been vehemently opposed to such a thing, one sought an opportunity to have one's college fees paid but had no other prospect than signing up, and so on). A question like: "Did you dress that way voluntarily?' uttered in ordinary circumstances, in which normal dress codes have been complied with, might prompt not a verbal response but a rapid glance to check out one's attire for blemishes etc.[95] Or it might be answered in the negative if one is wearing prison garb whilst still a prisoner whose status as such is not known to the questioner. 'Dressing' for the day is, then, in abstraction from local considerations of circumstance, *neither* voluntary *nor* involuntary. Such adverbs apply intelligibly only when a range of circumstances are in play.

Perhaps one source for the idea that 'voluntariness' is a candidate phenomenon for neuroscientific research and analysis is the notion that, since the 'involuntariness' of a bodily movement can indeed have a comprehensive neuro-biological explanation, then why not its opposite, a 'voluntary' movement? Some finger-flexes, after all, might be reflexes, whilst others can be components of, or even partially constitutive of, actions which are not involuntary at all. In flexing

---

[95] Stanley Cavell, "Must We Mean What We Say?" in Colin Lyas (ed.), *Philosophy and Linguistics* (London: Macmillan, St. Martin's Press, 1971), p. 137.

one's finger, one can be, *inter alia*, beckoning, shooting someone, etc., as we noted in the last chapter. But the 'one' here is not 'one' as a *body*, nor 'one' as a 'mind', but 'one' as a person. Neuroscientific explanations are explanations of (some of) the workings of (human) organs, not explanations of what and why people do what they do. Why have so many thought otherwise? Again, at least part of the answer is: Descartes' long, dark shadow still looms over us. Cook clarifies this issue very pertinently:

"Descartes introduced a highly extraordinary use of the word 'body'. He has to be understood to be using it always in the context of his distinction between *himself* and his body. So his use of the word is not at all like these: 'His body was covered with mosquito bites', 'His body was found at the bottom of the cliff', 'He has a strong body but no brains', and so on. In saying such things as these we do not use 'body' as the one side of a Cartesian distinction. We are not saying, for instance, 'His body, but not his mind; was covered with mosquito bites'. That would be utter nonsense. If I say that someone's body was covered with mosquito bites, I could also say 'He was covered, etc.' The word 'body' comes in here as part of the emphasis: not just his ankles and wrists, but his back and stomach, too. Again, in speaking of a corpse we can say either 'His body was found, etc.' or 'He was found dead, etc.' The word 'body' in the first of these is used to make the contrast between dead and alive. No special ontology need come in here... In these and in other ordinary cases our understanding of the word 'body' is tied in particular contexts to a variety of particular distinctions... and none of these provides a place to drive a conceptual wedge between Descartes and his body. But once again, this should not lead us to conclude: Then Descartes was *only* a body. For what distinction would that be making? It was not, after all, a corpse that wrote the *Meditations*."[96]

It is not one's *body* that flexes its fingers, it is one as a person who does this. In rejecting neuroscientific forms of explanation, we nonetheless court the risk of appearing to be defending *un*scientific forms. Our argument, though, hinges on the fact that there are many different kinds of explanation. The illusion of the supremacy of physiological-deterministic explanations is given by the

---

[96] John Cook, "Human Beings" in Peter Winch (ed.), *Studies in the Philosophy of Wittgenstein* (London: Routledge & Kegan Paul, 1969), pp. 123-24.

supposition that our commonsense explanations attempt to explain the same things (e.g., the players' 'moves' [note: *not* 'movements'] in chess and billiards). It is only on this basis that their apparent rivalry arises. The idea that neuroscience can displace our ordinary explanations of actions overlooks the fact that it does not give explanations for the same things as we ordinarily do, and when it strives to do so, as in the *cognitivistic* versions of neuroscientific explanation of the sort we have been discussing, it creates not explanation but confusion. It seems that if one insists that one has done something 'freely' one has entered a bid for exemption from the causal operations of the central nervous system, and, contrastively, the acknowledgement of neural causation seems to require us to deny that we ever do *anything* 'of our own free will'. Our position might loosely be termed a 'compatibilist' one, although we need to venture a caveat here: as this term has often been used in the philosophical literature, there has been scant regard for the fact that we are dealing with explanations of different things, not compatible explanations of the same thing. For us, as we will now argue, there is no direct confrontation between causal accounts of the functioning of the nervous system and intelligible – and correct – claims to have been 'able to have done otherwise than we did', to have done something 'voluntarily', etc.

'Folk Psychology' and Freedom

In developing our case, we shall need to examine the role of the notion that ordinary language users are possessed of a 'folk psychology' which may be shown to conflict with a genuinely (neuro-)scientific one. Large parts of our ordinary vocabulary are construed as hypostatizing immaterial entities such as 'belief', 'thought', 'intention', 'purpose', 'voluntariness' and so on. (One wonders what material form the hypostatization of immaterial entities takes, but we digress..). The claim is that such entities can have no role in explaining what and why we do the things we do – they can exercise no causal force, and so such entities have to go. Their elimination, in principle, paves the way for neurophysiological events to become the causal determinants of what we do, and the identification of such events will replace our 'folk psychology' which is the source of the belief that we are possessed of free will. Right away, however, a serious problem looms: eliminating the putative *explanans* (most if not all of our 'folk-psychological' vocabulary) actually transforms the *explananda*. For example, we would have to ditch expressions like 'crossing the street', since this expression, used to describe what someone in the middle of the street is doing, requires reference to the intended outcome of their purposeful movement, just as 'drinking a cup of coffee' implies the intended continuance of a course of action beyond the current sip. Nor could one 'cross the street warily', since to describe someone as doing this would attribute other 'mental states', such as expectations about the presence of risk, of attitudes of confidence in the means depended upon for carrying out the course of action, and so forth. It is not at all clear why it should be 'scientifically unrespectable' to describe someone as engaged in crossing the street or drinking a cup of coffee, nor why one should have any reservations whatsoever about being categorical that that is what they are doing.

Perhaps one reason for the confusion is a failure to distinguish between two uses of 'theoretical' in the context of characterizing our 'folk psychology'. Eliminativists propose that the concepts given in our 'psychological' vocabulary identify hypothetical or 'theoretical' items which explain observable behavior in the manner in which in some natural sciences there are postulated unobservable entities which explain observable ones. Note, however, that there is 'theoretical' in the sense of 'being part of an explanatory scheme' and there is 'theoretical' in the sense of 'exists, at this time, only in theory'. Consider the following analogy. That there was a mudslide explains why the village was devastated, but because 'mudslide' explains the damage, this does not make it an explanatory term. We think that there is no more reason to consider terms such as 'belief' to be theoretically explanatory in their nature than is 'mudslide' – not all explanations require the mediation of observables by unobservables, and that a person believes something and acts on the basis of that belief may be, like the mudslide and ensuing devastation, a conjunction of observables. Supposed 'folk psychological' notions (like 'belief') need not be *assumed* to be 'theoretical notions' in either sense of 'theoretical' – they are not expressions which theoretically postulate currently unobservable phenomena of unproven existence, nor are they expressions specialized in explanation but are ones which have many other uses than explanatory ones, and derive their explanatory power by virtue of those other uses. Thus, to eliminate folk psychological notions would not mean simply providing different explanatory terms for existing *explananda*, but would mean radically reconceiving the *explananda* as well. Some materialists, such as the 'methodological solipsists'[97], recognize this. Their materialist conception of science can only traffic in the physically intrinsic properties of organisms, in respect of both psychological causes and bodily conduct, but physical properties are not the only ones that organisms have – there are relational, conventional and contextual properties too, and such properties are properties of the *explananda* and of purportedly explanatory 'mental phenomena'. On these grounds, then, it would be a delusion to think that neural science can give better explanations of the things we currently regard ourselves as doing, or could provide substitutes for the 'intentional' vocabulary that we use in both identifying and explaining our actions. An honest proposal for cognitive neuroscience would surely feature a rigorous methodological solipsism, an attempt to purge all elements of 'folk psychology' from its conceptual apparatus, but this would mean that they could not claim to supply neurological explanations in replacement for existing folk-psychological ones – they would, perforce, substitute new *explananda* that are not coordinate with those formulated in 'folk psychology'.

---

[97] See, for example, Jerry A. Fodor, "Methodological solipsism considered as a research strategy in cognitive psychology" in John Haugeland (ed.), *Mind Design* (Cambridge, Mass.: M.I.T. Press, 1981).

Causes and Rules

Let us explore further the invocation of the notion of 'cause' in adducing explanations. Take the case of someone stopping for a traffic light. What someone does here can be explained causally, but what *kind* of causal explanation is given? When we say 'is explained causally' we often mean: an event brings about another, successor event which can be said to be its effect. But what kind of events are the events, and what is the connection between them? One event in our example is the change in the color of the light showing on the traffic signal. The other, successor, event is the increasing pressure of the foot on the brake pedal. It would look as though we have two physical events we can correlate. Does that mean, though, that we have a correlation of the wavelength of light with downward pressure from the foot? Sure enough, the light has a certain wavelength, which is what makes the light a light of that color, but it is not the wavelength of the light as such that even identifies the event. Still, we have a causal connection, but no one imagines that the fact that the changing of the light causes the breaking has immutable status, that the physical connection is an irresistible one by virtue of its physical properties. The mere fact that a color that we see changes does not compel us to behave in a certain way, and the fact that a light changes to red does not force us to stop the car. It is physically entirely possible, when confronted with a red light, to keep on driving: there is no physical compulsion to press the foot down on the brake pedal even though we want to keep driving on – we could do otherwise in response to the red traffic light than we do. However, our response to the red traffic light – to stop the car – is one which is *advisable* (not a concept to be found in physics). It is wisest to stop when the light is red since the consequences (physical, legal, etc.) that follow from ignoring it are potentially damaging. The red light causes us to stop not by virtue of its physical properties or any causal properties of its wavelength, but by virtue of its character as an event in human lives, namely the issuing of a signal. Its being a signal is not anything we shall establish from its physical properties as such – the traffic light is only so much wiring, plastic, metal, glass, etc., in a mechanical configuration. It has a physical position - those materials are assembled into a light display standing at the corner of the street – but it is the light's position in a system of conventions which makes it into a signal. The light is a stop light relative to various conventional ways in which human beings arrange their affairs, the part that authorities play in establishing and enforcing conventions, etc., and the use of those conventions to determine the value of various physical properties – the color red has the value 'warning' and green the value 'permission'. The changing of the light to red is not simply an event in the color spectrum, but is an event in a communications arrangement, one between the authorities and road users, and the change is a change in value, given that the lights are understood as sending a signal.

There is a tendency to think that explanation in terms of rules and explanations in terms of causes must necessarily be opposed, but there is no need to think that this is always the case. Sometimes it is, but not always. Thus, there is no problem in saying that the red light causes a driver to stop, but the status of the red light as a cause derives from the rules of the traffic system. It is only in terms of the traffic system that a red light can act as a cause of regularities in driver behavior. But note, the notion of 'cause' is different in the rule-governed context to what it would be in the case of, say, the physical transfer of propulsion from one billiard ball to another. The notion of 'cause' in the rule-governed case, and in other connections in human activities, is less like that of inexorable compulsion (or 'natural necessitation') and more like that of provocation or instigation. The traffic light instigates a response, but does not physically compel it. People may or may not be able to control their reactions to provocations, but the idea that they might and often do is not excluded. That one does not disregard the red light does not signify that one could not, for it is clear that a red light *as such* does not influence one's reaction. The word 'free' operates distinctively here also. One is free to do otherwise at the traffic light in the sense that one is physically unconstrained and has the capacity to press one's foot on the accelerator pedal and drive on into the road junction, but one is *not* free to do this without risk or responsibility – if something happens as a result of one's accelerating, then one is to blame. It is not solely up to any single individual to decide whether or not he is to blame for the accident that took place after running the red light. In a dueling system, you are free to issue a challenge to someone who has dishonored you, but you are not free to issue a challenge in the absence of a dishonor (if such a 'challenge' is issued, it will be invalid), whilst in our culture, without a dueling system, no-one is free to make a challenge at all because there is no such thing as a valid challenge to a duel. Words like 'cause' and 'free', then, do not always play the same part.

Some argue that a central aspect of a voluntary action is that it is an action which the agent did not need to perform, that the agent 'could have done otherwise' than to perform. The question of whether one 'could have done otherwise' is very often a question of what was within one's powers, and the contention that some things were within someone's powers does not contest his or her subjection to any natural law but rather respects it. Skid-control techniques, for instance, depend upon and do not defy physical laws, and one's possession or lack of possession of such techniques does not defy physical laws either. If one had known such techniques, one would not have had the accident on the ice that one had. As it was, in the real situation encountered, one could not have done otherwise because of ignorance of such techniques. One's claim to have been able to have done otherwise (e.g., to have been able to avoid the accident on the ice) is not a bid for exemption from causality, for it is not any kind of counter-assertion against a philosophical thesis about determinism. It is, rather, part of a distinction which we make within and between the things that we do, which we use to contrast the different kinds of situations in which we find ourselves: *viz.*, those within which we have the power to avert or to bring about some specific outcome from those in which we do not. Whether we had those powers is *not* established exclusively by (although it does not involve any defiance of) causal regularities in nature. In many other sorts of instances we say: 'I could not have done otherwise' to mean that it was not within our institutional power to take action, e.g., that one was not authorized to do X and therefore could *not* – legitimately or validly - do X, where X is a kind of action which can only be performed by an appropriately authorized person. Then there are those cases in which the issue pertains to *causal* powers: in respect of the causation of accidents, there are concerns as to within whose causal power it was to do certain things, whether or not a person had the causal power to take the appropriate evasive action to avoid the collision, and where the establishment of whether or not he or she had the causal powers involves considerations of the incident, speed, visibility, the mechanical condition of the cars, the road conditions, the drivers' conduct, and so on. Whether someone was to blame turns on what it was within his power to do, whether he took the action that was within his power to take. The need to make a distinction between cases in which one could, and cases in which one could not, do otherwise than one did, is not obviated by Laplacean arguments about universal determinism. It is, rather, dependent upon judgments about what is in conformity with physical laws, of what is physically possible, of the ways in which outcomes are causally brought about, of our own causal capacity to do things, as well as upon non-causal considerations, such as (e.g.) what the law allows, what persons in given social situations are entitled to do, or are excused from doing, etc. Giving up the expressions: 'I did it of my own free will' and: 'I could have done otherwise' would, then, be nothing but a sterile abdication from certain notations, for which we would require functionally exact equivalents in our lives.

The 'free will' issue, then, has everything to do with the practical, social exigencies of our everyday lives, and such exigencies are not abolished by neural-metaphysical speculation. Neither does adhering to such an expression involve contravening the well-established facts of neurophysiology about what happens in us when we make certain movements. If someone decides to type this word rather than that, and then his fingers execute this typing operation, his decision to type the word will only deliver its result if he relies upon the causal connections operating at the micro-physical level in his nervous system and their extension to his fingers as well as to the relationship between his fingers and the keyboard. We do not need to abandon the notion of a 'decision' here, and we certainly do not need to locate a 'decision' along the inner/outer dichotomy as something 'inner', solely in virtue of taking stock of the fact that 'doing what one decided to do' in this case is wholly reliant upon inner neural events and processes.

It is crucial to bear in mind, here, that our argument has been conducted solely in terms of what language-users can mean when they use expressions like: 'of my own free will', 'voluntarily', 'could have done otherwise', and the like, and *not* about what they might *believe*. The Churchlands, however, clearly think that what we can mean by the use of such expressions must somehow involve what we believe: "What the Marshall-Gurd duo and the two of us [Paul and Patricia Churchland] share is a quite deep if rather plain conviction. The facts are the facts; linguistic analysis may tell you what normal speakers believe, but it cannot be a reliable guide to facts about the world, to the real nature of things."[98] The facts are, indeed, the facts, and what speakers may believe may not consort with the facts, but this is irrelevant to *our* question, which is: what do speakers mean when they say such-and-such (e.g., 'I did it voluntarily') no matter what they may believe (e.g., about 'free will' and 'determinism' as *doctrines*). Failing to grasp this quite fundamental point has led many critics of 'ordinary-language analysis' to misconstrue the enterprise as a quasi-empirical review of what ordinary folk may think about this or that phenomenon. On the contrary: ordinary-language analysis (at least, as we understand its practice) elucidates the ways in which expressions are *intelligible* (or otherwise). Intelligibility is analytically

---

[98] Paul and Patricia Churchland, "Conceptual Analysis and Neuropsychology: John Marshall and Jennifer Gurd" in Robert N. McCauley (ed.), *The Churchlands and their Critics* (Oxford: Blackwell, 1996), p. 290.

prior to determinations of truth or falsity. The Churchlands do not attend *at all* to the analysis of what our words and expressions actually mean as these are used in the course of living our (largely linguistic) lives. Nor do they give us any reason to believe that speakers of the language *qua* speakers must subscribe to any philosophical doctrine at all for their words to make the sense that they make. We have already noted how the ordinary deployment of expressions such as 'voluntarily' commits no-one to the denial of causality, either in the nervous system or in any other material phenomenon in the world. One must avoid confusing mastery of a concept with possession of a theory, and one should not misconstrue our practical reasoning and discourse as part of our practical affairs in the world, in which intentional concepts have their indispensable role, as if they worked solely to comprise a form of (proto-)scientific theorizing *about* the world.

On Choosing

We now turn to a detailed discussion of the role of 'choice' in our lives. The concept of choice has been typically contrasted to the concept of cause and related (causal) concepts, and has been characterized as very much bound up with our concepts of 'freedom', 'voluntariness' and the rest. For example, one might ask: 'Did he choose to *X*?' and the reply might be: 'No, he had no choice in the matter. He was compelled to *X*, and this is a perfectly intelligible interchange. Certainly, if you are caused to, forced to, compelled to, do *X*, then choice cannot enter the picture. From here, it can appear that either (a) we are deluded whenever we say that someone has chosen to do something because everything that we do is really, fundamentally, caused by the operations of our nervous systems, or (b) we truly do choose to do certain things, and this means that some of the things we (choose to) do are exempt from any causal determination whatsoever, including, of course, neurophysiological causation. Here we shall argue that these are false dichotomies, and that accepting (as we must) the fact that our nervous systems do operate causally provides no grounds for doubting that we do, indeed (on occasion) choose (to do) things. We take it that if someone offers another a drink, and says: 'Beer or whiskey?' then the other has a choice. And he can choose. He can say: 'I'll have whiskey'. To which a response might then be: 'Islay or Highland Park?' The other says that he will have the Islay. Did he or did he not choose? And what did he do that made what he did choosing? A different scenario: someone says: 'Beer or whiskey?' and another answers: 'I don't know. I can't make up my mind. I just can't decide'. Now, he cannot choose in the sense that he cannot bring himself to say which drink he will have. Here, when asked the question, he cannot give a straight answer to it. Presumably, someone who would deny us free will, at least in the canonical form of the 'freedom to choose', will not want to suggest that after their arguments have been proven right no-one will ever offer us 'Beer or whiskey?' again? Or that we will have to respond: 'I cannot choose'. What is being proposed is that when someone says: 'Whiskey!' in response to the beer-or-whiskey option, or 'Islay' in response to the Islay-or-Highland-Park option, that even so he did not choose. But now notice that the theoretically-postulated-and-proven 'loss of our free will' does not alter our conduct. Hosts can still ask: 'Beer or whiskey?' and guests can still specify one or the other, but they will (according to the position of the determinist) not do so on the basis of free will. However, our capacity to choose in this instance consists in their being beer or whiskey to drink. If there is only beer to drink, then we cannot choose what to drink. We can still choose whether to drink.

Having a choice in such instances does not consist in one's being in any sort of special psychological or neurophysiological state, but being in a position in which one's host has put one. Choosing is *not* an antecedent animating force behind our actions, not an antecedent physiological occurrence, but is the very act of picking, or accepting, the Islay rather than the Highland Park (or vice versa). One chose, or picked, that one. In such a case, it is 'up to us' what we drink – it has been left that way by the host. If the host thrusts beer on us and insists that we drink it, then we cannot be said to have chosen the beer.

The idea which animates many theorists here is that 'choosing' is a kind of way of explaining actions, it being a hallmark of actions that we choose to do them, but, in our ordinary locutions, 'choosing' is *not* a general way of explaining our actions. It is, rather, the characteristic of certain kinds of actions in certain sorts of circumstances. When we get dressed in the morning, we do not choose to get dressed: what is the alternative here? However, we might choose which shirt to wear, but only because we have more than one clean shirt and there is no special dress code restriction placed upon us. We do not choose to eat, although we might choose what to eat, and when to do so. If we routinely eat lunch at the same time everyday, we do not choose when to eat, and if we routinely have the same meal, we do not choose what to eat. Obviously, in cases in which we choose a relevant issue is: what is the genuinely available alternative?

It might appear that our suggestion that we do not choose to get dressed in the morning is wrong because we do choose to get dressed. One could, the argument runs, after all *not* get dressed in the morning. What? And go to work? To school? Or not get dressed and stay at home all day and lose one's job or be expelled from school? One has no choice in what to do here if one wants to continue to lead a normal life in society and hold down a job or remain in school. It is not *up to us* what to do in these respects. But could it not be said that we are free not to get dressed and to go to work naked? Or not to get dressed and to stay at home all day? Well, if someone says that we are free to do these things in this connection, then his remark is tinged with a certain sarcasm – you are free to get arrested, give up your job or be expelled from school! Someone who, at work, says that you are free to resign might well be saying: if you offer your resignation, it will be accepted. It is, naturally, open to us to resign a job: this is because it is one of our rights or freedoms in our society – we are not indentured labor. Nonetheless, this does not mean that we are free to do, today, whatever we want to. Not, that is, if we want to keep our jobs or to remain in school…

The question: what is the alternative? has a lot of bite in connection with whether actions are ones where we can be said to be involved in 'choosing'. The idea that there is always an alternative is an attractive one in that we can always list different actions that are possible in response to any given set of circumstances. Instead of getting up, one could stay in bed. Instead of drinking the beer, one could refrain from drinking it. The point, however, is not whether there is some conceivably different course of action that could have been adopted in the circumstances, but whether these are alternatives available to the person doing the activity. Thus, if someone presses beer on another and insists that he drink it, then he is not free not to drink it if he does not want to risk offending the insistent host. It is, the host is insisting, not up to him whether he drinks the beer or not. This is what we mean by the host being an insistent one. To say that, nevertheless, it *was* up to us, that we could finally have refused, may be true – we are, perhaps, capable of saying No *in extremis* – but this is in the sense of ability, not of choice. One could say No and risk offending the host, but if one does not want to risk offending the host then one *cannot* say No. It is not, here, up to us. Someone who says: 'But you could have said No!' – very often with the implication that one *should* have said No! – does not care about the consequences of the action. But someone who is following a line of action precisely may care very seriously about the consequences of the action, and so it is not (or not entirely) up to them what they could do. We must scrutinize the kinds of actions and their relevant contexts to see if it makes sense to talk about alternatives available to their agents. Someone who eats lunch routinely at 12.30 does not choose to eat lunch at that time, nor does it assist to say that he or she is free to eat lunch at another time. The fact that someone eats lunch at a fixed time, who schedules his/her lunch for that time, does not then choose to eat lunch at that time. He/she eats lunch according to a schedule, and, once a schedule is in place, taking lunch at that time is not something which is chosen at all. If it makes any sense at all to say of such a person that he or she is free to take lunch at some other time, then this is a remark about such a person's entitlements: if you are not assigned a lunch period during your working day, then it is your entitlement to eat lunch at other times. However, if there is a set time for your lunch, then there can be no alternative times available to you. To say that there would be is to deny that there is a set time for lunch. Thus, being 'free' to choose is often a matter of not being subject to specific sorts of social restrictions.

An impatient response to our arguments might run as follows: we are not addressing the core issue of why a person opts for one thing rather than another, whether someone who 'chooses' something really chooses it, whether he or she is really free (of causal influence) and could have taken up the other alternative to the one actually selected. The impatience is misplaced, for the gist of the above discussion is that people do not assume that their actions are in any general sense free of restrictions – that their actions are in general instances of the exercise of 'free will' in the philosophers' sense. Moreover, implicit in the question: what is it that explains why people choose this rather than that? is the assumption that there could be a general sort of answer, and one that might displace any local, vernacular reason which someone might be able to give on some occasion or other.

It is precisely the point here that the philosophical problem turns on a trick: the trick is to get people to suppose that there is some kind of empirical content to disagreements such as arise in the free-will/determinism controversy. Thus, it is part of the trick to propose that neuroscience might make a difference in the dispute, usually on the side of determinism, by making neuroscientific discoveries that reveal facts which establish determinism and vanquish free will. However, what we are casting doubt upon here is whether 'free will' in the vernacular is at all the kind of thing against which determinist philosophers and other theorists polemicise or which other philosophers and theorists purport to defend. If the debate is a philosophical one, then 'free will' cannot be vanquished by the results of neuroscientific inquiries, because the content of the debate is not empirical whereas the results of neuroscience are. If 'free will' in the vernacular is being systematically misrepresented in philosophy, then it cannot be vanquished by philosophical polemics invoking neuroscience.

It is not at all essential to our collective, ordinary concept of 'free will' that it is something which defies causality. That there are many things which are logically not subject to explanation in terms of causes does not mean that there are, therefore, in any meaningful sense, exceptions from causality, occurrences which fly in the face of the laws promulgated by the successful natural sciences. It is the supposed general 'law of causality' which is at issue here and not any specific natural laws or specific, scientifically-established causal generalizations. Those who claim that accepting that people have the capacity for choice is tantamount to accepting the defiance of physical laws never tell us which ones are involved in the supposed defiance. Let it be specified just which physical/physiological laws there are which we ordinary folks defy when we choose, e.g., a malt over a blend. There are no specific laws at issue, only the Laplacean-inspired 'general law' of causality. Rid ourselves of the Laplacean metaphysics, and the whole problem evaporates, leaving the neurosciences perfectly intact and in order and leaving our choosings and voluntary conduct intact as well!

CHAPTER FOUR

CONSCIOUSNESS: THE LAST MYSTERY?

Readers who have followed us thus far in this book will be aware that our first reaction in considering the possibility that 'consciousness' might be a mystery, one of those topics lying at or beyond the limits of our understanding, is to look into the conditions that supposedly make it so intractable, to see whether there is a compelling need to set up the problem in the way that it has been, whether its identity as a problem depends upon the acceptance of a number of prior – and supernumerary – assumptions, and whether – even -- there might be 'solutions' to the problem already at hand. Perhaps, rather than being remote from all hope of finding the research evidence that might answer the question, we are actually now in possession of such information as we need to achieve [at least greater] clarity on the matter than its prevailing philosophical formulations allow.

A popular line of argument runs as follows: We have understood so much through the progress of science, there are few things left to understand, only the human mind remains (and that to a diminishing extent) a redoubt of darkness. We have already (do we not?) a good idea of the way that many mental phenomena may be understood, at least in principle. We can (can we not?) await the progress of brain science to fill out that in-principle outline of how the mind figures in human life (mainly in and through the workings of the brain). But, within this last redoubt, there remains the topic of consciousness, for which, as yet, it is claimed, we have no outline, in-principle, idea that seems a serious candidate for understanding this.

The intractability of the problem seems to consist initially in the fact that consciousness apparently does not fit into the framework picture that we have of how things in general, brains, and therefore minds, work. It is not just a matter of finding a space somewhere within that, so far highly successful, framework that creates the difficulty, however, but that the *prima facie* nature of consciousness is incongruous to that picture, and seems the sort of thing that is unsuitable to the general methods that have been used to build up the framework in place. If we take that method as the paradigm of what understanding something is, and take the *prima facie* character of consciousness as indicating its nature, then the conclusion is that consciousness is fundamentally resistant to our understanding, so much so that some will wonder whether it may even be impossible for consciousness to understand itself (unless, of course, we accept the only other alternative that is seemingly on offer, which is to assume that consciousness *must* fit with our paradigm of understanding, and that the *prima facie* nature of consciousness is *not* its true nature at all).

Consciousness for us is more of an 'Honest Houdini Problem'. Houdini used to have himself bound in straightjackets, chained, submersed in a tank of water, and have the tank tightly sealed, so that it would seem utterly impossible for him to escape. Everything used in his stunts was prepared so that things were actually easy to get out of, and to that extent Houdini's escapes were not honest ones. We will try to show that those who think that consciousness is a 'hard problem', even an *impossible* one, are like Harry Houdini to the extent of setting themselves up in a situation from which they cannot possibly escape. Unlike Houdini, however, their setting up of the problem has been genuine, they have not built any easy escape routes out of it, and so, also unlike Houdini, they are finding that they are inextricably locked into a problem they have entirely made for themselves.

'The problem' of consciousness as we see it is essentially this: Having set up a world view in which a narrow materialist interpretation of the natural sciences sets very rigid limits to what can be said to exist, those who depict 'consciousness' as a mysterious phenomenon find that they have extruded 'consciousness' from reality as they understand it – there is no space for it within the materialist world picture to which they unquestioningly adhere. However, at the same time, it seems that consciousness indisputably *does* exist and cannot, therefore, continue to be legitimately precluded from that world picture: some account of it *must* be given, and given in the standard terms. But neither can it be re-inserted because of the way in which they have conceived consciousness: they are attached to two unbending convictions, that the materialist world picture is the right one, and that consciousness is not the sort of thing that this world picture can straightforwardly incorporate. This is what makes the problem seem 'hard', even impossible. If the set up is correct, then something has to give, but, given the configuration of commitments, nothing really can: it must mean either finding an ingenious way of 'reconciling' the supposed nature of consciousness with the assumed materialist interpretation of science or giving up both of these unquestionable platform assumptions (because if consciousness does indubitably exist and does not conform to the materialist conception of what can exist, then the materialist assumption cannot be sound).

If, as we maintain, there is absolutely no need to accept either of these obstructing convictions, then the only 'hard' thing involved here is the effort involved in surrendering convictions that are so deeply ingrained, and, accepting that the apparent insuperability of the 'the problem' is entirely an artifact of the doctrines that state the problem.

We will put pressure on the idea that 'the problem' of consciousness is a scientific one, for we will argue both that 'the problem of consciousness' is not a single problem, and that the problems that are crucially constituent of it spring entirely from philosophical sources. It is not, therefore, a genuine problem at all. The supposed problem arises from continuing attachment to a variety of – rather ancient – independent philosophical preconceptions that have nothing to do with 'consciousness' *per se.* Our central case will be that the problem of consciousness does not represent the emergence of a new scientific challenge, but at its heart is the reappearance of venerable philosophical problems, most centrally that of *qualia,* those things that – in the empiricist philosophical tradition - provide the matter of our direct experiences, the impressions (or data) delivered by our senses.

The passage that follows very usefully crystallizes what the materialist understanding of the mind tells us, and is often and readily presumed as a widely accepted understanding of what it is that makes consciousness into a 'hard problem', explains why science has not yet come to terms with it, and why it appears, in the present, to be quite unable to do so. Simply, it seems that consciousness is something that just does not fit into the universe as that is understood by science.

> "In the view of modern science, the universe is fundamentally physical and existed and evolved for billions of years without any consciousness present in it at all. Consciousness, on this now commonplace view, is a very recent addition, a byproduct of the complex chemical processes that gave rise to sophisticated biological organisms. The question thus arises of how consciousness ever came to be. For it is clear that science describes the world purely in terms of spatial distributions of dynamic potentials to occupy and influence regions of space, without any reference whatsoever to the colors, sounds, feels, anticipations, meaning, and thoughts with which our consciousness is wonderfully filled. Moreover, the experiential qualities of our subjective awareness is so different *in kind* from the colorless, soundless, non-conscious spatio-temporal structures described by the physical sciences that *it seems impossible* to understand how such experiential qualities could ever be produced by the interactions of purely physical systems."[99]

Plainly, this passage is meant to provide a statement of the problem of consciousness as 'the hard problem', concluding that 'it seems impossible' to absorb consciousness to the materialist world picture (as though this were the

---

[99] Jonathan Shear (ed.), *Explaining Consciousness: The 'Hard Problem'* (Cambridge, MA: M.I.T. Press, 1997), p. 1

same as empirical science). However, the same passage surely gives the game away, for, on careful reading it proves to be written in very slanted prose that only selectively characterizes the situation it pretends to portray and exaggerates and misrepresents the purported contrast between 'the world as portrayed in science' and 'the nature of our conscious experience.'[100]

It is interesting that the passage sets out one solution even before it states the problem. Thus, we are told that 'in the view of modern science, 'Consciousness.... is a very recent addition, a byproduct of the complex chemical processes that gave rise to sophisticated biological organisms'. This seems to suggest that 'consciousness' is *no special problem,* that it is to be understood in terms of the general principles of chemistry and in accord with the understanding of the evolution of organisms. 'Consciousness' presents no special problem in the sense that there is no reason to suppose that any kind of break with, or modification of, the general strategy of the chemical and biological sciences is called for in order that they may encompass this development. We might note that 'byproduct' is, perhaps, an odd – slanted - choice of word, where 'product' might have done at least as well, though it would perhaps lack the rhetorical intimation of a diminution, in the scientific treatment, of something that we value: our consciousness.

Human Beings and 'Physical Systems'

But does 'consciousness' even present a problem, let alone a special one, in respect of the 'complex chemical processes that gave rise to sophisticated biological organisms'? Are we to suppose that 'consciousness' within the chemical and biological sciences is a single and singular development, involving the appearance of one distinct phenomenon, other than, and in addition to, all the

---

[100] Cf. Gilbert Ryle, "The World of Science and the Everyday World" in his *Dilemmas* (Cambridge, England: Cambridge University Press, 1954/1987), Ch. 5.

other chemical and biological developments that have given rise to 'sophisticated biological organisms'? Or should we see that the development of 'consciousness' would really require us to understand the chemistry and biology of 'sophisticated biological organisms' *per se*, to take in a diversity of scientific strands that contribute to the development of life, that lead to the evolution of the eye, the ear, the nose, the formation of sleep patterns, the development of the brain, and so on. If we go looking in the work of the natural sciences for accounts of 'consciousness' we may indeed find that these are – until quite recently – absent from its literature (at least, under that name, but as Ryle pointed out, topics that are definitely covered by the natural sciences are not necessarily identified by name). The recent literature begins to feature (unsuccessful) attempts to account for consciousness, but the idea that any further account than is already available in the scientific literature is actually needed may be misguided. When we look into the scientific literature, and fail to find identified treatments of the topic of consciousness, it may be not that this topic is absent, but that we are looking in the wrong place. Rather than looking for accounts specifically identified as being of the development of consciousness, we should be looking for studies of the development of living creatures, of the development of organisms that are reactive to their environment, and of the biological features that make them reactive in that way, such as the acquisition of organs like the eye, the development of stereoscopic and color vision etc., not to mention the development of organisms that are less dependent upon instincts and that are also more independent from the immediate stimuli of their environments – and much of this will involve us in attempting to understand the development of different kinds of organisms, not to locate a specific and distinctive feature of some organisms.

If we think of it this way, rather than it seeming impossible for science to account for consciousness, it would seem that some sciences are already a very long way toward enabling us to understand 'this development', and without causing even the slightest perturbations to their general investigative strategies.

We do not suppose that the understanding of animal chemistry and biology is complete, but do raise the question – and will continue to cast doubt upon the possibility – that the further development of this need proceed by adopting 'consciousness' as a problem. Certainly not 'the problem of consciousness' as it is currently constituted by essentially philosophical desiderata.

Shear's formulation has given the game away, in that its opening comment alerts us to the fact that there is an understanding of consciousness within contemporary science, and, if we construe that understanding as we do, there is no particular, and, certainly, no hard problem there. It also alerts us to the fact that Shear's remarks are an exercise in spin, an attempt to make it seem that 'consciousness' is scientifically mystifying. But, again, consider the manner in which Shear sets out this view, for he does not elaborate on what the problems with consciousness might be in terms of the issues specific to the chemical and biological sciences. The question arises, we are told, 'of how consciousness ever came to be?' as though it were, from the point of view of natural science, an unnatural kind of phenomenon, one that requires an unprecedented kind of scientific provision.

We are provided with a stark contrast, but not, however, a contrast that itself has any scientific character, but is only a crude and distorted contrast between the way in which 'science' (i.e., in this case, particle physics) portrays things and the way in which 'we', ordinary, most of us, presumably lay, persons experience things. On the terms of this contrast, we are left with a question as to whether the biological sciences are excluded from or included within 'the physical' sciences, for whilst we are purportedly dealing with how 'science' describes 'the world', we are offered a sketch of how things might seem from – supposedly - the point of view of particle physics, though we are invited to believe that this description is given by 'the physical sciences' generally. We ask about the possible inclusion of the biological sciences amongst these physical sciences, for the kind of description that 'science' purportedly offers is one that is provided 'purely in terms of spatial distributions of dynamic potentials to occupy and influence regions of space', in response to which we can only ask: is that how biology describes things? – fully confident that the answer is 'No'. (Ryle, noting the number and diversity of sciences, pointed out that in philosophy 'science' usually means physics and a bit of neurology – his remark has not been outdated by modern materialism. We have trouble with 'the world', too, for we can see that in the claim that this is how 'science describes the world' the appearance of that term will be understood to mean 'everything', and will seduce readers into supposing that such a mode of description – purely in terms of spatial distributions – is the only sort of *bona fide* scientific description that there is, and – if they have already swallowed the idea that science provides the only sorts of *bona fide* descriptions that there are – then consciousness will indeed appear a scientifically problematical matter: it will indeed seem as if it is something that is 'so different in kind' from the phenomena that science portrays that one truly cannot see how it could even be numbered amongst them.

The difficulty is an artifact of the slanted presentation of the matter, by concentration upon one way in which some of science describes some things. Expressions like 'fundamentally' in 'fundamentally physical' carry a lot of freight: we do not want to dissent from the claim that 'in the view of modern science the universe is fundamentally physical' either as a claim about modern science or about how things actually are, but we do want to be clear as to exactly what we are signing up to if we agree to it – after all, if we are being told that, in the view of physical science, the universe is fundamentally physical, then this is little more than a tautology. Similarly with: physical phenomena are fundamentally physical. But does 'fundamentally physical' mean 'only' or 'nothing but' physical? Or, as another possibility: there are *only* physical phenomena in the universe? Is Beethoven's birthday physical? Fundamentally physical? We are quite happy to accept that Beethoven's birthday is not part of the physical universe, at least in the sense that we have no idea where anyone would go looking for that in the way they would for a galactic core or the heart of the sun or how one could introduce talk of Beethoven's birthday into the very restrictive terminology of particle physics. We do not see, however, that we should accept that Beethoven's birthday is not part of the universe: why would anyone want to say that – does anyone want to argue that Beethoven didn't have any birthdays? But there is the trouble with saying that 'the universe is fundamentally physical' – we need to decide what is 'in' and 'out' of 'the universe' before we decide that 'the universe fundamentally' is this or that. We don't want to decide 'the universe is fundamentally this or that' *and then* start deciding what is 'in' or 'out' of it. But these problems exacerbate, and we should perhaps caution that we are not suggesting that there is some immaterial realm in which Beethoven's birthday *inter alia* might reside, but are questioning the utility of the undiscriminating notion of a material real as an all-inclusive one.

If we describe some things 'purely in terms of dynamic spatial distributions' then we shall be describing them in very different terms than we otherwise would (as when describing how a glorious sunset looks, say), so it is hardly surprising that taking the two ways of describing them and subjecting them to stark comparison they will seem very different indeed. Before we worry about different 'kinds of things' we might, then, wonder about different kinds of descriptions. Isn't the attempt to square the materialist circle more a matter of trying to understand two descriptions that are of admittedly different kinds by simply matching them, one against the other, providing an almost assured method of bewildering ourselves? Unless we understand how the 'frameworks' within which these kinds of descriptions can be made themselves differ and relate we will perhaps think that they are at odds when they are not: which does not mean that they are compatible instead, just that they are different. Compare the description that a witness to a crime gives of the offender – he is white, age about twenty two, blond haired etc. – with that given by the offender's mother – he is a good boy, he always looks after me, etc. They are different descriptions, and whilst both are of the same individual we might – if in the kind of mood in which the passage from Shear is written - wonder whether they could possibly both be descriptions of the same person. But of course they are, for one is a description of what the person looks like, whilst the other is a description of his character: the first description is designed to assist the police in finding the offender, the other is perhaps given in consideration of whether the individual really can be guilty of such a bad deed or about how he should be treated when he has been convicted. We would not feel, in such a case, the inclination to wonder well, which is he, six feet tall and blonde, *or* good to his mother? We would not be inclined to think, either, that we could find out these things about him all in the same way: one can find out the facts about his height and hair color just by looking at him for a few seconds, but one finds out about his character by relating to him over a long time, seeing what he does and how he treats other people.

That a science makes no mention of some topic or phenomenon does not signify that it thereby denies their existence. Why should anyone think this, except as a strange prejudice? For example, economics 'describes the world' in terms of consumer preferences and the like, and makes no reference to, for example, the home addresses of the consumers with the preferences. Are we therefore to conclude that consumers have no homes, though not because they are homeless, but, rather, because the notion of 'having a home' is not a *scientifically acceptable notion* (because it is not a scientific notion, i.e., not one that it took a scientist to produce)? We might insist, then, that economics describes the world purely in terms of its particular ensemble of technical concepts (in which case 'home' would drop out of its vocabulary), but how are we to understand the restriction in the vocabulary used in the 'descriptions' provided by economists? We could understand that in much the way that Shear seems to understand the specialist – the 'purely physical' - vocabulary of physics, as involving an insistence that there really are (only) the kinds of phenomena identified in that vocabulary, which converts the understanding that 'home address' is not really useful for the specific, specialized purposes of economics into the idea that, if economics does not say they do, then people do not have homes.

The word 'description' often serves as a 'success' word, having the sense of saying correctly how something is. Thus, we have the seeming implication that the way in which particle physics describes 'the world' carries the suggestion that any other kind of description – not confined purely to the distinctive vocabulary of particle physics – must be incorrect. Further, since what particle physics describes is 'the world', are we to think that it describes the whole world, and all that's in it, in these few words (and where are the words that particle physics uses, are they themselves amongst the phenomena numbered by this (bit of) science – is 'word' a term in particle physics, or does particle physics happily and unproblematically avail itself of words that its own theories do not acknowledge? And is this really a problem for particle physics? If particle physics does describe the whole world, then any other kind of description will seem impossible, for it will be a different kind than the (only) correct description, using terms that are not merely not present in, but are to be understood as excluded – outlawed – from particle physics. The difficulty, if we accept the way this is being set up, is that consciousness seems to involve the sort of thing that is *strictly* excluded from the world of nature, the world of nature-according-to-science. But isn't this only because we are buying into a string of not-always-explicit assumptions?

How are we thinking of what 'science', i.e. particle physics, does here? Are we thinking of it as actually doing what *metaphysics* tried to do, namely to give us a vocabulary in which to speak of all that there really, ultimately is? But why should we think of particle physics as some kind of fulfillment of metaphysics? – except, of course, that doing so will enable us to go on as though a metaphysical reading of the results of particle physics was quite in order. Can we not think of the empirical sciences as breaking away from metaphysics, perhaps because the problems that metaphysics tries to ask are ones that cannot themselves be solved? Why should we think that 'science' does solve these problems if it rejected them and does not itself attempt to solve them? Is the problem that is being raised here itself a scientific one? Of course not! It is not a question that turns upon what the results of particle physics, *qua* particle physics, themselves show (i.e., that there are such and such particles, with such and such properties). The question at stake here is 'how to construe the results of particle physics philosophically?' That is, in relation to questions such as: 'should particle physics be given such a special place amongst the sciences that its results can, singularly, be reported as telling us (entirely and exclusively) 'how the world really is''? That question will not be answered by looking more carefully into the science's results, for it is one that pertains to what we can rightfully say about those results (whatever they happen to be). To deny that particle physics occupies such a singular place is not in any way to 'demote' it from its unquestionably highly successful position amongst the sciences, but only to suggest that its relationship to the other sciences, and to things that we ordinarily say, is rather more complex than is suggested by this (actually very) crude idea that is being offered as a generally accepted one. That this *is* widely accepted, and not merely a perverse idiosyncrasy, may be the one thing in Shear's account that is not wholly questionable.

Should we think that there can only be color photographs of people? A color photograph clearly shows what people look like, so does this mean that a monochrome snap, which differs from the color one, therefore cannot show what people are like (at all)? Obviously, we do not normally think in that way. A black and white photograph can show us all sorts of things about what a person looks like, though they do not show us that the shirt the person is wearing is pink, that the tie is red, and so on. So long as we understand the difference between the two kinds of photographs there is no reason to think of them as presenting us with the choice as to which one must be accepted as showing us what people look like, and which must therefore be entirely rejected. The logic of a position being reviewed here would be that we *could* decide, because black and white snapshots show us people in black and white, that therefore color photographs cannot possibly show them as they (really) are. Naturally, we all understand that color photographs show some things about how people look that black and white snaps do not, but that there are some things about people that both black and white and color photographs can show. Whilst we may, for the purposes of particle physics, be restricted to its 'pure' vocabulary, why does it follow that we must retract the vocabulary that we previously – and for quite other purposes – used to talk about the phenomena that particle physics talks about? Is not the way in which particle physics talks about these phenomena just a different - even a very different – way than those in which we otherwise topicalise them.? Why should the fact that the home addresses of store customers is quite irrelevant to the needs of economic theorizing lead us to propose putting an end to identifying home addresses? Assuredly, economic theorists do talk about the same individuals as we do when we identify them and give their home addresses, but the way in which the economist talks about those individuals differs from that in which we – and which they too – do so in other contexts. The specific identities of 'consumers', including their places of residence, is just an irrelevance to the interest that economic theorists wish to take in those same individuals that we know personally (just as the geometer is not particularly interested in this circle that we have drawn on the board, in when it was drawn, how long it has been up there, and so on, but only in its geometrically relevant properties, and the way in which it resembles other circles.)

As for the claim that 'science' describes 'the world' 'without any reference whatsoever to the colors, sounds, feels, anticipations, meanings, and thoughts with which our consciousness is 'wonderfully filled' is surely only true of particle physics, and not true of other parts of physics or of astronomy (a discipline closely interlinked with physics and highly dependent on particle physics as well as a frequent user of color photographs), nor is it true of another major natural science, biology. It is only true of particle physics that it makes no reference to any of those because particle physics talks about phenomena – particles - that themselves are colorless, and that do not see, hear, feel or expect anything, nor do they have thoughts and opinions.

Is it not the case that, in Shear's remarks, we are coming up against that old philosophical distinction between primary and secondary qualities, with the idea that certain properties – size, weight, molecular composition – are intrinsic to the object, are part of it, whilst other properties – color being a notable example- do not really belong to the object at all, but exist, rather, in our minds only? Certainly, debates about color realism continue to thrive in the present. Is it surprising that the world of microphysics features structures that are colorless and soundless, for we are, after all dealing with phenomena on an incredibly small scale, where part of understanding that idea of scale – of understanding what we have learned from physics - surely involves appreciating that they are much too small to see, and that they are phenomena that occur, after all, on a much smaller scale than the wavelengths of light and sound encompass – the wavelengths of light and sound together with our human biology fixing what we (unlike dogs, say) can see and hear. Surely it is no part of microphysics to claim that the fact that the particular constituents of their discipline's phenomena are colorless and soundless implies that the phenomena of which they are constituent must be colorless and soundless too. The difference *'in kind'* is surely so great because it is between the medium sized dry goods world that we can all take in and the (for many of us, surely, in a literal sense) inconceivably small size of the world that particle physics talks about. Particle physics does not – does it? – present this world, the micro-world – as though it were the same world as that in which we go about our daily business? The micro-world is surely presented as being far removed from our daily world in terms of scale, and as being undetectable with our sensory apparatus (that we can't see quarks is itself a fact of physics, to do with the size of particles and the wavelengths of light etc.)[101]   Particle physics may not include the concept 'color spectrum' in its own – very specialist – vocabulary, but that does not leave it entirely disconnected from the other concepts of physics, for, in the way we have just been indicating, its placement relative to the rest of physics (and relative to our daily experience) involves just such concepts as 'wavelengths of light', 'sound waves', and the rest. For, of course, other parts of physics incorporate quite direct reference to 'the color spectrum', 'visible light' and 'sound waves', whilst astronomy identifies 'red dwarfs' and 'red shifts' as well as 'white giants', and biology treats the colors of animals and plants as evolutionary products that play an important role in affecting their adaptability.

Physics would not, and surely should not, endorse the argument that things became colored only when creatures with color vision evolved, since this would be to temporize with the primary/secondary qualities distinction. Whilst sensitivity to the color spectrum may be a relatively late development in the history of the universe, arising only some time after evolution had begun, the color spectrum is not itself an evolutionary concept, and the emission of light on the wavelengths of the color spectrum is something that originated during the expansion of the universe, not in the course of biological evolution.

We are wary that the kind of post-positivist materialism that we are opposing is not the only angle from which our approach to things might be severely reproached, for there are all kinds of 'constructivists' on the watch for anything that seems to 'privilege' the natural sciences as providing a picture of what is 'really there'. These last are apt themselves to be wedded – albeit unwittingly – to something very close to, if not identical with, the primary/secondary qualities distinction, being much concerned to distinguish what

---

[101] Recall here the ambiguities attaching to 'what we can see' discussed in connection with some observations of Pinker in our Introduction.

is 'intrinsic' to a phenomenon, in contrast to that which is (only) attributed to it by us. What we had to say about the fact that 'being colored' antedated the origin of color vision might well seem the worst kind of post-positivist provocation to them, but our own position cannot be located on the grid of positional possibilities they are capable of drawing. Our remarks on physics, biology etc, are what we call 'grammatical' or 'conceptual', are comments upon what are (or seem to us to be) the intelligible ways of speaking that can be found in one or other of the many regions of discourse that there are. If we say that 'it is – seemingly – correct in physics and astronomy to talk about light emissions within the visible band as being generated at a relatively early stage after the Big Bang', it would be quite wrong to take this as a comment endorsing the correctness of the physics that says that. We have, of course, no competence in physics or any of the other natural sciences, and are simply in no position to either endorse or contest the scientific value of the claims that one or another science makes – our endorsement of particle physics would be as scientifically worthless as any other philosopher's. The correct way to understand us is as saying that, as far as contemporary physics is concerned, these are acceptable ways of speaking of such phenomena as light and color. The ways in which one can talk about the temporal origins of light are just different from those that are (in biology) acceptable for talking about the origins of color vision, and it would, therefore, be a serious mistake to conflate the two, and to suppose that the timescale for talking about the generation of light within the visible spectrum have to be integrated with that for talking about the origin of color vision. Thus, our resistance to the materialist way of setting out what 'science' says, and where 'consciousness' fits in arises from the conviction that such remarks are, themselves, of a grammatical character (whether those who make them would accept this or not) but that they seem inaccurate or misleading characterizations of the grammar in question, of what is intelligibly said in the different scientific disciplines, and therefore of what can intelligibly be further said about what those disciplines might show. Thus, the protestation that 'it seems impossible to understand how such experiential qualities could ever be produced by the interactions of purely physical systems' seems to us to arise from the failure to get a clear grasp upon the ways in which different parts of the wide diversity of disciplines called – or calling themselves – sciences fit together or operate independently. The difficulties may be presented to us as those of finding room for 'consciousness' in a world picture which is (or, key word, seems to be) at odds with what 'science' will allow could possibly be the case, and may seem, therefore, to present a true difficulty, that of wedging into a pretty thoroughly worked out and exclusive scheme a kind of phenomenon for which this scheme has hitherto made no room whatsoever. If that were so, then perhaps it *would* be a 'hard problem', but it is at least as plausible to think that the difficulties follow from the ways in which the purported description of 'the world according to science' simply short circuits the difficulties and complexities confronting the derivation of any such thing. After all, this last sentence may invite us to think that it would be 'impossible' to see how 'experiential qualities' could 'ever be produced by the interaction of purely physical systems'. Everything in this remark hinges upon what 'purely physical systems' are presumed to be, i.e., how this expression is being used. Are human beings purely physical systems within the meaning of the act? Or, which is presumably much the same, are there any human beings? 'Human being' is certainly not amongst the concepts of particle physics, and if we take those as the measure of what there is, then there are only purely physical systems, and no human beings. It is, however, a cliché about modern physics that it needs to attempt to unify the two different theories that encompass the very large and the very small, the world of microphysics and that of the universe as a whole – but if that is so then physics does not insist that there are only microsystems, and there is no reason, then, to think that it must insist that there is nothing between the very large and the very small, and, therefore, no reason to exclude the existence of human beings, but human beings are not microsystems. Either, then, we can have it that there are human beings, but since they are not explicitly recognized within particle physics, they must be something other than 'purely physical systems', and that, therefore, 'purely physical systems' are not the only kinds of things that there are. Alternatively, we can accept that human beings are 'purely physical systems' and we accept that they do have color vision, hearing and the like, then, the conclusion would be that: purely physical systems manifestly do have such capacities, and there must therefore be something wrong with the use that has been given to the expression 'purely physical systems' so as to encourage us to think that it was 'impossible' (no less) for them to be capable of stereoscopic color vision and so forth – since such things patently do have these capacities. Of course, if we accept this, we are not accepting that any 'purely physical system' is capable of these things, but that only certain kinds of them – human beings and a range of other kinds of living creatures – are. Trivially, that has a lot to do with their physical structure, but one that cannot be described at the level of microphysics, with their possession of eyes, ears, noses etc. The development of these features of the organism presents, surely, no problem of massive discontinuity for the natural sciences, where they are already well accommodated and, presumably for the purposes of some sciences, well understood. The transitions involved between the stories told by one natural science and another do not involve the yawning gulf we have been invited to suppose confronts us. The transition between inanimate matter and animate forms is not itself *entirely* understood, but this is not because anyone in the relevant sciences imagines that an understanding of animate beings must in any way defy the principles of particle and other kinds of physics (though it may depart from those presently in place). Nor does anyone suppose that the development of the eye, the ear, 'radar' in bats – whilst it might present an important transition in the evolution of particular forms – presents a vast scientific gulf, for, of course, the development of these is just part of the evolution of the diversity of species that now inhabit the globe.

If human beings are 'purely physical systems' and are the kind of 'purely physical systems' that have not only the kinds of physical structures that detect sounds, discriminate colors, and so on, and if they are also accepted to be 'purely physical systems' that have long evolutionary histories, then it is quite apparent that some of the natural sciences already understand a very great deal about how these capacities have arisen in 'purely physical systems' and, in accord with their disciplinary remits, they do so in 'purely physical terms.'

If, however, we think that a purely physical system must be conceived only at the level of description available to microphysics, then we will, of course, have very considerable difficulties in seeing how the interaction of 'purely physical systems' of that kind might produce the 'experiential qualities' with which our (physics confounding) consciousness is so 'wonderfully filled'. It might, indeed, be impossible to achieve any understanding of this, but more because we have, in setting the matter out in that way, divested ourselves of the understandings that otherwise prevent this kind of mystification from ever getting a toehold.

Our own arguments could be alleged to leave us open in this way: that we have emphasized the extent to which the development of eyes, ears, noses and finger tips is well understood – though perhaps in the loose, programmatic and evidence-impoverished way that much evolutionary science is confined to – but that we have thereby evaded the very thing that is the problem, and that is not itself encompassed (as yet) by the biological sciences – including the neural ones – namely the consciousness that is (presumably) the upshot of these physical processes. What is the puzzle, and what the sciences now need to take on board, is the existence of 'experiential qualities', or, in other, and largely interchangeable words for the purposes of such discussions, the awareness of colors, sounds, odors and textures. It is this that there is no scientific provision for, and it is only here, in the context of the natural sciences so far, that the hard problem appears. These 'experiential qualities' are missing from the natural sciences, and therefore from the world it portrays, and the difficulty is, now, of introducing a phenomenon that those sciences have not, as yet, made serious efforts to come to terms with. We are unconvinced, however, by any of this, and the following sorts of grounds engender our refusal to buy into the problem – making it entirely an imagined problem, as far as we are concerned.

Once again, much depends upon accepting a very rough and ready, indeed, rather primitive conception of what it is that science has so far achieved, and what it cannot now do, a description which depicts everything in ways which suggest immense difficulties without considering whether there is any real necessity to describe them thus. Without doubting that there is much about the physics and physiology of sight, sound, touch, and smell that remains to be investigated, we can nonetheless dispute whether the (further) consideration of 'consciousness' calls for some profound topical and strategic break with work so far. That is, we don't accept that 'consciousness' is yet to be investigated. Insofar as there is sense and point to talking about investigating 'consciousness', this is already being done by studies of sight, sound, and by those of the bodily clock, the chemistry of sleeping and waking, the effects of drugs on the nervous system and so on. We insist on this partly because we are not persuaded to buy into the idea that consciousness 'has a phenomenology', and that it is this which provides something that both needs to be explained but that is, seemingly, elusive of our scientific reach (as if the various sciences were not, in their various ways, always and already trading on their 'phenomenological' access to color, sound, etc.). In fashionable terminology, there is 'something it is like' to be a bat (or a human being, or any other conscious creature) but can we possibly say, can we possibly capture, what whatever it is like *is like*. It is *the quality* of consciousness that is not mentioned or captured in the descriptions of ear drum vibration or, more generally, and using Quine's way of putting it, the effects of irradiations on our sensory surfaces.

Michael Tye writes:

"I taste a lemon, smell rotten eggs, feel a sharp pain in my elbow, see the color red. In each of these cases, I am the subject of a very different feeling or experience. For feelings and perceptual experiences, there is always something it is *like* to undergo them, some phenomenology that they have. As the phenomenal or felt qualities of experiences change, the experiences themselves change, but, if the phenomenal or "what it is like" aspects disappear altogether, then there is no experience left at all. I shall say that a mental state is phenomenally conscious, just in the case that there is some immediate subjective 'feel' to the state, some distinctive experiential quality"[102]

We certainly don't want to challenge the claim that Tye can distinguish the taste of lemons, detect the smell of rotten eggs, feel pains in different parts of his body, or see many things that are colored red. What we do doubt, however, is whether what he goes on to say in this paragraph adds anything {except repetition and/confusion) to the statement of these uncontested facts. Does the second sentence say anything other than that our sense of smell is different from the sensation of pain and from the deliverances of our color vision? Does 'In each of these cases, I am the subject of a very different feeling or experience' really mean anything different than that it is Michael Tye who has tasted the lemon, felt that pain when he struck his elbow, saw the red light just in time to stop the car - is that what his being 'the subject of a very different feeling or experience' means?

The same question arises with regard to the next sentence: 'For feelings and perceptual experiences, there is always something it is *like* to undergo them, some phenomenology that they have'. This could be a non-controversial remark, virtually a reiteration of what has been said in Tye's first sentence, that smelling rotten eggs is not like feeling a pain in your arm, and that both of these are different from seeing the red sky at dawn (though, of course, watching a beautiful

---

[102] Michael Tye, *Ten Problems of Consciousness: A Representational Theory of the Phenomenal World* (Cambridge, MA: M.I.T. Press, 1996), p. 3.

dawn sky develop is surely an experience, not one of our feelings – though it may have associated feelings – whilst the pain in the elbow is something that is felt). But should we be led by these reformulations into thinking that they are amplifications, that Tye is saying more about the fact that these things that he has tasted, smelled, suffered and witnessed are the sort of thing that almost any one of his readers will also have tasted, smelled etc?

> "As the phenomenal or felt qualities of experiences change, the experiences themselves change, but, if the phenomenal or "what it is like" aspects disappear altogether, then there is no experience left at all. I shall say that a mental state is phenomenally conscious, just in the case that there is some immediate subjective 'feel' to the state, some distinctive experiential quality".[103]

It seems that he is aiming to say more, to tell us what the nature of a conscious mental state is, but consider, first, that the claim that that there is no experience left if the phenomenal qualities disappear really says only that if we do not feel anything in the elbow then there is no pain, if we do not smell the laboratory gas then there is no 'smell of rotten eggs', and that if we do not see the red sky, the red light, the red curtains etc. then we do not see anything red. The concluding sentence, taken on its own, can at best only be a summation of the triple reiterations of the same point, that our senses of vision, smell, hearing, taste, and our sensations too, are different from each other, and that, further, that these senses yield different deliverances, that the smell of rotten eggs is different from the smell of a cooking meal (the smell of the meal varying with the kind of meal it is), that the sound of a punk band is very different from that of a progressive rock one, and that neither sound much like a jazz quartet, and so on. But whilst the sentence is a reiteration of what everybody knows it is surely not a felicitous or particularly perspicuous one. It does license the confusion that, we think, Tye wants, which is that there is some "immediate subjective 'feel' to the state, some distinctive experiential quality" that is over and above the sensation, the smell, the

---

[103] *Ibid.*

taste and so on, and that is the 'something that it is like' to have these sensations, smells, tastes and viewings, something that (and very much so to speak) it feels like to smell rotten eggs, or to look into the red sky. Insinuating this will service the illusion that consciousness is elusive, that we ought to be able to describe what it is like to smell rotten eggs or to see something red, and we ought, perhaps, to feel that we should be able to say what it is that makes this a perception of red rather than a sensation of pain or a smell of wet straw - after all, it is we who are having these 'subjective feels' and we can tell one from the other, so we should be able to say what enables us to tell those differences. But any such suggestion is gratuitous to the matter formulated to imply it, and represents (by omission) a mischaracterization of the role of expressions such as 'I can smell rotten eggs' and 'Those tiles are green' in our language. It is, clearly, the case that these are the means of describing our experiences, sensations, feelings, etc., not the description of only the materials of our experience, perceptions, sensations and feelings, which then await *a further* description of the experience that encounter with those materials generate. To say that it is a smell of 'rotten eggs' *is* to say what the smell is like, and to differentiate that smell from other smells - the smells differ by virtue of being the kind of smells that they are, and we can say what it is like to smell something by saying what that something smells like. Thus, the answer to the question 'What do rotten eggs smell like?' can be straightforwardly answered by exposing someone to rotten eggs: *that* is how they smell. Indeed, we can describe how rotten eggs smell by comparing them with other smells – sulphurous gas smells like 'rotten eggs', so if you are familiar with that gas then... And, of course, one can become refined, complicated and elaborate, not to say poetic, in the kinds of descriptions and comparisons that one can make of, for example, smells: consider wine tasters and whiskey connoisseurs. The temptation to think otherwise resides in making it sound as if to describe the smell is one thing, and to describe the experience of the smell is another, but to describe the smell *is* to describe 'the experience', and we do have resources (of variable richness) for saying what the smell smells like. If we are drawn to the idea of giving yet further description, of describing what it is to smell the smell of rotten eggs, then we shall indeed find ourselves without resources to give such a description, and if convinced that they ought to be available, we will then begin to think that there is something that is evading our descriptive efforts, that somehow we simply cannot capture the 'what it is like' to smell rotten eggs.

We are suggesting that it is hardly surprising that there is no other, ready vocabulary in which to 'describe our experiences' since there has been a failure to notice that this job is done by the vocabulary we already have available. There is a confused idea of what it is to describe an experience in circulation here. We learn how to tell the difference between one smell and another by smelling them, not by identifying them in accord with some description which tells us how the smell of coffee should smell, and how we are to recognize. It is because we can identify and differentiate smells that our characterizations of them get going in the first place. The idea that there is any further identifiable difference between 'the experience of smelling' and 'the experience of hearing' should, we think, be seen to be equally meaningless – there is no way in which we 'tell the difference' between hearing something and tasting something, hence there is nothing that could play the role of telling us what the difference between seeing a color and feeling a pain is – that we see one and feel the other – that we see this color and feel such a pain in that place - is the difference. Perhaps we can intensify appreciation of the emptiness of formulations such as "a mental state is phenomenally conscious, just in the case that there is some immediate subjective 'feel' to the state, some distinctive experiential quality" save as less perspicuous formulations of the facts that we have tasted lemons, smelled sulphurous gases, and so forth, by suggesting that if indeed there is 'something it is like' to have this immediate subjective 'feel' then it ought to make sense to say that there is something it is like not to have this immediate subjective 'feel', but, of course, it does not, and so the difference that this latter formulation marks is, quite simply, that between being capable of seeing, hearing, smelling, tasting etc, and not being capable of that.

It should now be clearer why we deny that there need be any special division of science with 'consciousness' as its subject matter, though this does not involve us in denying the existence of anything. 'Consciousness', as deployed in Tye's case, which is by no means idiosyncratic, turns out to be no more than a contrivance which locates the varied capacities of sight, hearing, taste and smell within a single collection, so as to convey the impression that there is something common to them other than the fact that they are our sensory modes. Recognized as identifying those varied capacities, it can then be seen that 'consciousness' is far from being a *new* topic for the sciences – do we need a 'new science of consciousness' – let alone insisting that it is an intractable mystery when it identifies only a range of topics (sound, vision etc.) that are already well catered for within the sciences (was one of Newton's early and great contributions not on opticks?), and that, far from presenting us with impenetrable mysteries, are already well understood.

If our argument is right, we are very far from being in the position of having to attempt to insert a new subject matter, consciousness, into a science which is ostensibly unable to accommodate it; but we appreciate that our argument thus far is unlikely to seem, to those we would dissuade, to be a really persuasive one. They are likely to regard us as – at the very least –evading the difficulty, which is that whilst there might be abundant scientific work on vision, taste, hearing, smell, etc., across different disciplines including physics and neuroscience, we are none the less ignoring the fact that the smell, the visual appearance, and the audible texture of phenomena are not present in those sciences. More seriously, we are perhaps – and perhaps deliberately – overlooking the real philosophical significance of Tye's remark that: "In each of these cases, I am the subject of a very different feeling or experience" – the sentence makes reference, of course, to a subject of these experiences, and it is that subject which is both the possessor of consciousness and that does not appear in the natural sciences – where, there, is the room for the subject and the subject's awareness of its experiences?

We are trying throughout to dispel a philosophical picture of 'the mind', and when we deny that there is need for a 'phenomenology of consciousness' we are denying that such a project is a really meaningful exercise, but we are not thereby in any way bringing into doubt that people are conscious or conscious of or aware of things. That these things are so does not compel us to think that they must imply the existence of some unified mental phenomenon which must be distinctively provided for in any putative 'science of the mind', over and above the studies of the diversity of sensory modes (mainly) and their interrelationships that are already under way. The supposition that we need a phenomenology is, we now attempt to show, merely the perpetuation of the hoary old supposition that we have been criticizing above, to wit that there must be some kind of 'representation' of the outer world 'within' the mind. This 'image' might be termed 'our experience of' the world, but it serves much the same purpose as the idea of a 'representation', that our capacity to respond to an external world requires that that environment be matched by something in our 'mental realm', something that corresponds to what is 'out there' but mediates or substitutes for our perception of that which is out there. Thus, the proposal for a 'phenomenology of consciousness' - though it may be anything but materialist or reductionist in intent – nonetheless risks preserving the conviction that there must be an identifiable 'inner representation' of any worldly counterpart.

'In the Mind' Does Not Signify: In Psychology's Remit

At the outset let it be plain: in denying the necessity for – indeed, in strictest terms, the possibility of – a 'phenomenology' we are, as always, disputing the intelligibility of a philosophical proposal, not attempting to legislate what kinds of things there are. Denying that there can be a 'phenomenology of consciousness' is not, therefore, denying that people can, as they ordinarily do, 'describe their experience', but what they do when they do that is not the sort of operation to be carried out in a 'phenomenology'. The possibility of the latter cannot, therefore, be presumed on the basis of the reality of the former, for that actuality is entirely independent of philosophical partisanship. Once again, to reach the point at which a 'phenomenology' in the proper sense can be proposed requires building on a set of *a priori* philosophical assumptions.

Another impulse propelling people toward the idea of an 'inner representation' is the desire to capture the topic of 'mind' for the discipline – science, even – of psychology. This might seem an odd thing to say, but it should be remembered that the idea of psychology as 'the study of the mind' has only recently been restored to repute. Prior to the 1950's, and the influential – but deeply misleading - interventions inspired by Noam Chomsky (and others) around and after the middle of that decade, psychology was not the science of mind but 'the science of behavior'. We have no enthusiasm for behaviorism, being apt to feel that its intrinsic deficiencies were not its worst feature, for these held sway only temporarily. Its worst effect was to prepare the way for the 'mentalist' reaction, to appear to set things up in such a way that, given that the conception of psychology as 'a science of behavior' was manifestly inadequate, the only and obvious alternative was to (re)turn to the idea of a 'science of the mind'. How specifically does this latter turn bear upon present considerations? By implying that whatever might be considered 'mental' aspects of human life, whatever might be thought of as things done by or involving the mind, should naturally be deemed part of the subject matter of the science of psychology – thus, for example, perception is such a kind. Therefore, any matters which have to do with 'perception' must involve some sorts of occurrences 'in the mind', for they are supposedly 'mental' or 'psychological' phenomena.

But this kind of logic, propelled as it is by prior assumptions about what 'the science of psychology' must be, is what we are very reluctant to accept. We do not accept that understanding how people are able to perceive, or perhaps fail to perceive, certain kinds of phenomena involves any reference to any authentically 'psychological' phenomena. That persons may or may not be able to perceive what is on show when viewed through a microscope, in the skies to be seen by the naked eye, or discerned in a painting ordains no specifically 'mental' allusion. It is not the working or the failing of any 'psychological' mechanisms that facilitates or inhibits their capacity to make appropriate identifications of what is – in these cases – before their very eyes. In all these cases it is, rather, the availability to them of certain techniques – sometimes quite elementary, at other times not – that are part of – not the mind – but of the sciences of physiology and astronomy, or of aesthetics. Thus, the capacity to 'perceive' a constellation in the sky depends upon simple techniques that enable one to pick out and interrelate some of the stars in view and give them a name. We do not, either, think that a psychological explanation is needed for the fact that there are stars in view when we look up at the night sky, though neither are we suggesting that any techniques are necessary to see those lights (though a good deal of background scientific information is needed to see that they are stars, in our modern understanding of what stars are). Explanations to people about how to discern the important and telling features of an artistic achievement involves teaching them about *paintings,* not about eyeballs, nervous systems, and so forth. Consider the case of Noam Chomsky's reallocation of the description of the grammar of languages to 'the study of mind'. Presented as a consequence of scientific advances, Chomsky's disciplinary re-allocation is much better viewed as a matter of definitional gerrymandering. It pivots upon the simple *commonplace* fact that we can and do speak of people 'knowing' languages – as simple as most of the facts Chomsky appeals to in justification of his inflation of the modest notational innovations his actual linguistic work involves into a purported revolution in our understanding of the mind. Follow Chomsky in this, and you will immediately be invited to believe that it follows that the study of language is the study of what people know, and knowledge surely resides in the mind! However, it is not as if studying 'knowledge' as a mental condition was some kind of substantive psychological enterprise, since the study of 'what people know' turns out to be, after all, studies of that which they know. In other words, in Chomsky's case, the study of that language which is what it is that people know is to be formulated in....why, *grammatical* terms, of course. The basic tools of Chomsky's linguistics are parsing and paraphrasing, perfectly ordinary non-psychological practices. Of course, Chomsky's relentless and ingenious self-promotion does get more complicated than this, but, since we do not really treat 'in the mind' as a particularly informative expression in such discourses, we do not see that anything is really added to 'the study of language' by making it 'the study of knowledge (of language)', and take it that 'what people know' is the language, some of which is surely its grammatical principles - then the study of what they know is (in part) the study of those principles, not any states of mind (not least since 'knowledge' is not a state of mind). Take a skeptical view of the career of Chomsky's further reasoning, and it seems to take this quite unconvincing course: that the study of language is not the study of languages but of something else, entirely, which is 'language' and is putatively a neurological structure of the brain, which is supposedly the embodiment of something called 'universal grammar' but which is not to be identified with any of the languages people actually speak (encouraging others to hold that it encodes a language called 'mentalese'[104]). The upshot of his, however, is effectively to retract the initial, motivating claim that the study of language is the study of what people know, but 'language', the neurological structure, is not anything that, in any intelligible sense, speakers

---

[104] It is worth noting here that, many years after it was announced, the study of 'universal grammar' remains a largely programmatic proposal, there being little specification of the actual form of that grammar.

know[105]. In the sense in which they, ordinarily speaking, 'know English' people certainly do not know 'mentalese' (the name given by Fodor to the supposedly innate 'language of thought'). However, when one is confronted with a contemporary textbook in Chomskian linguistics one encounters a large number of preliminaries about science, about the mind, about innatism and rationalism and the like, but when one gets down to business, what is one actually confronted with but 'grammar', attempted (abstract) descriptions of the acceptable forms that the arrangement of types of words may take in a language. One can, of course, say that the study of language is 'of the mind' insofar as a language is part of culture, but that is to use the expression 'the mind' in a very different way, one that would encompass the study of theatre, music, scholarship or other topics. There is no need to think of these as 'mental phenomena' or to imagine that their portrayal is any kind of specifically psychological affair.

The purpose of the 'digression' on Chomsky was to make the point that there is an attempt to appropriate subject matters for the – largely - imagined science of psychology, with the appropriation of 'grammar' being a prominent and influential case in point. The point about their being no 'phenomenology' of consciousness is very much a parallel to this, it being our claim that the proposal for a 'phenomenology of consciousness' is an attempt to identify something 'in the mind' that can be studied.

Phenomenology of Nothing

The idea that there is something – consciousness – to be studied is not something derivative from the phenomenological tradition alone, but as much a successor to a very old standby of the empiricist tradition, that of sense data, of

---

[105] To evade some of these difficulties, Chomsky switched from 'know' to 'cognize', but this is the same order of evasion as the hybrid 'mind/brain' and gives away the fact that one does not need 'know' at all – and does not therefore need any substitute for it, either.

'the qualia', the appearances yielded by our sensory apparatus, from which we may infer or attempt to construct inferences about what, if anything, is behind them in the way of external objects. We have immediate acquaintance with the 'qualia', they just show themselves to us, and if we are to have knowledge of anything beyond the qualia, of what may exist external to and at a distance from our senses, then we must be able to 'construct' or infer from the qualia to whatever phenomena they represent. Thus, again, the way in which a problem is set up 'transports' the qualia inside our mental world, for these are (from a good empiricist skepticism, only possibly) the upshots of the irradiations on our nerve endings that Quine talks about, and therefore follow from any contact we might be having with the external world. In the empiricist scheme, too, we can describe the qualia entirely independently of whatever it is, if anything, that stimulates the appearance of the qualia. The kind of mental content that protagonists of qualia might envisage may be very different from those who advocate 'representations' but the idea that there is a counterpart 'in our minds' to whatever there is 'in the world' is the same across very different traditions, and everywhere supports the idea that there is a need, therefore, for a description of that mental content, and an associated idea that there is a need to provide it with a location and/or a function within our mental economy. But if there are no representations, no qualia, then there is no need to give an account of them as 'part of the mind'.

Again, we repeat, we are not trying to deny that people see things across the street, that they have red spots before their eyes, that they have looked on Whitney Houston plain, or any of these things, for that these things are so is the common position-neutral site of all the philosophical positions. We are dissenting from the philosophical construals that are set upon these commonplaces, in particular, from the idea that there is a need for some kind of mental mediation between Whitney Houston and our sightings of her. Up to now we have been emphasizing the way in which the philosophical tradition presses toward the conviction that mediation is necessary. Now we want to show that these pressures can and should be resisted.

We have no doubt that the convictions we are questioning are very stubborn, that there will be strong resistance to the idea that we have really confronted, let alone liquidated, the 'something that it is like' issue. We are not aspiring to do more than chip away at the multiple conceptions which underpin the formulation of that problem, and fully expect the problem to rear its head again after the immediately preceding arguments. That our 'subjective experiences' arise from our molecular nature is not something that those we are arguing with would deny for they would characteristically wish to be materialists. That is their problem with consciousness, for the 'material' origins of consciousness are of course what give rise to our 'subjective experiences', but those themselves are seemingly of an immaterial nature, affirmation of their existence seemingly giving rise to a commitment which is inconsistent with the prior, and more fundamental, materialist one. Hence, from this point of view, there is a problem, and it is the one which therefore confronts, in a thoroughly perplexing way, the very presuppositions of the materialist project: there is an 'explanatory gap' between the facts of our physical states and the (presumptively consequent) subjective experiences. It is easy enough to see how the story told by molecular science (though it may have much work still to do, especially in understanding the brain) traces the material impacts on our sensory system, traces the further effect of light falling on the retina, of sound waves agitating our inner ear, etc., but it is difficult to see where in this story there appear either the subjective experiences that are associated with these processes or, worse, the subject whose subjective experiences these are.

The explanatory gap is, for us, no less illusory than the other problems we have tried to defuse, and is no less traceable than the others to philosophical origins, and this particular kind of puzzlement is surely traceable to the classic source of Cartesian influence. Whilst it may be the ambition of contemporary materialists to expunge Cartesian *dualism* from philosophy of mind, as we noted earlier, it is nonetheless their practice to attempt to do so in the terms that Descartes initially set out for thinking about these things. We are, at this point, almost certainly struggling with the poisonous inheritance of the conception of the mind as something 'inner', and the derivative assumption that, therefore, the relation between the 'inner occurrences' and the external situations to which we respond requires some kind of mediation, involves some 'representation' which appears on this – the hitherto 'inner' – side of the inner/outer divide. The materialist declines Descartes dualism, but preserves his inner/outer division, and therefore finds the conclusion that the mind must be the brain compelling, and therefore must be some kind of molecularly constituted phenomenon. It must be so for, of course, the mind is (as in the classically Cartesian assumption) a series of inner workings in the head, but the only inner workings a materialist can find in the head are those of the brain.

The deeper issues, which we cannot go into here, then, between the Wittgensteinian and Cartesian traditions with respect to the 'brain sciences' is not, in any way, to contest or aim to prohibit neurological studies, but to insist that this post-Cartesian story does nothing to clarify understanding of the relationship between the results of such inquiries and our understanding of how people go about their affairs. Thus, we cannot find the materialist conclusions at all compelling. Although even a little brain science clearly shows that there is a great deal of electro-chemical activity on the part of the brain, the conclusion that the study of this will reveal the 'nature of the mind' depends upon the Cartesian assumption that the mind is 'inside the head'. That prior assumption is necessary to give force to the supposition that since (in a materialist world) there is and can be nothing else in the head except the brain, therefore the brain must be the mind, there being no other plausible candidate. Then, of course, there must be moves to 'materialize' the inner representations, to locate the place within the workings of the brain where these are to be found. (It is worth noting here that 'functionalism' is a way to try and deal with the problem that nothing specific is readily to be identified with these). Still, for someone captivated by the conviction that there must be something that it is like within the mind, the problem will remain – where is the experience itself to be sited within the materialist account? For something like that is surely not to be found in the world-according-to-science as the materialists understand it, and yet, nonetheless, and, for them, undeniably, there is something that is 'something that it is like' which is actually there.

We have certainly not denied that people smell things, that they see things, that they hear things, that they taste things, and so on, but have tried, above, to explain that the idea that 'there is something that it is like' to see things etc, is not a perspicuous way of talking about these matters. Again, we will deny that there is a subject for science, 'consciousness', but, again, we will not be making absurd denials of commonplace truths.

No Explanatory Gap To Bridge

The 'explanatory gap' is, to put the issue crudely, that we need an explanation for the experienced contents of our consciousness, we need an explanation for the phenomena which comprise the 'inner representations' of the smell, color, flavor or whatever, in the form that those present to us as subjects as our sensory modalities. When we say that there are no contents to 'consciousness' we are not, then, saying that no one smells anything, sees anything or tastes anything, and we are certainly not saying that people are like the supposedly imaginable zombies that will be introduced shortly, that their smells, sights, tastes are either illusions or epiphenomena that must be excluded from the molecular story. We are saying the ideas we are trying to deny follow from a wrong way of understanding (a) what the molecular story needs to do and (b) how the molecular story works.

Let us try and explain our point about consciousness by analogy to the case of the contents of the visual field. If we deny that the visual field has any contents, we are attempting to deny that a standard philosopher's way of talking about the visual field is at all helpful, however much it means to be so. Our denial, strictly formulated, is this: the visual field has no contents in the sense which many philosophers suppose that it does. What we are contesting is this kind of idea: that there is, out there in the world, an array of phenomena with which our visual system is currently interacting. The physical inputs from that exterior array are being fed into our nervous system, and it is the activity of the nervous system that is generating an inner representation of that outer situation, and it is the upshot that those nervous system processes generate that constitute our visual field. Thus, the contents of our visual field are the representations generated by the nervous system. *Ergo*, our visual field is inside the head, is part of the nervous system.

Gilbert Ryle long ago explained to us why this kind of argument could only appear convincing as a solution to the problem it sought to resolve if subject only to the most thoughtless acceptance. Here is the initial puzzle: how can we see the external world? Answer: we don't. What we see is an inner representation of the external world. But how does this help us to be clearer about what it is to be able to see something? Being told that we see something 'outside' ourselves might seem troubling and the trouble might seem to be alleviated by saying that what we see is 'inside' ourselves, not remote, but directly accessible to us – but the real puzzle remains, how is the idea of seeing something inner easier to understand than seeing something outer – the idea of 'seeing' has remained unclarified throughout. And it is just this kind of problem that remains unresolved, that troubles those who feel there is an explanatory gap. Hence, we are rejecting the idea that there is any content to the visual field in this sense only. We find the story leading to the inner representations that exhibit the visual field unconvincing. Of course, we do not doubt that the visual field has contents in the sense that one can respond to requests to describe the contents of it, can distinguish between things which currently are within the field, and things that previously were or are not yet in the visual field. Thus, if asked to give such a description one might talk about the car park outside the office window, the cars parked in the car park, the people walking through the car park, the lamps that are meant to illuminate it, and so on. Indeed people's visual fields have contents, but visual fields are not, themselves, any part of the physical world. My visual field is no more a part of the external world than it is a state of inner imagistic representation in my inner one, and all that is present in my visual field is whatever is out there, outside the office window, in the car park, and so on. My visual field is not a kind of place, where anything can be located, and which would be distinct from and, therefore, located elsewhere than, outside the office window, in the car-park etc. My visual field is not a kind of place, and therefore, there is no need to suppose that if this place is not 'outside' then it must be 'inside.' The visual field *is* nowhere in *that* sense, for the expression 'visual field', as we all use it all the time, refers simply to whatever it is that I can see from my current vantage point, and it is demarcated not by any kind of boundary in space but by the range of my vision, by what it is possible to see from here. So, describing my visual field is simply a matter of describing what I can currently see, looking from here, and looking that way, and the contents of that visual field are simply the things that I can see whatever they are. Thus, what I am describing are not my inner representations but, rather, the view from my office window (and no one would, we hope, object to talking about such a thing as the view from my office window, or engage in an effort to figure out where the view from my office window is – is it in my office, in the window etc?). Describing the contents of the visual field, in this case, is a matter of describing the car park, the cars and so on. In this sense, the visual field has contents, but we do not need to find any separate location, distinct from looking out of my office window, and looking toward the car park, for either the visual field itself or the contents of it. But this is a very long way from accepting that there is any such thing as a visual field or any such thing as the contents of it in the sense that philosophers might be tempted to think of it - as they are, indeed, inclined to think of consciousness and its contents (for, of course, the visual field would be, on their convictions, part of the content of consciousness). We have made plain that denying that consciousness has any contents – and that there is a necessary scientific task of accounting for those contents – is a denial that consciousness has contents in the sense that philosophers seek for such things. Of course, we might talk of the 'contents of someone's consciousness' but this would – as with the visual field case – be merely a matter of describing what they are conscious of, what they are aware of, attending to, thinking about – it would be a description of, e.g., the music they are hearing, the food they are eating, the perfume they are smelling. We surely do not need a scientific specialty to teach us how to describe music, food or the effects of a perfume in scientific (molecular) terms. In this sense, there is again no work for a 'new science of consciousness' to do.

These then are some reasons, sourced in the Cartesian tradition, for thinking that there is an explanatory gap, but there is a sense in which the impression of an explanatory gap involves a misunderstanding of how scientific explanations explain. It would be a calumny, in the light of all we have said, in this chapter and others, to suggest that we are in any sense against science. We are against what seem to us misrepresentations of science. The fact that it is done in the name of science and accompanied by dogmatic insistence upon the decisive importance of science does not mean that it thereby renders an accurate understanding of science. Those who protest that there is an explanatory gap, it seems to us, are making a mistake akin to that made by someone who imagines that there is a problem in explaining how loud speakers work: they might think that there is an explanatory gap, a yawning one, between the description of this relatively simple machinery, and the way it produces vibrations in the air: how can these relatively uncomplicated arrangements reproduce such a vast variety of intricate, delicate and musical sounds. But the gap is an imaginary one, and they have simply failed to see that there is nothing more to explain – given the principles that govern the operation of the loudspeaker system then *that is* the explanation of how it generates the sounds that it does. The failure to see that the description of how our visual system works is the explanation of how we are able to observe what we do, and that there is no additional work to explain why whatever we might see is present in our visual field in the way that it is. To understand how the color spectrum interacts with the visual system *is* to understand why this color sample is red, and nothing further is needed to explain why it is that red looks red rather than green etc., for, of course, those things are just the effects of the color spectrum and our visual system. It is not that being unable to say why red is this color rather than some other color is something that defies the capacity of our science, for insofar as that is an intelligible issue at all, it is one which has already been dealt with by the science, when that is properly understood.

Further, a point whose relevance we will elaborate next, we are not fooled into thinking that the omission of a space and the insertion of a slash between the words 'brain' and 'mind' betokens the existence of any effective and worked through argument that legitimates the unity seemingly indicated by this facile typographical sleight. The postulation of the mind/brain looks to us like a confession of confusion, not a fix for it. If it is not compulsory to adopt this fusion of the two words by typographic fiat, then the idea that there is a need to describe the brain at the level of a series of mental operations also evaporates. The idea that there is a 'level of description' of the workings of the brain which is necessary, and which describes not merely physical but 'mental' operations, such as those of, e.g., thinking, or, more generically, of 'information processing', has (although controversial) been a great asset to many materialists in seeming to demand the mind/brain unification, and thereby provide a technique for incorporating 'the mind' into the materialist world view: the mind involves only a certain kind of (relatively abstract) description of the workings of the brain, of the 'operations' the brain performs through its causal workings. An uncountable number of contemporary thinkers have been carried away by the hallowed idea that the mind is busy about the handling of images or representations, and that the operations that need to be described are those of generating and transforming representations. The idea that there is an 'inner', i.e. 'mental', counter-part to the 'outer' world (its representation) has the tempting initial appearance of solving the problem of the relationship between these two otherwise dissociated realms. But these assumptions, and their necessity, are all of philosophical provenance, and it is this that needs to be questioned. If the brain is not carrying out these 'mental operations' then there may remain much to be found out about how it, the brain, works, but there will be nothing to be determined as to how it 'carries out' the tasks of thought.

There has been a philosophical slide in the understanding of the mind from thinking of it as identical with 'consciousness', through a series of steps – often announced as 'scientific' advances – into supposing that 'the mind's' operations are largely 'unconsciously' carried out. Part of the reason for this has been the conviction that 'the mind' is an ensemble of states and processes, and that these must be located and identified (and must, of course, prove to be 'material' states and processes if there are to be any such things at all). Relatedly, and another part of the rationale, is that introspection turns up empty with respect to these mental states and processes. People are not conscious of these states and processes, but – given the assumption that 'the mind' must consist in states and processes (since there is nothing else – unless one goes for 'fields' – for them to consist in) then the fact that they cannot be identified by those who must have them dictates that they are not to be considered conscious, and must, therefore, be unconscious. An easy and encouraging thought is that since there is so much for the mind to do in relating our inner representations to the complexities of the external world, and in such ways as to administer the operation of our bodies to provide timely and therefore often instant responses to the environment, these processes must just run too quickly for our consciousness to capture them. Withdraw the assumption that the mind is a constellation of states and processes, and this sequence of thoughts disintegrates. However, grant the sequence for argument's sake, leaving then the question: but where does 'consciousness' fit in here? What are consciousness's own operations, and how do they purportedly relate to those of 'the mind's' other operations being carried out in the brain? The term 'unconscious mental processing' seems to us merely a superfluous coinage, of no more real use than talking of digestion as 'unconscious food processing'.

The idea that there is a need for a description of the brain at a 'mental' level can be encouraged by the example of the image that light creates on the back of the retina, which image is inverted. Since the image presented to the brain is upside down, and since the world as we view it is 'the right way up', it seems clear that the brain must carry out operations that (somehow) turn the image on the retina upside down again. But this all assumes what there is no need to assume, which is that the image on the back of the retina plays any kind of role in vision. There is an attraction to do so if one is attached to the idea of 'representation', of course, for here there appears to be a specifically identifiable one, albeit one that requires the kind of 'functional' treatment of mental operations that re-work the spatial layout of that image, with it being – since the image is a visual representation - the visual properties of the image that require transformation. However, this supposes that the image as such is not causally inert in vision, a mere by product of the causal impacting of light on the retina, for if that is so, then the fact that the image is 'wrong way up' is inconsequential to vision. That is, it is not the visual shape of the image that the nervous system is responding to but the distribution of light's impacts across the rods and cones constituent of the retina, and the causally chained sequence of electro-chemical reactions which the causal impact of the light causally initiates. In short, if this is so, then there is just no need for a level of description of brain activity which captures a set of corresponding operations which transform a presented inverted image of (say) an upright triangle into a perceived image of an upright triangle. The image is, of course, a product of the physics of optics, of the interaction of light and lenses, but the fact that this results from the crossing of the paths of beams of light does not mean that the existence of an image on the retina is anything but an adventitious occurrence relative to the physics of vision. The enunciation of the necessity for a 'functional level' of description – brain activity in this case at least – seems only an effort to evade the fact that the description of brain activity for scientific purposes does not need to provide other than a physiologically causal account, that the language of 'folk psychology' (or 'cognitive science') is simply superfluous to these.

Are we not now coming to the same position as the 'eliminativists', insisting that the neural sciences should stick to causality, and that they have no need to draw upon 'folk psychology'? To the extent of insisting that the study of the brain is a neurophysiological inquiry, and has no need for a 'functional' re-description of brain activity in 'mental' terms, we are, but the difference between us and the 'eliminativists' is that we do not think that this implies the elimination of 'mental' terms, their displacement throughout by neurophysiological descriptions, our adoption – in everyday use – of the latter in preference to the former. But then the eliminativists suppose that the 'mental' terminology is a failed theory of brain activity, whereas we never supposed that it was any such thing. The eliminativists and the functionalists agree in assuming that our mental vocabulary is a candidate description of brain activity, but disagree over whether neuroscientific research will vindicate those descriptions or fail to do so. We reject their common assumption. Our disagreement with them arises over whether it is the nature of our 'ordinary language' as such, and specifically, that encourages the view that it is a candidate description of brain activity, or whether the ordinary language only does this when viewed in the light of their post-Cartesian assumptions about the mind which, even more importantly, are really assumptions about the nature of language that we all speak. Which brings us back to our running theme, that they key problems arise long before, and really have nothing to do with, the evidence from the brain sciences that are (occasionally) introduced. When one arrives at the point where they are brought in, there everything turns not upon the evidence *per se,* but upon the way in which that evidence is brought in and presented (as with 'the image' on the retina).

To reiterate: Saying that someone is conscious involves saying that they are awake, that they react in normal ways to the situation, as opposed to being asleep or knocked out, and their reacting in the normal ways involves using their sight, hearing, touch, sense of smell and taste. Far from being impenetrable mysteries to the biological and brain sciences, these senses are already massively investigated as are the mechanisms of the body clock that put people to sleep and wake them up, along with the chemistry of soporifics etc. The state of mystery is rather imperiled here. One does feel differently when one is dressed than when one is naked, but it does not thereby follow that one is conscious of the socks that one is wearing on one's feet, of their contact with one's body. Being 'conscious of', rather, involves, is closest to, paying attention, noticing or being aware of – thus a sound may have been present in the vicinity and audible to one before one becomes conscious of it, before one notices, for example, that one's car alarm is going off. And there is a perfectly good sense of 'unconscious' in our ordinary language too, involved with when we do things without being aware that we do them – some are involuntary things, as when one is unconscious of the fact that one's face is twitching or grimacing in a certain way, and others are rather more habitual, as in shifting gears when one drives the car – one does these things unconsciously (though one is not unconscious when doing them, nor are they done by one's unconscious).

But do we want to identify 'mind' with 'consciousness'? Well, we don't want to identify 'mind' with anything, so we do not want to follow Velmans in supposing that: "'mind' refers to psychological states and processes that may or may not be conscious".[106] One tack seems to be to threaten our apparent autonomy by invoking a specter of our neurology as causally determining what we do, and enabling the elimination of our (so called) intentional vocabulary, but the strategy of argument seems to work the other way around, with the extension of our so-called intentional vocabulary into domains where causal description and explanation would seem to be entirely appropriate and appropriately exhaustive, to wit into the workings of the brain. Whilst this maneuver may appear to be licensed by the identification of 'the mind' with 'the brain' it simply seems to beg questions about why the brain should seem to be the site of psychological processes, conscious or otherwise. We are certainly not conscious of the workings of the brain, but that is very different from assigning to the brain a set of unconscious tasks to do. Assuredly the input of light into the retina stimulates reactions in the brain, and the causal character of these reactions clearly has much to do with how we see – and with other things such as how we maintain balance and the rest – but why suppose that the inputs and effects, considered in that way, need to be described in other than straightforwardly causal terms – why imagine, as Velmans does, that it is necessary to follow "current conventions in the psychology of perception" and "assume that the brain constructs a 'representation' or 'mental model' of the what is happening based on the input from the initiating stimulus, expectations, traces or prior related stimuli stored in long terms memory and so on". (113)   Might not one as well put scare quotes around 'constructs' as around 'representation' and 'mental model'? One could say that putting matters in these terms is heuristically useful, that treating the brain as if it carries out 'mental processes' such as 'creating representations' and 'making constructs' and 'producing mental models' is helpful in focusing and organizing research into the physiological reactions (not psychological processes) that occur in the brain, but that would, of course, undermine the project of contemporary philosophy of mind which advances such ways of talking as literal ones. There is no disagreement but that a lot is going on in the brain that has to do with why we don't keep tripping

---

[106] Max Velmans, *Understanding Consciousness* (Philadelphia: Routledge, 2000), p. 7.

over, why we sometimes fail to recognize things and so forth, but there is certainly reason to be circumspect about taking such cognitivist terminology seriously. After all, it begs the basic question that the Cartesian tradition never really resolved, which is why anyone would suppose that the existence of 'inner representations' made the apparently puzzling nature of our relation to the world around us any less puzzling. If we find it puzzling as to how we are capable of recognizing the situation in front of us as the kind of situation that it is though we can, for example, plainly see and hear what is going on, then why should it be thought persuasive that we can understand that situation by way of an inner template that 'represents' that situation? To return to Ryle, it is surely no less problematic that we can understand 'the model', the 'inner representation' as that we can understand the situation that the model purportedly stands for. The puzzlement was with the notion of understanding and to be told that we understand X's in terms of Y does not answer the question as to why we need Y's to understand X's nor how it is that we understand Y's themselves. Do we not need models to understand Y's, and so on in endless regress?

Velmans wants a better phenomenology of our consciousness, and proposes a notion of a reflexive relation between, for example, what is perceived and our perception of it – the cat is perceived as out in the world, where the cat is. The trouble with phenomenology, however, is that whilst it recognizes that consciousness is 'directed', intentional in Brentano's sense, is often rightly said to be consciousness of something , it nonetheless supposes that the experience, the consciousness, can be – so to speak – peeled off from the thing that it is experience of and that, therefore, there is something that provides the subject matter for 'psychological' investigations – how does the cat, which is 'external' to the perceiver's body, get to be perceived *as* external, for example? But isn't this merely because consciousness is presumed to be being mediated, and that is what the representations are? Talking about the cat being perceived as being out there in the world, and about the reflexive character of consciousness, does not, however, give or really avail a direct answer to the question: what is it that is perceived? Is it the cat, or is it an image of the cat? The necessity for an image is imposed by the desire to make the consciousness itself (and not whatever the consciousness is consciousness *of*) the focus of study – to study the cat that one sees could not be considered a psychological investigation, and so one needs to isolate the putative psychological element for investigation. This psychological element must reside 'in the mind' for it to be isolable from the 'initial stimulus' that, by 'mental processing', is eventually perceived as 'the cat on the mat by the door'. One must have a 'visual representation of the cat' in order to see 'the cat'. But does one see 'the visual representation of the cat'? But this can drive us back to other Cartesian necessities, the 'inner eye' that, not being any kind of eye, nonetheless visualizes -- and seems to us much more mysterious than the visual faculty involving two eyes that it purports to explain. Does not perceiving a visual representation require exactly the same things as detecting any visual phenomenon, and does the inner representation not, therefore, simply require the duplication of the supposed psychological processes?   But the visual representation is 'in the brain' and not something that the person with the visual representation in their brain actually sees – "the information in her own mental model is translated into something that she can observe or experience - but all she experiences is a phenomenal cat out in the world...While she focuses her attention on the cat she does not become conscious of 'having a mental model of a cat' in the form of neural states. Rather, she becomes conscious of what the neural states *represent* –an entity out in the external world".[107] Is she conscious of the 'content' of the neural states, that 'content' being, so to speak, what the neural states provide as representation – is she, then, conscious only of the contents of her brain? Or is she conscious of a mental image that the visual representation creates in her consciousness? Is she conscious of an image of the cat, but an image of the cat as being outside in the world? Or is she conscious of the cat itself? But if she is to be that, is she then conscious of two things, her mental image of the cat and

---

[107] Max Velmans, *op. cit.*, p. 114.

the actual cat that her mental image represents? Or is she mistaken in that her experience is of the neural states that have been 'translated into something that she can see and observe' or of whatever it is that these have been translated into when she thinks that it is the cat in the external world that she sees.

Mention of 'the phenomenal cat' , which is 'all she experiences', gives the game away – we are back to creating work for a supposed science of psychology, that of explaining how the brain-and-mind or the mind/brain or the mind's conscious and unconscious processes creates and manipulates a series of images that are deemed necessary not because there have been identified any image creating and processing neural elements, but because of the way that experiencing is set up, of the felt need to have something on 'the hither side of perception' that can be (so to speak) directly perceived and which can then be used as a means for the 'indirect' perception of whatever is outside in the world. All of this, further, presupposes that the brain can recognize a phenomenon from its input – it must, if it is to construct a visual representation, recognize that of which it is to produce a representation, identify the correct kind of representation required for the kind of thing that is providing the initial stimulus, namely the cat, and then the brain can help *us* recognize the cat by inputting this into our consciousness? Why is it not enough – and much simpler – to say that a certain configuration of neural states are produced by the input of the kind of visual stimulation that seeing a cat cross one's path causes, than to say that these neural states comprise a visual representation of a cat? Deeply, too, the problem is that of attempting to bridge the gap between the world 'inside our heads' and 'the world outside it' which is a more important Cartesian division than the mind/body split in many ways.

On 'Qualia' and Zombies

What need is there for 'qualia' as the material of conscious experience, which is itself the same as asking: what need is there for consciousness since consciousness seems to consist in the presentation of qualia? Much of a human organism's 'information processing' is supposedly done without accompanying qualia, so why can't all of it be accomplished in that way? Put differently, are zombies logically possible?[108] Could there conceivably be creatures that are materially indistinguishable from regular human beings but that are without consciousness?

'Materially indistinguishable' purportedly encompasses one or more of the forms -- physical (as in molecule for molecule identical), behavioral and functional – that are variously appealed to as providing the specification for a zombie. Asking the zombie question is imagined to pose a test case for the correctness of the materialist doctrine about the reducibility of mind to brain states. As such, it reproduces the assumption upon which the materialist approach depends, that human beings are mechanical information-processing systems, and the consequent puzzlement about the supposed presence of 'qualia'. It highlights the fact that, from this standpoint, the conception of consciousness is at odds with the conception of 'mechanical information-processing systems'. The zombie question can ostensibly focus this issue by asking: 'does consciousness play any role in relating the physical inputs (which are the impacts of the environment on the organism) to the physical outputs (which are the bodily movements of the organism)?' The transformation of the one into the other is a product of the lawlike relations between them, and the mind is to be understood as merely a mechanism which, mechanically, effects such transformations in accord with the relevant laws, hence 'consciousness' is apparently anomalous here since, even if it

---

[108] Zombies are debated in innumerable sources, including these: A. Cottrell, "Sniffing the Camembert: On the Conceivability of Zombies", *Journal of Consciousness Studies*, Vol. 6, 1999: Daniel Dennett, "The Unimagined Preposterousness of Zombies", *Journal of Consciousness Studies*, Vol. 2, 1995: O. Flanagan & T. Polger, "Zombies and the Function of Consciousness", *Journal of Consciousness Studies*, Vol. 2, 1995: Robert Kirk, "Zombies versus Materialists", *Proceedings of the Aristotelian Society* (supplementary volume), Vol. 48, 1974: Robert Kirk, "Why There Couldn't Be Zombies", *Proceedings of the Aristotelian Society*, Vol. 73, 1999 and N. J. T. Thomas, "Zombie Killer" in S. R. Hameroff et al. (Eds.), *Toward a Science of Consciousness II: The Second Tucson Discussions and Debates* (Cambridge, MA.: M.I.T. Press, 1998).

is a medium for such transformations, why is it distinct from all those transformations that are the product of the physical workings of the mind of which the mind's possessors are quite unaware? 'Consciousness' seems a gratuitous outcropping of the 'unconscious'.

Since the work that materialists assign to the mind is so extensive and requires such high speed processes, it seems clear that all this work could not possibly be done by consciousness (especially since the expression 'information-processing' has been extended in such a wide way). Our conscious attention is limited, our step by step thinking is insufficiently rapid to get through all the sequences postulated to direct our actions, so it must follow that the work that has to be done cannot be done by consciousness – hence the need for an 'unconscious'. This need is the product of a cycle of philosophical reasoning. The mind is equated with conscious thought and conscious thought is treated as the regulator of bodily conduct. It is noted that our actual behavior is not all the product of conscious thought – the more impressive finding in reports of studies of introspection is the poverty of their contents – therefore our conscious thoughts cannot generate *all* our conduct. The mind has been defined as identical with conscious thought, so if the mind is to explain our conduct that kind of thought must be supplemented by another kind of thought, an unconscious kind. This is the vital move in the creation of the mind/brain hybrid, since it retains the idea that the mind is identified by thinking, but introduces a new concept of 'thought'. The relation between 'conscious thought' and 'unconscious thought' is that they are imagined to be involved in exactly the same kind of 'processes' – the only difference is in their respective loci. The only candidate for the locus of unconscious thoughts must be the brain,[109] and this, taken with the assumption that the processes of thought are the same throughout the mind, are identical in

---

[109] No one seriously questions that the way, e.g., our visual system works depends upon the workings of the brain, but the idea that an 'unconscious' is involved is a result of supposing that the brain's work is best described as a species of thought, which is the point at issue here.

both conscious and unconscious modes, readily licenses the functionalist idea that the workings of the brain can be described in terms of thought processes.

If it had been appreciated that the (again) Cartesian picture of the mind as comprised of conscious thought which explained our bodily comportment was a doubtful way of conceiving 'the mind' to begin with, then this sequence of steps would not have followed – but they were taken. Now, the cycle completes itself, and role for more than '\unconscious thought' becomes a problem for the materialist project.

We have been arguing that there are no such things as 'qualia'. To what, exactly, does that commit us? It should be apparent that our arguments are conceptual (terminological) and not ontological. When we deny that there are 'qualia', we are certainly not claiming that people who report that they have seen and heard the things that they report that they did indeed see and hear are mistaken (except and unless certain circumstances can be shown to make it clear that that they were). The main thing that we argue is simply this: that the notion of 'qualia' does not contribute to, nor does it assist in the clarification of, our understanding of whatever it is that we can both see and hear (and smell) etc. That conception is an artifact of purely philosophical theorizing.

The remainder of this chapter will be given over to attempting to cast doubt upon the way in which the significance of the natural science's *extant* achievements and results are misunderstood. We have – all of us, not just us personally – been invited to participate in a thought experiment, in which we imagine two creatures that are 'molecule for molecule' identical to each other *but* that are nonetheless different. One of those creatures might be one of us, and it possesses consciousness, has the (supposed) subjective experiences of taste, smell, etc., whilst the other lacks these: the other is a *zombie*, shambling around, but bereft of any awareness of its world. We are supposed to conclude that, since such is at least an *imaginable* state of affairs, then molecular identity could be irrelevant to the presence in one case of 'consciousness', posing a problem for the materialist position. The trouble with this thought experiment, as with so many others, is that it is a jerry-built construction, set up in such ways as to essentially beg the questions that it is supposed to help us address (not a very thought*ful* experiment). The idea of the 'zombie' is fine in a George Romero film, just as the idea of vampire is wonderful in the works of Bram Stoker and Joss Wheedon, but *ask yourselves* whether you are at all clear on how the idea of either zombie or vampire is supposed to work – what really is the difference between a vampire and an ordinary human being except that the former is said to be 'undead' – just how does 'undead' relate to wide-awake and thriving? As for zombies, well, they are allegedly dead but walking around. Do they have sensory awareness? Well, they follow people around and try to grab them, they can detect where their food is (they are allegedly dead, with – one can only presume – cessation of all metabolic processes, but *they must eat?*). So, do zombies *see* their prospective lunch or not? And if not, how do they detect the presence of a possible free lunch? It won't do to suppose that they have some other sense than sight that allows them to do this, for that just begs the question. The zombie – and this is just how we are to imagine them for the purposes of the thought experiment - is lacking in *all sensory awareness,* hence it cannot be that they detect things by any such sensory awareness. So, if they have no sensory awareness, *how do they manage to behave as if they do* (albeit, perhaps, somewhat less delicately than in our own normal case)? So, here is the question that the zombie case begs: are we to imagine that the zombies *behave entirely as if they have exactly the same kind of sensory awareness as we all do* but do not have any such thing? They can read out the words on this page (presumably) but cannot see these words?

It might seem that we are not really understanding the thought experiment, rather than succeeding in locating its flaws. Here is what we mean: the point is that according to the (real) sciences we are made up of molecules, and those molecules behave according to laws. Given that they are in an initial state, then one can apply those laws, deterministically or probabilistically makes no difference to the issues, to predict the future state of those molecules. In the picture according to science, the creatures are only configurations of molecules, and they are, in that respect, *identical.* Thus, one could take their current configuration, apply the laws, and predict their future behavior. This will be (within the bounds of probability at least) also identical (by definition). Therefore, the zombie and the person behave exactly the same even though one has, and the other does not have, consciousness. Really? Is this *seriously* meant to be a construal of what the natural sciences actually tell us about *human beings?* Does this line of argument not just beg the question about whether the idea of human beings as 'just' configurations of molecules is a proper projection of what goes on in physics?

There are so many flaws in the reasoning here we hardly know where to start. Let us return to our line of argument where we ask about the zombie that is reading our words from the page just as we do. But *is* the zombie doing the same as we are doing? Well, we could say that it is, and operating from the point of view we are otherwise opposing, argue that the mistake we have been making is in supposing that we should take ourselves as the measure of the zombie. What physics tells us is that the zombie should be the measure of us. The zombie is molecule for molecule identical with us, and is reading out the page of text, but it is doing so *without consciousness.* Our mistake would be to maintain that this is different from what we are doing when we read out the page, for *we* are doing that by virtue of our consciousness. But why suppose that, for science is telling us that we are molecule for molecule identical with the zombie and are doing the exact same thing - producing exactly the same sounds – as the zombie, and our behavior must be explained in the exact same way. Therefore, it is our presumption and illusion that we are reading the text off the page, but, of course, our production of sounds *must* be explained by the causal laws acting on our constituent molecules, and, therefore, in the same way in both cases, i.e., without any reference to consciousness.

Isn't this ridiculous? And doesn't it show a strange idea of how the scientific laws that we do have actually work? The zombie argument only repeats what it assumes, that description and explanation at the molecular level would be the appropriate one for understanding what we are doing when we read a page of text (or *don't read* a page of text as the zombie argument would have us imagine). The real question, remember, is not: is this assumption legitimate? The real question is: is this assumption one that the molecular sciences make? Are the philosophers who set up the zombie thought experiment so-to-speak speaking for science, as they no doubt like to think they are, or are they just making up an argument about science? We, it should be clear, suspect the latter. Here is the fact: the assumption that the zombie thought experiment can be seriously set out just begs the question. In other words, can it really be imagined that there could be – *under our science* – a zombie? Well, recall, the question it is meant to help us tackle is whether the notion of 'consciousness' is superfluous to science, but it might as well be seen as confronting this question: is *life* a superfluous notion to science? Can something be molecule for molecule identical with a living human being and yet be a zombie? There is no requirement, for the thought experiment, that the zombie be considered alive, and therefore on its terms, something that was dead could be molecule for molecule identical and would have to behave in the same way as something living. Setting that question aside, we can equally ask: but, under the laws of our science, could something be molecule for molecule identical with us and not have 'conscious experiences'? Could something have a molecule-for-molecule-identical visual system to ours and yet see nothing at all?... and so on. What license does anyone have to suppose that the laws of molecular behavior carry this kind of implication? Presumably, the assumption which is actually made in the natural sciences is that a creature with molecule-for-molecule identity with a normal person *would* (unless there was something very wrong with those laws) have the full apparatus of visual, aural etc, capacities – not the other way around. The zombie *could not be* molecule-for-molecule identical to a sighted person etc. Further, the idea that we and the (impossible) zombie were doing the same thing would not be a valid one, for, obviously, we *are* reading the text from the page, whereas the zombie would not be doing that since it cannot see the page, and, again, we must conclude it could not be molecule-for-molecule identical, because there would have to be a difference in the effect that light has on the zombie than it has on us (and how could that be under general laws governing molecular behavior?). As we say, this involves a very strange attitude to scientific laws, presuming that we can envisage a situation which is very different from what our scientific laws allow, and yet which is covered by those same scientific laws (the twin-earth thought-experiments being subject to the same complaint)?

But are we ourselves not begging the question, for the molecular sciences (conceived as functioning as the equivalent of metaphysics, to tell us what there really or ultimately is) make no mention of consciousness? First of all, molecular science is *not meant* to explain the behavior of conscious people. It is meant to explain the behavior of molecules, and it is only by a crassly behaviorist *reductionism* that it is imagined that people are only large configurations of many molecules whose behavior must be understood entirely and only as involving the complex application of the laws that shift molecules around. Of course, from the point of view of molecular science, that is all that a human being can be, but that is not because molecular science has found out what human beings really are. It is just the fact that we refuse metaphysics, and thus the idea that there are (metaphysically) real natures, that has prevented us from supposing that what something (really) is is the same as what it is made of. Hence, we do not read the statement 'Water is H20' as saying anything other than 'Water is [made up of] H20': molecular science tells us what anything that is made of something must be made of, namely molecules, but it does not thereby tell us that there is nothing else but molecules. There are so many *other* things about human beings that are *irrelevant* to what it is that molecular science is interested in and competent with. *Insofar as* - and isn't that the important qualification? – human behavior involves the movement of molecules, then it must be subject to the laws of molecular science, but who has ever denied this? The issue is about how far that 'insofar as' extends - those who *imagine* molecular science delivering exhaustive explanations of everything about human activity are at the very least *far beyond where the actual molecular sciences are,* and are envisaging developments in directions which, at present, the actual molecular sciences give very little sign of even attempting to go. Therefore, the fact that 'consciousness' does not get mentioned in science turns into: it does not get mentioned in *molecular* science, but then, the sensible question is: why would you think it should, since molecular science is not dealing in phenomena of the sort where reference to 'consciousness' would be involved. Sure enough, *from the point of view of molecular science,* there would be no difference as to whether two identical molecular configurations differed with respect to one's being conscious and the other not, but the fact that *it makes no difference to molecular science* just does not translate into *there is no difference.* It makes no difference to the TV repairman what we watch on the television, but there is a very big difference between programs we will and will not watch. In other words, *our* assumption is the same as that which is the actual assumption of the natural sciences, that our 'subjective experiences' of seeing, smelling, tasting, all arise from our molecular constitution and are perfectly well understandable in terms of this and that *the kinds of things that scientists are interested in about such things* can indeed be comprehensively understood in scientific terms. But this takes no toll on our contention that 'consciousness' is not reducible to a molecular phenomenon.

CHAPTER FIVE

MEMORY: EXPLAINING CAPACITIES VERSUS EXPLAINING PERFORMANCES

Cognitive neuroscience, as portrayed in *Wet Mind* at least, is a hybrid discipline inasmuch as it is based upon the premise that the theoretical constructions with findings advanced within cognitive psychology can productively be synthesized with results drawn from basic neurobiology. Those findings which have been of special concern pertain to brain lesions which have been found responsible for various impairments in conduct (e.g., an incapacity to recognize people's faces, or to recollect numerical information of certain sorts). One explanatory structure characteristic of a good deal of work in cognitive neuroscience may be termed "inverse inference".[110] The theorist presents the neurobiological evidence linking a specific lesion to a specific kind of performance failure and argues that the neural region in which the lesion has been discovered is causally implicated in the production of the normal, well-functioning performance under consideration. We shall return to discuss this mode of explanation in relation to memory phenomena further on. For the moment, we shall simply note that, while it is reasonable to explain a loss of memory capacity or a reduction in some other 'mental' capacity specifically by reference to a neural lesion, one cannot simply reverse this procedure and imagine oneself having thereby explained, e.g., some specific recollection by reference to the functioning of the unlesioned region in question. We shall refer to this as 'the failure of inverse specificity', and we shall argue that this point is rarely acknowledged as the logical constraint upon neural explanations that it is.

---

[110] A good instance of this can be found in S. M. Kosslyn & O. Koenig, "Memory" in their *Wet Mind: The New Cognitive Neuroscience* (N.Y.: Free Press, 1995), pp. 358-359: "We speculate that associative memory depends in part on the superior, posterior temporal lobe, if only because patients with lesions in this area often appear to have disrupted associations."

138

'Memory', as depicted in cognitive neuroscience, is often supposed to be both foundational and ubiquitous. Consider the following passage from Kosslyn and Koenig:

> "Memory plays a critical role in many - if not all – aspects of cognition. Indeed, memory figured centrally in all the abilities discussed in the previous chapters [movement, language, reading, vision]. It lies at the heart of our ability to understand written and spoken language because it enables us to identify words, to ascribe meanings to visual or auditory patterns, and to integrate the meanings of individual words into connected discourse. Similarly, it is critical in movement and writing, in recognizing the face of a friend, in forming mental images, and so forth." [111]

The picture presented here is one of persons having to remember the meaning of the words they use as they use them (or *before* they use them?) having to 'identify' the words they speak or read as they speak or read them, having to recollect what the objects and events are which populate their surroundings as they go about the business of their everyday lives. Persons are even to be supposed to have to ongoingly remember how to walk or to manipulate objects, and also to 'recognize' the familiar faces of their friends whenever they encounter them! Truly, remembering, on *this* account, is accorded a range of roles in our lives which would be quite remarkable if it could actually be rendered intelligible! Simply put, the ascription conditions logically required for the concept of 'remembering' or of 'memory' to apply are absent in these routine cases of ordinary human activities, achievements and capabilities.

What has gone wrong here? For one thing, this series of conflations and over-extensions appears to derive from a failure to unpack the grammar of recollection verbs. One does not 'remember' ordinary words and their meanings when one utters a sentence in one's native tongue, for one knows these words (how to use them) without having specifically to recall them. Exercising one's

---

[111] S. M. Kosslyn & O. Koenig, *ibid.*, p. 341.

capacities to speak, read and navigate through one's everyday settings is *not* a matter of continuously recollecting things to oneself.

In tandem with the foundational conception of memory we find the familiar 'storage' theorizing: memory 'representations' are said to be 'stored' in yet another subsystem, which we called associative memory, and that associative memory contains a wide variety of different sorts of information… we will focus on the subsystems that allow us to enter various types of new information into memory."[112] Memory is here, oddly but typically, depicted both as *that which is stored* (in the form of 'representation' or 'information') as well as *the store itself* into which the representations/information have/has been deposited. The topographical metaphor is soon literalised: the memory subsystems are (eventually) to be mapped onto neural regions via inverse inferences from lesional effects.

Norman Malcolm has pointed out that 'representing' is a normative notion (contrasting with '*mis*representing'): discussing an earlier but logically similar mode of theorizing about memory 'storage', he wrote:

> "How could there be physiological evidence in this matter? Is it really possible that *the brain* should employ symbols, rules, descriptions? This is something that *people* learn to do in learning language…. Errors are made and corrected… Given correction and more examples, the child will begin to apply the words correctly. What does it mean to say that the child applies them *correctly*? It means that its use of those words conforms to the practice of the community of speakers in which the child is reared. How does *the brain* of a person or animal fit into this picture? Is a brain a member of a community of speakers? Does it say things?…Does the brain, in the beginning, make mistakes; or is it always right?"[113]

---

[112] *Ibid.*, p. 342.
[113] Norman Malcolm, *Memory and Mind* (N.Y. Cornell University Press, 1977), pp. 208-209.

Since 'representing' is representing *correctly*, it seems as though one must be committed to claiming that neural states and processes possess normative properties, and this is absurd. Neural states and processes occur, not 'rightly' nor 'wrongly', 'correctly' nor 'incorrectly, whereas to represent is to do so correctly, i.e., not to misrepresent, and to inform is, likewise, not to misinform. Hubert Dreyfus has short shrift for the deployment of the notion of 'information' in cognitive science, arguing that it is invoked to bridge a gap which is logically unbridgeable, that between depictions of neural functions in neurophysiological terms and ascriptions of 'person-level' predicates (such as 'remembering'):

> "The brain is clearly an energy-transforming organ. It detects incoming signals; for example, it detects changes in light intensity correlated with changes in texture gradient. Unfortunately for psychologists, however, this physical description, excluding as it does all psychological terms, is in no way a *psychological* explanation. On this level one would not be justified in speaking of human agents, the mind, intentions, perceptions, memories, or even colors or sounds, as psychologists want to do. Energy is being received and transformed and that is the whole story."[114]

In order to graft a 'psychological' account onto neurophysiological data, recourse is made to the notion of 'stimulus information'[115], and the subsequent processing, storing, retrieving and transforming of such 'information'. However, if the input to the nervous system is energy "then it is only necessary that it be transformed into other energy [e.g. photons transduced into ion flows along the optic nerve] – the processes in the brain are surely physical from beginning to

---

[114] Hubert Dreyfus, *What Computers Still Can't Do: A Critique of Artificial Reason* (Cambridge, Mass.: M.I.T. Press, 1993), p. 177

[115] It is striking how often theoretical recourse is made in cognitive neuroscience to the behavioristic concept of the 'stimulus' and even the familiar pairing of 'stimulus-response'. It is also significant how frequently 'stimuli' are conflated with 'object' or 'event' as well as identified with energy quanta impinging upon receptors. See, e.g., Kosslyn & Koenig, *op. cit.*, pp. 347-47, 380-81, 452, 455, 457, 461, and 471-74.

end. Matter-energy can be transformed, reduced, elaborated, stored, recovered, and used, but it will never be anything but matter-energy." [116]

Construing matter-energy in terms of 'information' permits a slippage into the ordinary notion of 'information', of that which is informative, which reports news or facts, narrates events, etc., as in 'information about X', or '...that Y is the case', and so on. But *this* conflation of a technical with an ordinary use, mere slippage between 'information' in the information-theoretic sense, and 'information' in plain English, does not work to bridge the conceptual gaps between the physical descriptions of energy inputs and their physical consequences in the cortex on the one hand and 'psychological' descriptions of what human agents can do. Dreyfus is adamant: for him,

> "The language of books such as those by Miller et al., Neisser, and Fodor is literally incoherent. On almost every page one finds sentences such as the following:
> When an *organism executes* a Plan *he* proceeds step by step, completing one part and then moving on to the next. [117]
> Here all three levels exist in unstable and ungrammatical suspension.'When an *organism* (biological) *executes* (machine analogy, borrowed from human agent) a Plan *he* (the human agent...) 'Or, one can have it the other way around and instead of the organism being personified, one can find the mind mechanized." [118]

Cognitive neuroscience can be (partly) defined in terms of these very conceptual moves which Malcolm and Dreyfus rightly disparage. Recall our earlier question, according to which our focus should be upon "the subsystems [neural] that allow us [human agents] to enter various types of new information [machine analogy] into memory [construed as a neural region on the analogy with a computer's buffers]". Precisely the same unstable and ungrammatical

[116] *Ibid.*, p.181
[117] Citing Miller, Galanter & Pribram, *Plans and the Structure of Behavior* (N.Y.: Holt, Rinehart & Winston, 1960), p. 17.
[118] *Ibid.*, p. 179.

amalgams are being advanced here as in the earlier, AI-based, versions of cognitive science.

Let us consider in more detail the commitments entailed by construing memory both as stored information about the past and as the 'subsystems' which house the stored information. The problem arises: how is memory *itself* being explained when we confront the problem of how the system directs the selection of memories from within its store? Presumably, it would have to remember the contents of the store in order to deliver (retrieve) what is stored there. But if this is so, then memory is being presupposed in the very effort to explain memory. This displacement of the problem is a familiar pattern of argument that we meet throughout this book, and in this case, as in others, nothing has actually been explained at all.

How does the cognitive neuroscientist actually synthesize his theoretical schemes with data from the neurosciences themselves? Here is a sample (again from Kosslyn & Koenig):

> "The memory formation subsystems rely on a set of anatomical structures roughly in the middle of the brain, the principal members of this set being the *hippocampus* and related cortex), the *limbic thalamus*, and the *basal forebrain*. Damage to any of these structures greatly impairs an animal's ability to store new information in the memory...the entorhinal cortex ultimately receives perceptual input in multiple perceptual modalities. A lesion in one or more of these structures typically results in memory deficits that are particularly evident when the subject tries to learn new material...The hippocampus sends information to many parts of the brain... The hippocampus not only is involved in storing new representations of stimulus properties, but also plays a critical role in storing associations between representations."[119]

The actual neuroscientific data upon which such elaborate conceptual structures are erected turn out to be quite modest: they are findings about the

---

[119] Kosslyn & Koenig, *op cit.*, pp. 344-5.

effects of structural damage and lesions in the various named neural regions upon a person's (or animal's) capacity to acquire new forms of behavior. We can have no argument with such findings. However, nothing in these data strictly supports the elaborate psychologizing overlay which is imposed upon them: nothing here requires nor entails any reference at all to "storage", "information", or "representation", nor, indeed, in some cases, even to "memory" itself. Indeed, the theoretical proclivities at work in cognitive neuroscience tend vastly to outstrip the punctate appeals to the deliverances of good, old-fashioned neurophysiological research. Are we here arguing against any form of what we have earlier termed 'inverse inference'? Not at all. There are perfectly reasonable versions of such inferential operations in the basic neurosciences. Consider the dopamine hypothesis which seeks to explain the occurrence of auditory hallucinations by postulating an overproduction in certain regions of the brain of this particular neurotransmitter. This hypothesis was derived from a process of inverse inference: various phenothiazines administered to victims of auditory hallucinations were found to decrease the levels of dopamine naturally generated within the brain. Insofar as the pharmacological suppression of dopamine levels could be correlated to the reduction of the auditory hallucinations, it seemed entirely reasonable to investigate the actual levels of dopamine being naturally produced within the brains of auditory-hallucinating patients to discern the extent to which a pathological overproduction was occurring. The evidence is so far inconclusive[120], but the investigation is both coherent and *a priori* plausible in its explanatory force.

---

[120]   See, e.g., M.M. Mesulam, "Schizophrenia and the Brain", *New England Journal of Medicine*, Vol. 322, No. 12, 1990, pp. 842-45. For an illuminating account of this methodology and the development of the hyperdopaminergic theory, see Ian Creese & Solomon H. Snyder, "Biochemical Investigation" in John C. Shershow (ed.), *Schizophrenia: Science and Practice* (Cambridge, MA: Harvard University Press, 1978), Ch. 6. Paul R. McHugh and Phillip R. Slavney write: "The discoveries that amphetamine prolongs the effects of synaptically released dopamine and norepinephrine and that drugs effective in the treatment of schizophrenia block dopamine receptors in the brain have contributed to the

In cognitive neuroscience, however, matters are rather different, and in efforts to explain *normal* memory functions in human agents, we confront a radically different context for this sort of inferential operation. Ryle once warned against a similar style of reasoning in the psychology of his day. Arguing that whilst it is reasonable to pose questions such as: what sorts of factors can impede our estimations of shape, size, illumination and speed, for example, nonetheless, "we feel that the wrong sort of promise is being made when we are offered corresponding explanations of our correct estimations... Let the psychologist tell us why we are deceived; but we can tell ourselves and him why we are not deceived." [121] He goes on:

> "The classification and diagnosis of exhibitions of our mental impotences require specialized research methods. The explanation of the exhibitions of our mental competences often requires nothing but ordinary good sense, or it may require the specialized methods of economists, scholars, strategists, and examiners. But their explanations are not cheques drawn on the accounts of some yet more fundamental diagnoses." [122]

These remarks have achieved a certain notoriety over the years since they were first published and assessed They appear to restrict the role of specialized psychological explanation to the *abnormal*, the defective, the 'impotencies' rather than the competences exhibited in our conduct, leaving the commonplace, commonsensical, and ordinary ways of living and acting immune to psychology's explanatory efforts [whereas what they actually do is remark upon the

---

proposal that the pathologic mechanisms involve biogenic amine neurotransmitters. Abnormalities in dopamine metabolism, dopamine receptors, or both, for example, may represent the pathological disease mechanisms responsible for a subgroup of schizophrenic illnesses." In their "The Schizophrenic Syndrome", *The Perspectives of Psychiatry* (Baltimore: Johns Hopkins University Press, 1986), p. 65. For a recent critical assessment of the generality of the hyperdopaminergic theory, see Robert M. Julien, "Antipsychotic (Neuroleptic) and Antiparkinsonian Drugs" in his *A Primer of Drug Action* (N.Y.: W. H. Freeman & Company, 1995), Ch. 11, esp. p. 272.
[121] Gilbert Ryle, *The Concept of Mind* (Harmondsworth: Penguin University Books, 1973 – original publication date 1949), p. 308.
[122] *Ibid.*

appropriate role of neurological causation in explanations of our performances]. Neuroscience, for example, is perfectly competent to explain memory *deficits* of certain kinds, but, on Ryle's view, is not logically capable of 'explaining' our ordinary, successful recollections of events, places, objects, and persons. Is this just an arbitrary – even reactionary, anti-scientific - restriction upon the proper objectives of a human science? We think not. Let us approach the issue systematically, focusing upon mundane memory phenomena.

The first point which we need to establish is that Ryle was not opposed to *all* efforts to explain "normal functioning" – e. g., of mechanical devices. Some philosophers have read his remarks to rule out explanatory accounts of normal functioning *tout court*. But this was *not* their point: his argument was directed against efforts to create the impression that there is a need scientifically to explain conduct where such conduct is not in fact in any need of explanation, let alone of the scientific kind. He certainly would not have countenanced the idea that one could not, for example, explain the normal capacity of a vehicle to travel at 100 miles per hour by reference to the tuned-up state of the engine, the refinements involved in the engineering of the carburetor, the honing of the pistons, and so forth. However, he would certainly have objected to efforts to 'read back' into disrupted neural functions anything like 'representations' of phenomena. The missing ten feet of train-track lines can be appealed to in explaining the two-hour delay in the train's arrival without our having to attribute its tardiness to any loss of 'representations' of its journey, or of the time-table, etc., within the missing segment of the train-track.

Ryle's target was quite specific: the explanation of ordinary, routine, unproblematic human conduct does not require specialized accounts. We should seriously consider the implications of the fact that human agents are not routinely preoccupied with explaining their own and others' conduct. Why is this the case? Largely because such conduct, insofar as it conforms to community norms, rules and standards, is self-explanatory, or, to put this another way, explanatorily transparent. I have no need to explain why I stop at a red traffic sign (unless to someone unfamiliar with such symbols) simply because the rule is known-in-common and unworthy of comment. The student who indicates that he wishes to ask a question in class by putting his hand up is doing something according to the rules of classroom conduct and therefore in no need of special explanation. We must remember that explaining is a mode of problem-solving: No problem, no need for an explanation.

The rules and standards involved in our everyday affairs equip us not only to *see* what someone is doing but also, and quite routinely, to tell *why* he or she is doing what he or she is doing. It is the rule-departing (defying, deviant, breaking, violating, etc.) conduct which may tempt us to seek some form of explanation. And explaining an action is itself a mode of conduct. Explanation is a functional, problem- and context-dependent operation. It requires certain conditions to obtain for its intelligibility and appropriateness to be vouchsafed. In the domain of 'memory phenomena', what sort of explanations could qualify as logically appropriate, and what sort of explanations might actually qualify to do the work of genuinely explaining?

In order to fix some of the parameters involved in this discussion, let us consider (1) the nature of genuine memory phenomena as these are available to us in our everyday lives, and (2) the nature of explanatory enterprises pertaining to human conduct and capacities, and the role which they play in our lives. In determining the logical space available for 'explanations of remembering', we can return to our main theme – cognitive neuroscientific endeavors to 'explain memory' – and see to what extent they jibe with, or violate, the logic of the phenomena of interest. To put this point in different terms, we shall be inquiring into the pre-theoretical characterizations of memory phenomena among human agents, in order to specify the *explananda* which cognitive neuroscience sees itself as addressing, and we shall be asking: are the *explananda* properly described, and, if so, what sort of explanation (if any) can they legitimately require? We start out from the premise, that we assume is shared with our adversaries, that stipulated versions or arbitrary characterizations of phenomena cannot qualify as genuine phenomena-to-be-explained.

In what ways do 'memory phenomena' actually enter into our lives as active human agents? What *are* 'remembering', 'recollecting', 'recalling', 'memorizing', and so forth? Clearly, these verbs are not interchangeably predicable of human agents. That which one recollects is not necessarily that which one has memorized: that which one recalls is not simply that which one knows and has not forgotten: that which one has memorized is not necessarily that which one has recollected. We can now begin to discern an array of *diverse* predications, falsely (because misleadingly) subsumed under a unitary rubric such as: Memory. To complicate matters further, we can identify cases of, *inter alia*, remembering *to do* something, remembering *how to* do something, recalling that something *is* the case, recalling that something *was* the case, recollecting that something could be, might be, may be, will be, the case; remembering that/what/why/who/when/where ...., [123] and so on. To use the language of ethnomethodology for a moment, we can say that these are *occasioned*, situated and practical accomplishments, not interior accompaniments of the host of other things we are capable of doing, although some of these will undoubtedly presuppose the capacity to recollect, etc.. Now, the issue presents itself starkly: what is the exact nature of the *explanandum/explananda* for 'memory models' in cognitive neuroscience? This issue is rarely, if ever, addressed in rigorous terms.

---

[123] Note that some uses of these constructions ('remembering that...') can have *future* orientations, as when one remembers next August 17th will be one's first anniversary. One can recall what is scheduled to occur next Tuesday, when the next performance is to be held, where one will be next summer, and so on. Too much emphasis is placed upon 'past events, objects and experiences' in cognitive approaches to the phenomena of memory.

Theorists settle for a generic rubric, failing to specify the range and variety of contextual phenomena subsumed, phenomena with quite heterogeneous features. For example, my recollection of an appointment can be manifested, *inter alia*, in my suddenly stopping what I am doing and rushing to catch a train to see someone, or in my mentioning to time and place I intend to meet someone, or in my asking my secretary to call the person to cancel the appointment, and so on. [124]

Let us now turn to consider the actual nature of explanations for non-defective memory phenomena as these are provided in our quotidian lives, and see to what extent there are *residua* amenable to some sort of scientific explanatory quest. We insist upon the polymorphous nature of memory phenomena. To elaborate: we may be interrogated as to why we recollected that thing *there and then*; we may be asked how we could possibly recall *that* datum; we may be asked on what basis we are confident that we remembered that event *as such-and-such*, and so on. Note that all such inquiries presuppose problems and problem-contexts for their intelligibility. And there are ranges of credible vernacular replies (defeasible, of course, in their particular applications) to such legitimate queries. But note that, for example, there is no sense whatsoever to a query such as: how did you remember, when you signed your check, that your name is N.N? Unless, of course, N.N. was suffering from amnesia and yet signed his check with his name... But that, as Ryle pointed out, is the exceptional case: the normal case does not require any explanation at all.

To these arguments, the typical riposte is as follows: vernacular accounts for such phenomena are all very well, but what do you construe as the role of the

---

[124] See P.M.S. Hacker, "Memory and Recognition" in his *Wittgenstein: Mind and Will (Vol. 4 of An Analytical Contemporary on the 'Philosophical Investigations')* (Oxford: Basil Blackwell, 1996), p. 495. Cf. Norman Malcolm, *op. cit.*, p.75.

central nervous system in accounts of accurate recollection? Explanations for recollections as these may be adduced in our every day lives presuppose that 'normal conditions apply', and these conditions naturally include the 'normal' functioning of an intact nervous system. Cognitivism, however, insists upon much more than this: there is supposed to be, within the CNS, a 'representation' of an event in the past which was personally witnessed. Wittgenstein addresses this sort of claim in the following:

> "An event leaves a trace in the memory: one sometimes imagines this as if it consisted in the event's having left a trace, an impression, a consequence, in the nervous system. As if one could say: even the nerves have a memory. But then when someone remembered an event, he would have to *infer* it from this impression, this trace. Whatever the event does leave behind in the organism, *it* isn't the memory. The organism compared with a dictaphone spool; the impression, the trace, is the alteration in the spool that the voice leaves behind. Can one say that the Dictaphone (or the spool) is remembering what was spoken all over again, when it reproduces what it took?" [125]

The memory of the event is (in examples like these) the correct account of the event, which took place in the past, and was personally witnessed (observed, noticed, etc.) by the one making the memory claim. This cannot be what has been deposited in the organism, since no one believes that everything that one witnesses and subsequently remembers is given an explicit characterization at the moment of witnessing, by the witness, in words, symbols or other media of representation (as must be the case for a dictaphone to work). Thus, as Wittgenstein remarks, whatever (if anything) has been left behind 'in the organism' it cannot itself be the memory, the recollection. Moreover, the exact nature of the role of the stored 'representation' in the occurrent recollection is unclear: does it operate to furnish a prompt in the form of an image? a sequence

---

[125] Ludwig Wittgenstein, *Remarks on the Philosophy of Psychology, Vol. 1* (Eds. G. E. M. Anscombe & G. H. von Wright: Trans. G. E. M. Anscombe: Chicago: University of Chicago Press, 1980) para. 220.

of expressions? It cannot, as in the cognivitist account, simply be a causal (neural) event, since this would preclude construing it as, in fact, a 'representation'. Representations are, roughly, representations *of* something, whereas, by contrast, causal events are not 'of..' or 'about' anything. Whatever theoretical stipulations one might advance to answer this question, *none* of them can satisfy the requirement for which the storage model has been created in the first place - the explanation of the remembering. This is because there is no one, unitary or unique phenomenon we could call 'the remembering': the same event in the past may be differentially characterized for various audiences, purposes and contexts. And images and symbolic expressions do not *intrinsically*, in and of themselves, determine their sense, and they do not come with self-labeling guarantees of either the date or the period of the initial occurrence which they purport to depict.

Wittgenstein comments: "One might almost marvel that one can answer the question 'What did you do this morning?' – without looking up historical traces of activity or the like. Yes; I answer, and wouldn't even know that this was possible through a special mental process, remembering, if I were not told so." [126] The natural, spontaneous act of recounting what one has done upon being questioned about it is not something which stands in need of any theory of special mental processes (and we must bear in mind that Wittgenstein has elsewhere, and often, drawn our attention to the grammatical fact that 'remembering' is not a process verb at all[127]). Indeed, here the remembering is manifested in the correct account given, and not in something anterior, interior or accompanying the conduct of telling the other what one did.

---

[126] *Ibid.*, para. 106.

[127] Cf. Ludwig Wittgenstein, *Philosophical Investigations* (Trans. G. E. M. Anscombe: NY., Macmillan, 1968), paras. 305-6.

Remembering X, that X occurred, or was the case, is characteristically contrasted to remembering-how-to do this or that (e. g., recalling yesterdays' newspaper headline is contrasted to remembering how to swim or how to ride a bicycle). The former are construed in cognitive neuroscience to require "propositional" representations[128], whereas the latter are (rightly) understood to be abilities or capabilities, and are not logically suitable candidates for 'storage' theorizing (since one cannot 'store an ability' *in* anything). This contrast, however, is misleading (and, in one sense, grammatically incorrect). In the 'recollection of the headline' case, for example, it appears to allow a space to open up for stored items or units of (propositionally-expressed) 'information' which are (somehow) 'retrieved' from the store and subsequently uttered in words, phrases, expressions, or in visual depictions on paper, etc. From our point of view, however, an occurrent articulation which correctly specifies yesterday's headline still consists in the exercise of a capacity, albeit of a different kind from, e.g., remembering how to swim as manifested in swimming again after many years. 'Recalling that X' is the exercise of an ability no less than, although in a different sense from, 'remembering how to play poker'. No doubt various neural structures and processes facilitate the exercise of this ability, but neither the ability itself nor the product of its situated exercise need be postulated as themselves 'stored' in the brain, nor anywhere else. Latency does not entail locality, any more than retention entails storage.

Cognitive neuroscience, like its AI-based precursor, computational cognitive psychology, trades heavily upon the device of the flow-chart to depict the properties and relations theoretically representing 'mental organization', typically connecting dimensions of this putative 'organization' to 'inputs' (perceptual, experiential, etc.) and 'outputs' (behavior, activity, communication, etc.). Although a good deal of genuine scientific work successfully employs

---

[128] E.g., Kosslyn & Koenig, *op cit.*, p. 344 and *passim*.

'idealizations' and simplifying 'models' to facilitate experimental extrapolations and to subserve specific, substantial applications to real cases, we do not find that the flow-charts and diagrammatic portrayals in cognitive neuroscience fulfill these functions. The impression conveyed, nonetheless, is one of a specification of linked domains within the sphere of the 'mental' ordered in such a manner so as to be construed as (potentially) isomorphic with linked regions in the cortex. This isomorphism is a check to be cashed at the bank of lesion-based neurobiological research, in global and/or piecemeal fashion. Kosslyn and Koenig present us with such a flow-chart figure[129], in which box compartments are arrayed and linked to one another by arrows. In each compartment there are labels identifying the independently specifiable domains of phenomena: Decision, Associative Memory, Perceptual Encoding Subsystems, Memory Formation and Stimulus-Response Connection. The vectors linking up these domains are open to very different kinds of interpretation: either weakly (e.g., as: 'is linked to' or 'is connected to') or strongly (e.g., 'is causally related to'). The figure purports to depict "the general structure of the memory system".[130] 'Input' to the Perceptual Encoding Subsystems is registered by an incoming arrow, even though the actual nature of what is to be counted as 'input' varies across the scheme. Outgoing arrows from this compartment extend to the compartments labeled Associative Memory, Memory Formation and Stimulus-Response Connection. Double-direction arrows linked up the compartments labeled Associative Memory, Memory Formation and Decision. A single outgoing arrow emanates from the compartment labeled Stimulus-Response Connection (presumably indicating 'Output'). Our colleague Michael Lynch has subjected graphic and other visual construals in the social sciences to critical scrutiny.[131] For Lynch, "an analysis of diagrams and related illustrations in theory texts shows that labels, geometric boundaries, vectors, and symmetries often are used

---

[129] Kosslyn & Koenig, *op cit.*, p. 343, Figure 8.1.

[130] *Ibid.*, p. 342.

[131] Michael Lynch, "Pictures of Nothing? Visual Construals in Social Theory", *Sociological Theory*, Vol. 9, No. 1, 1991, pp. 1-21.

to convey a sense of orderly flows of causal influences in a homogeneous field."[132] He notes that "theory pictures" can have communicative functions which are often difficult to decipher because the ontological status of the components is either opaque or incommensurable (as are 'Decision', a person-level achievement, and Perceptual Encoding Subsystems', a hypothetical construct presumably referring to a cognivistically-described neural system), and the vectors linking them (in our figure, represented diagrammatically by arrows) are of varying status. For example, in the textual discussion relating to our figure, Kosslyn and Koenig depict the relationship between some of their arrow-linked compartments in widely varying terms, such as: "are critical for", "are relevant to", "plays a role in", etc. In Lynch's terms, such pictures are not iconic, because they do not deploy conventional symbols visibly related to a spatial configuration, nor do they represent definite perceptual experiences. Nonetheless, they create an illusion of definiteness, conceptual distinctness and determinacy of relationships. This is especially pernicious in the realm of so-called 'mental' phenomena such as memory, decision, perception and conduct, because the proclivity to reification, to assigning misplaced properties of concreteness and independence, is already powerful. The proliferation of such figures promotes the further illusion that one order of mapped organization of discrete phenomena may be related systemically to another. Just as, in fact, the hippocampus is physically connected to the septum, the hypothalamus, the anterior thalamic nucleus and the amygdala, we are encouraged to think that such actually connected neural structures (or whichever ones are identified by the theorist) somehow might embody or correspond to the connected 'theoretical structures' purporting to depict 'the general structure of [*inter alia*] the memory system' given in the flow-chart scheme.

We maintain that, far from being legitimate scientific idealizations of concrete phenomena (whether observable *or* unobservable), flow-charts of

---

[132] *Ibid.*, p. 1.

'cognitive' factors such as those which adorn the texts of cognitive neuroscience do not and cannot function in this manner. Such flow-charts, in which heterogeneous and complex predicates and constructs are given as *names* in compartments, linked by arrows (again furnishing a false sense of determinacy and consistency of relationships) whose textual interpretations are actually very diverse, render merely ineffective emulations of scientifically useful devices, not their serious introduction.

Finally, we take issue with the general conception of the brain (or its constituent parts) as a 'micro-analyst' of environments of persons. We could add that we also take issue with the prior cognivitist assumption that human agents are, as they act, interact and communicate, themselves continuously operating as 'micro-analysts' of their environments and of each other's conduct, that they are engaged in continuous interpreting, decision-making, abstracting, disambiguating, matching, storing, and the rest. The projection of these *occasional human practices* to the interior, 'mental' realm, ripe for theoretical reduction to neural operations and functions, is at the heart of the cognivitist enterprises, old and new. A principal basis for the resurrection of what Ryle disparagingly termed "the intellectual legend", according to which all conduct flows from mental operations and inner courses of theorizing, was probably the work of Noam Chomsky and his challenge to the behaviorist tradition. For Chomsky, language acquisition and use derives from the possession of an unconsciously represented theory of the structure of a language. Later, and in concert with the first generation of cognitive psychologists whom he influenced, such a picture was extended to other areas of human ability, including perception and conduct more generally. This picture animates and inspires the current efforts to combine findings from neurobiology with 'information-processing' theorizing. However, if one refuses to personify neural states and processes in the interests of a theoretical stipulation, if one rejects a picture of human agents as relentlessly

155

engaged in activities for which the ordinary ascription criteria are not satisfied[133] and if one maintains a clear sense of the logico-grammatical distinctions between verbs of personal predication and the appropriate terms of neurophysiological description, the conceptual edifice of *cognitive* neuroscience can be judged for what it is: a redundant sequence of stipulative glosses erected upon the hard data of neurobiology. Neuroscience does not need cognitivism, for there are no ontological gaps to be bridged, no explanatory power gained, and only chimera emerge from the attempt to link the two.

---

[133] The attribution to persons (or to their brains) of predicates such as: 'deciding', 'interpreting', 'analyzing', and 'abstracting' (etc.) in the absence of their satisfying public criteria *in situ* for their attribution is a counterpart to the (Cartesian) claim for the 'invisibility' of such actions and achievements and their 'location' in the hidden 'mental' interiors of persons. The postulation of ongoing 'cognitive processes' as informing our quotidian conduct trades upon the same failure to grasp that the 'inner' stands in need of outward criteria, as Wittgenstein argued. Only in certain circumstances does my conduct license the attribution to me of 'deciding' or 'analyzing' or 'interpreting', for these are *practices* and not mere processes, let alone 'interior' ones. The latter notion of interiority derives as well from over-extrapolating from the fact that one may *occasionally* conceal one's 'interpreting' (etc.) from others.

CHAPTER SIX

DISSOLVING THE 'PROJECTION PROBLEM'

Proponents of the cognitive sciences claim to have identified a central problem confronting attempts to understand pattern recognition, and learning more generally, and also to have advanced what they argue is a uniquely adequate approach to its solution: the 'projection problem'. Essentially, this is the problem of explaining the human capacity to discern general patterns from the presentation of one or a few cases or instances. In what follows, we will try to demonstrate that this putative problem is an artifact of the assumptions underlying its formation, ones which exhibit various philosophical misconceptions about the nature of instruction and learning.

Sources of the Problem

Jerry Fodor has been one of the most vigorous and provocative advocates of the position that Chomsky's generative-grammatical conception of language, involving as it does the notion of 'projecting' an infinite number of sentences from a finite set of components and rules, must be extended in its general form to explain how children acquire the capacity to recognize new instances of *any* phenomena on the basis of an exposure to only a small number of instances, instances which may differ multifariously (within varying latitudes) from one another. For Fodor, this issue can only properly be understood by the postulation of abstract, generative 'mechanisms' in the mind/brain. Other related versions of this 'problem' have been termed: the problem of 'going beyond the information given'; the problem of 'invariance extraction'; the problem of 'perceptual constancy'; the problem of 'stimulus generalization'; the problem of discerning 'the same in the different'; the problem of 'rule finitism'; the problem of 'token-to-type subsumption', or the more general problem of 'inductive inference'.

Take the case of tune 'Lillibullero' (an example Fodor chooses because it is used by his arch-nemesis, Gilbert Ryle). Fodor writes:

"... one can recognize the tune when it is played on a warped record, transposed, played as a waltz, played as a march, and so on and on. It is important to bear in mind that, from a strictly acoustical point of view, the capacity to identify the tune in these various guises amounts to an enormous but highly specific tolerance of distortion. on the one hand, to recognize a tune played at half speed on a phonograph with the volume turned down is to be able to recognize it in spite of the simultaneous alteration of pitch, amplitude, and temporal relations."[134]

The same point applies to visual as to aural phenomena: "Cubes look like cubes however they may be rotated. Faces look like faces whether they are smiling or frowning, whether they are upside down or rightside up, whether they are seen in profile or full on..."[135] From such (indisputable) observations as these, Fodor concludes that any serious accounts of visual and auditory perception, pattern recognition and learning more generally, must be bound to come to terms with the fact that training generalizes to objects that may only quite abstractly be related to the initially given object (in the way that the diversity of all the forms – typographical, hand-written, etc. - in which letters of the alphabet can be represented are nonetheless all instances of the same letter and all visually identifiable as such). The achievement of recognitional constancy appears to Fodor to require the postulation of very abstract conceptual schemata and equally abstract mechanisms of application – these provide the means of *projecting* from the instructive instance(s) to *all other* instances of the same. Subsequently, other cognitive theorists pursued the same theme. Franks formulated the 'projection problem' in this way:

---

[134] Jerry A. Fodor, *Psychological Explanation* (London: Random House, 1968), p. 25.
[135] *Ibid.*

"Just as in the case of language... novelty in perception has important implications for pattern recognition. Environmental events rarely, if ever, are exact copies of previously experienced events. Every 'A' (or 'chair') we encounter probably differs in greater or lesser degree from previously experienced instances. In pattern recognition, as in language, there is essentially an infinitude of possible instances of any perceptual/conceptual class. Grammars are formulated as generative recursive systems to characterize the unbounded set of potential sentences.Likewise, in pattern recognition, an adequate characterization of our knowledge would seem to involve some sort of generative recursive structures."[136]

Gunderson, a critic of cognitivism, remarks that the 'projection problem' is "*the* central problem of pattern recognition".[137] He continues:

"That is, the problem which arises when one actually tries to enumerate characteristics (implicitly operative or otherwise) of objects belonging to a certain class in a way that permits variation and novelty amongst members within that class and at the same time excludes obvious non- members from that class. For example, it is natural to presume that an adequate account of our ability to recognize the written character 'M' would explain why and how certain characteristics of M's enable us to see both m and M *as* M's".[138]

Referring to the work of Chomsky, Ziff, Katz, Fodor and Postal (all participants in the tradition led by Chomsky, though with various degrees of withdrawal from Chomsky's initial positions over their subsequent careers, including, we might add, Chomsky himself), Gunderson states: "What these writers call 'the projection problem' is roughly synonymous with the problem of

---

[136] J. Franks, "Toward understanding understanding" in Walter B. Weimer and David S. Palermo (eds.), *Cognition and the Symbolic Processes* (Hillsdale, N.J. & London: Lawrence Erlbaum Associates, 1974), p. 241.

[137] Keith Gunderson, "Philosophy and computer simulation" in Oscar C. Wood and George Pitcher (eds.), *Ryle* (London: Macmillan, 1971), p. 316.

[138] *Ibid.* Note here that Gunderson has some trouble establishing exactly what the problem *is* in the domain of letter-recognition. After all, an 'M' is upper-case and an 'm' is lower-case. In this sense, they are *not* the same. Gunderson appears to be in the grip of a misleading analogy: that between a number and a numeral that expresses it (e.g., 'four' as '4' or as 'IV', etc.). But there are no 'abstract letters' for which there might be tokens of types or classes. The idea that 'M' (upper-case) is the *same letter* as 'm' (lower-case), then, begs the question: for what purpose(s)? After all, we *distinguish between* upper-case letters and lower-case letters for a variety of sound reasons.

formulating the rules underlying what may be conveniently viewed as our syntactic-semantic pattern-recognition competence".[139] We shall return later to consider some of Gunderson's objections to cognitivist efforts to 'solve' the 'projection problem'.

In beginning to disentangle what we believe are fundamentally conceptual issues in this discussion, we shall first consider Fodor's position in which, in its initial articulation, was developed in opposition to Gilbert Ryle's anti-intellectualist account of 'recognition'. Ryle's general line was that the rationalist tradition to which Chomsky and his cohorts have affiliated themselves was based on misconceptions about the whole range of matters they choose to identify as 'mental', assuming that they needed to postulate some set of operations taking place 'in the mind' (or, following current parlance, the 'mind/brain'). Fodor regards Ryle's line as manifestly refuted by arguments such as his own, although, as we shall see, Fodor can only maintain this conviction by persistently begging the questions Ryle raised). Thus, Fodor refuses to accept Ryle's argument that hearing a tune or melody 'according to a recipe' so as to distinguish it from other tunes or melodies is a matter of 'hypotheticals' of the following kind:

> "… if, after hearing a bar or two, he expects those bars to follow which do follow; if he does not erroneously expect the previous bars to be repeated; if he detects omissions and errors in the performance; if, after the music has been switched off for a few moments, he expects it to resume where it does resume; if, when several people are whistling different tunes, he can pick out who is whistling this tune; if he can beat time correctly; if he can accompany it by whistling or humming it in time and tune, and so on indefinitely."[140]

In comparable ways, people can pick out 'the same letter' though it is inscribed in different handwritings, in different type faces, on the page and on a vast advertising hoard, just as they can pick out the same face though it has

---

[139] *Ibid*., pp. 320-01.
[140] Gilbert Ryle, cited in Fodor, *op. cit*., p. 23.

changed over the years. For Fodor, however, 'having the recipe' for recognizing a tune (or the capacity to recognize re-presentations of the same visual phenomenon) is to be construed mentalistically as more like having the sheet music in one's head rather than like having one recording of the tune or, in the visual case, having a picture or other visual template mentally stored to act as a means of comparison with things appearing in the visual field. Matching a recording or a template is, indeed, a grossly oversimplified notion when we reflect upon the range of variations we can subsume under one class or type. It is this realization that gives Fodor's plea for 'very abstract mechanisms' its initial appeal. And, moreover, we think that he is right to note that Ryle's invocation of the notion of a 'recipe' "very nearly gives the show away"[141], but *not* because we think that it is in the least conducive to Fodor's 'internal' conceptualism. Fodor's line is this: one can give an account of some of the information a hearer employs in recognizing a tune if one allows oneself such abstract concepts as 'bar', 'note', 'measure' and 'tempo'. Such musicological concepts are abstract in the sense that they have, by and large, no simple acoustic interpretation:

"... once the recipe story is made explicit, it is indistinguishable from a quite elaborate conceptualism. That is, it is unclear how to account for the ability to recognize identity of type despite gross variations among tokens unless we assume that the concepts employed in recognition are of formidable abstractness."[142]

But surely Fodor is not suggesting (is he?) that to recognize 'Lillibullero' a hearer must be an amateur musicologist? Ryle may well have put out a hostage to fortune in his use of the notion of a 'recipe', but that scarcely lends itself to Fodor's elaboration. The first point to note is that, while Fodor takes note of Ryle's insistence that 'recognize' is an achievement verb[143], and not a performance or process verb, he fails to explore the deep implications of this

---

[141] Fodor, *op. cit.*, p. 27.
[142] *Ibid.*, p. 28.
[143] *Ibid.*, p. 16.

logico-grammatical point. Ryle held that, generally, the mistakes of his mentalist opponents resulted from under-estimating the differences between kinds of words, thus, for example, supposing that words which apply to things people do – such as 'run' and 'see' – are all of the same kind, being words which name some 'process' – since 'run' does identify a process, and because 'see' looks like the same kind of word it must do the same. Thus, 'seeing' must be some kind of process, and there is a need for a scientific (psychological) account of the processes involved in seeing. Ryle insisted that if we pay attention to the way in which we use the word 'see' and related expressions when we actually speak the English language, we will come to appreciate that 'see' is not a *process* kind of word at all. Something is indeed 'going on' when somebody runs, but 'win' cannot be a word on the same kind of level as 'run', for nothing is going on (except the running) when someone crosses the finish line first: 'win' is a 'result' or 'achievement' word, i.e., one that says what results from or is achieved by a performance like running – one has got to the finish line before other runners because one ran faster. Ryle makes this contrast to argue that 'see' is in most of its uses in English more like 'win' than it is like 'run'. But what connections can 'see' have with 'achievements'? With those such as (correctly) identifying or picking out, for example: someone can look at (more of a performance expression) something without seeing it because, e.g., one does not know how to pick it out.

Fodor is fully prepared to grant that it must be 'Lillibullero' that the orchestra or stereo is playing in order for the difference to be established between "having recognized the tune as 'Lillibullero'" and "incorrectly supposing oneself to have done so".[144] What he wants to insist upon is the following: the fact that it was 'Lillibullero' which was being played is obviously not a *sufficient* condition for recognizing 'Lillibullero' as the tune which was being played, thus a cognitive psychological theorist may legitimately argue that it is certain (yet-to-be-specified) mental events or processes which determine whether or not the tune *is*

---

[144] *Ibid.*, p. 17.

recognized (or that the letter is seen to be an 'e', say). By analogy, even if there really are robins present in the garden, is it not the occurrence of the relevant mental events or processes in the mind of the individual looking out into the garden which makes the difference between perceiving the robins *inter alia* and not perceiving anything at all?

Fodor's Problems

There are several problems which arise with Fodor's espousal of cognitivism here. The first has to do, again, with the achievement-character of recognition. As we have noted, one important feature of an achievement verb is that it *contrasts with* a process or performance verb. It is more akin to arriving than to traveling, more akin to winning than to playing. Yet Fodor seeks to somehow 'decompose' recognition into two aspects: one, the *correctness* feature (a hallmark of an 'achievement' here) and the other a *process* feature (those postulated inner 'mental events or processes'). This cannot logically work, because whilst '*trying* (perhaps unsuccessfully) to recognize something' can indeed comprise various sorts of 'processes' (but none of them need be construed as 'mental'), actually recognizing something cannot. Fodor is, characteristically, underestimating the complexity of relations amongst different kinds of verbs, and this would be tantamount to seeking to partially processualize an achievement verb, akin to claiming that, say, now being at one's destination (having arrived) is partially also a matter of also *doing* something *in addition* to being there. The second problem with Fodor's position is that he believes that abstract concepts must be involved in recognizing things, and that these concepts are mentally housed and activated when applied to the phenomena recognized for what they are. The idea that recognition and perception must involve the extraction of some abstract essence (say, of 'Lillibullerohood') and its subsequent 'fitting' to an instance or token is a familiar metaphysical thesis in modern philosophy, to which Norman Malcolm (another persistent critic of the mentalist tradition) has provided the most appropriate challenge. He argued that if we claim that the way that someone knows that something before him is a dog is by seeing that the creature 'fits' his Idea (his Abstracted Essence) of a dog, then we must also ask: how can he know that *this* is an example of 'fitting'? In a way similar to that which Ryle often employs, Malcolm is highlighting the oddity of the sort of explanation that mentalist cognitivists think they are giving, asking whether these really make the thing that the theorists originally found puzzling any less puzzling, or whether they simply relocate the same problem, as though it were easier to understand how people can recognize what they see if it is suggested that 'recognizing' is something that takes place inside the mind, leaving it unresolved as to how the 'recognizing' works. In this case, if one is puzzled by the capacity to understand how someone can recognize another instance of something they have seen before just by looking at it, how can that puzzlement be eased (as cognitive theorists claim that it can) if one supposes that one has some sort of mental picture of the sort of thing that one consults in order to see if the instance matches the general picture (or 'recipe'). How is it any less problematic (in *their* terms, since *we* do not think that the issue is at all problematic in the way they conceive) to recognize that this instance matches a general picture than it is to recognize that this instance resembles that previous? Taken seriously, this line of argument can only lead to an infinite regress: if one is postulated to need a general procedure to perform a cognitive operation, then one will need a further general procedure to apply to those cases in which one makes use of the general procedure, *and so on*. At some point, to end this regress, one will need simply to affirm that what is done is done without further general guidance, but in that case why not make the 'stopping point' at the very beginning of the chain of thought about recognition before one has postulated the internal, general process? The introduction of the idea of an abstract general guide to recognition is simply a detour around, not a solution to, the original 'problem'.

"What guides his judgment here? Does he not need a second-order Idea which shows him what it is like for something to fit an Idea? That is, will he not need a model of *fitting*? ... An infinite regress has been generated and nothing has been explained."[145]

Rorty has suggested that Fodor's distinction between abstract and concrete properties of phenomena has led him astray in his analysis of recognition. He remarks:

"... nobody thinks that 'constancy' requires postulating 'abstract' mechanisms in photoelectric cells or tuning forks. Yet is there any difference between middle C and 'Lillibullerohood' save that we have dubbed the former a 'concrete acoustic quality' and the latter an 'abstract similarity'? We could specify a thousand accidental features (timbre, volume, presence of light, color of the object emitting the sound) which the tuning fork ignores just as the Lillibullero-recognizer does."[146]

Rorty's point is that supra-physiological models of the sort to which Fodor and others aspire are not only incoherent, they are otiose: since the concrete-abstract distinction is relative to a given database (as is the simple-complex distinction), postulating 'abstract' concepts as required in recognition "would not occur... if we did not already have the whole Cartesian bag of tricks in hand."[147]

Can a satisfactory response to what *animates* cognitivist and mentalistic conceptions be given? Recall: for Fodor, it is the human restriction on the tolerance for variation, distortion and novelty which motivates his theoretical enterprise. Is there a *non*-cognitivist account that might be given to explain this? Let us return to consider Gunderson's critical assessment of cognitivist approaches to recognition. He reminds us that "... human recognition does occur within a context which very often plays a crucial role in determining how

---

[145] Norman Malcolm, "The myth of cognitive processes and structures" in Theodore Mischel (ed.), *Cognitive Development and Epistemology* (N.Y.: Doubleday, 1971), p. 391.
[146] Richard Rorty, *Philosophy and the Mirror of Nature* (Princeton, N.J.: Princeton University Press, 1979), p. 233.
[147] *Ibid.*, p. 232.

something is recognized as being a certain sort of thing".[148] Focusing upon letter recognition for his examples, he notes that, for example, it hardly matters given the second letter in CATS AND DOGS whether the apex is closed, since the context disperses all doubt as to whether an open apex A were an H or not an A. He continues:

> "More emphatically, trying to decide whether an H-A-shaped inscription with either an open apex or converging sides is an A or an H in isolation is obviously an idle decision, since there is clearly no right choice to be made. Such decisions would have the flavor of real choices only if made against a background of real alternatives."[149]

Again:

> "... if we recognize the second to the last letter in the sentence 'The cow chews cud' as an almost closed u, and not as a somewhat open o, it will no doubt be because of what we know about the meaning of the word 'cud' and the meaning of the word 'cod' (as well as what we know about the eating habits of cows)."[150]

Clearly, then, there is a major obstacle confronting cognitivist efforts to explain human recognition competence(s) in terms of abstract features/concepts stored in minds or brains. Even allowing for the (theoretical) possibility of compiling a gigantic encyclopedic representation of 'what people know', it appears that, for many cases of recognition, *negative* background knowledge would also have to be codified (e.g., that cows do *not* eat fish), and *that* does not look in the least auspicious.

---

[148] K. Gunderson, *op. cit.*, p. 322.
[149] *Ibid.*
[150] *Ibid.*, pp. 323-24.

Can the Problem be Dissolved?

Having now reviewed the nature of the 'projection problem', adduced evidence of its ubiquity in modern cognitivism, and discussed a few of the more prominent objections to the cognitivist 'solution' to it, we turn now to a systematic discussion of its possible 'dissolution'. A good place to start is with the very initial formulation of the problem. According to Fodor, we confront a problem of giving an account of the n+1th case of recognizing that 'this' is a case of 'that', given that we have only, so far, seen variable cases of 'this's' and not every possible or imaginable instance. We will argue that this is fundamentally a pseudo-problem, established by the acceptance of a wholly contentious (but often unrecognized) presupposition about the nature of *learning* and about the *character* (and *role*) of the cases involved in learning (e.g., that something is a case of a 'this').

When we learn a tune or to identify the letters of the alphabet, we do not simply learn *this playing* of that tune as though we were engaged in a one-off event. This would be tantamount to claiming that, when we learn to drive by being guided and corrected by our driving instructor as we drive around a familiar neighborhood, all we are learning is (how) to drive around this particular neighborhood. However, when we are really learning to drive, we are learning to drive just about anywhere! When we are learning to drive around a particular neighborhood, if we lack the generality to drive around *other* neighborhoods, then we have only learned some rote procedures. The fact that when we learn to drive in circumscribed circumstances this can equip us to drive *tout court* is one that seemingly escapes our cognitive theorists. When we learn a tune, we learn how to tell when it is played in various possible ways. To learn to recognize the letters of the alphabet, we are learning to recognize these letters as *standard* letters in the alphabet, not to recognize just *these* letters as written out, and when we learn a tune we are not learning to recognize only the tune *as we first heard it played*.

Note in this connection Franks' misleading remark about the failure of environments to supply 'exact' copies of originals in terms of our learning what is what – not that Franks has provided us, or could provide us, with any *context-free standards* for what might count as an 'exact' vis-à-vis an 'inexact' instance. This is another case of the failure to grasp the point that learning to recognize something as what it is involves a *generality* built into our primary learning paradigm. That is, we do not learn to tell that just *this* (the original sample or samples) is what it is (are what they are) but that this *and* countless likenesses are cases of the same thing.

When we are taught to start the car by turning on the ignition we can learn, from the one instance, how to start the car on any subsequent occasion (given no faults that affect the ignition) and how to start many other cars as well, and we can do this for the simple reason that the ignitions in automobiles take an enormously standardized form. Further, when we are being taught it is not difficult to see what kinds of considerations are relevant to the determination of what it is that 'starts the car' – it is putting the key in the slot and turning it (using a hand, of course) but whether the hand is wearing a signet ring, whether its nails are well manicured, whether they are dirty, and so on, has nothing to do with 'starting the car by turning the key in the ignition slot'. When our instructor starts the car, it is clear that, *in the instruction scenario*, he is not just starting the car but showing us how to do the same thing and it is equally plain to us that the fact that it is the instructor who is starting the car does not matter because *that person's* doing it is not constitutive of the criteria for 'doing the same thing' – another person can 'do the same thing' here.

There are, in addition, issues about the strictness with which 'the same thing' is to be identified. Consider the strictness which applies to reciting the order of letters in the alphabet or proceeding through certain kinds of arithmetical computations, as opposed to the comparative looseness with respect to the recognition/transcription of those letters in handwriting – the identification of an 'a' does not require close resemblance in print font or handwriting styles. As well as learning 'the relevancies', one learns that there are – or that there are not – tolerances in the identification of 'the same' as part of learning how to identify the instance used in instruction, training, learning: i.e., we learn how to understand and apply its particular paradigmatic status. We can pick up on Gunderson's remark on 'context' and generalize that into Wittgenstein's point about 'stage setting' in relation to Fodor's impoverished assumptions about the learning situations of children. Ryle indicated some time ago, in a much-neglected paper[151], that the tradition emanating from the work of Noam Chomsky characteristically treats child learning as a matter of solitary inductions governed by innate (universal-grammatical) rules.

"In that real life that Chomsky and Vendler are too scientific, or too un-ecological, to recognize, Tommy ordinarily has a mother, father, brothers, sisters, uncles, aunts and playmates. Some of them are (hush!) actually fond of him, as he is of them. They like helping him and bringing him on; he demands and delights in their intended and unintended guidances, examples and stimulations... They recite to him, and then prompt his return-recitations to them; they provide, wittingly and unwittingly, what he models his own actions, accents, intonations and nascent phrases on; they challenge him, race him, practice him, test him and correct him... they *show* him the delivery of rhymes, numerals, letters of the alphabet, street-names; they applaud and laugh at his earliest puns and word-coinages; they feed his nascent hunger for consecutive prose with bed-time stories; and they listen with fond patience to his own first self-invented stories. Their disappointing misunderstandings and non-understandings of him teach him to try to employ safeguards against such disappointments; following their examples, he tries to avoid or correct equivocations, ellipses and indefinitenesses."[152]

Solitary inductive operations? "Rubbish!" says Ryle: "Does he learn hide-and-seek, snap and football by solitary inductions? Or does he learn to play

---

[151] Gilbert Ryle, "Mowgli in Babel" in Konstantin Kolenda (ed.), *On Thinking* (N.J.: Rowman and Littlefield, 1979).
[152] *Ibid.*, pp. 101-02.

initially strange but thrilling games with other children by whole-heartedly playing them?"[153]

Wittgenstein's point that understanding the act of 'naming' something presupposes a great deal of stage-setting in the language employed can be developed by noting that preparations, orientations and assistance in learning circumstances provide for the nature of what is being learned – e.g., one understands that one is being shown not John starting his car on the 14th of June 2002 at 1.07pm, nor even how *John* starts *his* car, but how one starts cars. Moreover, one learns to understand a lot about what cars are, how they (minimally) work, etc., within which the technique for starting them is to be defined. Someone who draws a *shape* in instructing someone in the alphabet is not drawing 'this line' but is drawing a shape, and not just any old shape, either, but (e.g.) *the shape of the letter 'e'*. To benefit from such instruction requires that one be clued into what is going on in the situation, one's prior understandings giving one extensive guidance as to what it is about what is being done that matters relative to grasping the lesson or course of instruction. Understanding the initial instructive instances *is* understanding how to 'extend' to other cases. Having understood the instructive instances there is nothing more to learn or to figure out.

Muddles about Learning

We are essentially confronted by another of the Chomsky/Fodor school's exercises in theoretically motivated fact reversal. The deep assumption – deriving from a metaphysically peculiar view of the role of science in our understanding, and especially about the role of generalities – is that the process of learning must be the same throughout, that 'mechanisms' of learning (which are partly assimilated to 'mechanisms' of perception) must operate in the same way from the start, that the capacity for learning is basically unchanging throughout life and,

---

[153] *Ibid.*, p. 102.

ultimately, throughout the history of the human species – with the result that absurdities of the sort John Searle complains about (e.g., that people must have had the concept of 'carburetor' in Neolithic times) can arise. This is, of course, fact defying since it is indisputably plain that an individual's capacity to learn varies over the course of his or her development, that the capacity to learn *builds upon* what has been earlier learned, that what has previously been learned can modify the capacity for further learning. Thus, we instruct small children by way of very basic reactions, and we use these reactions to teach them some basic bits of language, and having taught them some basic reactions and bits of language, we can then use these reactions and bits of language to teach them something more complex, and we can, when we have taught them sufficient language, use the language itself to teach them a lot more. Of course, a child at birth does have the capacity to learn a language, and we would not doubt that the capacity to learn a language is innate in the human species (though we doubt that anyone has ever seriously doubted this, even *tabula rasa* empiricists whose excesses provided a pretext for the return-excesses of the Chomsky/Fodor school). However, the possession of the capacity to acquire something must not be conflated with the possession of the thing one has the capacity to acquire. That a nuclear bomb has the capacity to destroy a city the size of New York does not mean that somewhere about this bomb, a constituent part of its molecular structure, must be: the destruction of New York City. To say that the bomb has the capacity to do something is to provide the sort of thing Ryle described as 'semi-hypothetical': it says what will happen *if* certain conditions are satisfied. The claim that the bomb has the capacity to destroy a city the size of New York is simply to say something (true) about its physical construction and about the kinds of effects that its features would generate under certain conditions. To say that a child has, when it is born, the capacity to learn and understand a language is to make a predictive statement that is based upon nothing more than that the child is a human being and human beings normally, in overwhelming proportions, grow up and learn to speak. To have the capacity to do something that requires certain resources does not mean that one has any of the resources necessary already available! Why should one think that? Unless one is wedded to the idea that one cannot understand anything *de novo*? Fodor, alas, is of this persuasion.

Many of these problems are, at base, actually rule-following ones (hence the link we mentioned earlier to 'rule-finitism'). A common mistake is to treat the acquisition of a rule (for identifying letters, for spelling words, for distinguishing tunes, etc.) as if it were a matter of learning an extension of cases to which it applies, instance by instance. Rather, we would argue (as one of us has elsewhere[154]) that, given the distinction between *correctly* identifying something and *thinking that* one has, albeit incorrectly, rules become relevant to such matters. However, learning rules here is a matter of picking up general standards that can apply to instances where the 'instances' themselves are internal to the relevant rules and not problems for the application of independently and separately specifiable rules. To have grasped the rule *is* to be able to identify the instances correctly. The latter is a criterion for the former, and not an independent matter at all. To think that rule acquisition and following is wholly distinct from instance-determinations leads to a falsely postulated gap – a gap between the rule and its applicable instances. If there is no such gap (and we insist that the notion robs the concept of a 'rule' of its sense here), then theoretical efforts to bridge it are otiose. Of course, this is far from denying problematic or borderline cases. It is not to deny, either, that cases might arise in which the application of a rule becomes contentious. We have learned to call small, eight-legged creatures with such-and-such features 'spiders' – what are we to say of the Amazon explorer who returns with a creature in every other respect like a spider but which has twelve legs? Note, however, that this problem is utterly dissimilar to Fodor's 'projection problem'. It is, rather, a matter of making a decision whether to continue using the word in the way we have been or to change it and allow it to

---

[154] Wes Sharrock and Graham Button, "Do the right thing! Rule finitism, rule skepticism and rule following", *Human Studies*, Vol. 22, 1999, pp. 193-210.

subsume a case that it did not previously subsume. Is the 'projection problem' perhaps a lurking residuum of the idea that the meaning of a word is its extension, the assortment of things for which it 'stands', or that it names? Is it tied up with the idea that the items identified by the word must all have something or some things in common, must all be identifiable by the recursive application of some principle of identification? But if – as Wittgenstein pointed out – there is no 'single thread' running through the uses of a single word, no common characteristic that identifies all the items that may be subsumed under it as instances of the thing it names, etc., then the mastery of a term's employment cannot be a matter of extension but must be an *ad hoc* affair. Further, the decision with respect to the twelve-legged 'spider' may be based on a number of criteria, and there may be grounds both for and against going one way or the other. There may be a marked element of arbitrariness in deciding to give criteria other than 'number of legs' the decisive role: one could do as well as the other.

There is a strange sort of metaphysics, we believe, which animates much of the philosophical discussion of the projection problem. It is one which would assert (with Franks) that 'everything is different from everything else'. Our point would be that determinations of similarity and dissimilarity are facilitated by *contexted* standards and local purposes. Indeed, as Wittgenstein observed, the same is true for claims that "this is the same as that".[155] Detecting the 'same' in the 'different' is not a generic task nor even a generic capacity which might pose a tractable empirical problem for neurophysiology to tackle. There is a motley of cases with indefinitely varying features which one might construe as identifying samenesses or similarities and the converse. And if any actual (as distinct from theoretically stipulated) problems of detection or determination arise, their solutions will be discerned in the history and circumstances within which they arise, not by inspecting the brain or central nervous system.

---

[155] Ludwig Wittgenstein, *Philosophical Investigations* (Trans. G. E. M. Anscombe), Oxford: Blackwell, paras. 215-16.

CHAPTER SEVEN

FETISHISING 'SYNTAX'

'Speaking intelligibly' is a human capability sometimes thought by neuroscientists to require a special sort of explanation from them. Producing and understanding meaningful utterances is widely construed as a complex endeavor, and the sort of explanation to be adduced is one in which mental or cognitive processes are central. The initial assumption is seemingly obvious: speaking intelligibly is a matter of uttering sounds in specific sorts of sequences which can be understood by others. The sense of any utterance is a function of the meanings of the words uttered and the order in which they are articulated. It is clear that to delete (or to add) one or more words, or to rearrange their order, can result in a change of sense or in nonsense (even babble). Hence, it is thought, speaking is essentially a compositional process involving the realization of a prior 'semantic intention' (Dennett) in sequenced strings of words. A crucial component of utterance-production, then, is asserted to be its syntacticity. In what follows, each facet of this intuitively plausible thesis will be subject to critical scrutiny and found to be seriously deficient. The major point under contention is the very idea that there are rules of sentence-formation which cover all possible, grammatically well-formed and intelligible ones. Linguists (and philosophers) have for years played around with the combinatorial tolerances of various words and expressions in an attempt to determine the general possibilities of combination throughout a given language, but the basic notion that sentences can be analyzed in terms of lexical combinatorics is rarely challenged. In confronting this issue, it is as well to begin back at square one.

Syntax is one facet of the analysis of the use of language which focuses upon the order of words in phrases, clauses and sentences. Children have learned in school for many generations how to 'parse' sentences into such categories as 'noun', 'adjective', 'verb', 'preposition' and 'adverb', amongst others. In the contemporary intellectual scene, however, 'syntax' has assumed a strange sort of priority in linguistics as well as in cognitive science. The origin of this focus is in Charles Pierce's trichotomy of linguistic analysis into the dimensions of 'syntax', 'semantics' and 'pragmatics'. This trichotomy lives on in contemporary linguistic theory, largely thanks to the efforts of Noam Chomsky. For Chomsky, 'syntax' is divorced from 'semantics'. His major (now classic) example for such a separation is the sentence: 'Colorless green ideas sleep furiously'.[156] On its face, this sentence looks – in terms of the correspondence in the sequence of word-classes from which the words in each sentence are taken - like the following: 'Lazy brown foxes jump sluggishly'. According to Chomsky, the former nonsense sentence has a parsing which can be represented quasi-algebraically as follows: 'S (sentence) = Adj. + Adj. + Noun + V + Adv.'. In this analysis, Chomsky is clearly drawing upon a parsing which would be appropriate for the latter sentence, viz. 'Lazy (= Adj.) + brown (=Adj.) + foxes (=Noun) + jump (=Verb) + sluggishly (=Adv.). His point is that *both* (sorts of) sentences have the same syntactic structure which is adequate for a well-formed, grammatical English sentence, but one is nonsense and the other makes sense. Thus, he concludes, grammaticality can be distinguished from intelligibility. If this seems a fine point, this instance should serve as a reminder of the way in which, in general within the cognitive sciences, and in Chomsky's case in particular, great castles of claims are built on the slightest illustrations.

However, the problems start here because there is absolutely no warrant for the syntactical parsing accorded to the nonsense sentence (if it can even be considered a sentence at all). 'Colorless green ideas sleep furiously' makes no sense in the English language (nor in any other language) – it is, so to speak, 'nonsensical all the way down'. After all, one might argue that 'Colorless green ideas' is the name of a rock-band, hence forming a compound noun. The

---

[156] Noam Chomsky, *Syntactic Structures* (The Hague: Mouton, 1957), p. 3.

specification of what this combination of words actually amounts to 'syntactically' is entirely up for grabs. As many crazy 'interpretations' of what this nonsense might amount to could dictate whatever syntactic analysis might then be defended. But none of them could be warranted *independently* of such 'semantic' considerations. Consider the following two sentences: 'Time flies like an arrow' and 'Fruit flies like a banana'.

> "The word 'time' here may be either a noun, an adjective, or a verb, yielding three different syntactical interpretations. (To see how it could be one of the latter two, which are perhaps less perspicuous, compare: 'Fruit flies like a banana' and 'Time runners with a stop-watch'.) The only way to choose between these possible interpretations is by recourse to the semantic context, either that of the surrounding sentences, or the vaguer and much vaster one of general information (e.g., there are not any things called 'time flies'). This means, of course, that we cannot treat the semantic level as simply dependent on the syntactic.'[157]

We shall return to this theme – the putative 'autonomy of syntax' – further on. It looms large in modern efforts to argue for a relationship between 'grammaticality' construed as a specific, encapsulated, skill, and brain function. However, 'grammaticality' is a much more problematic concept in this context, and much less tractable to any sort of neurophysiological-reductionist account, than is commonly portrayed in much of the academic literature with which we are currently bombarded.

The mentalist orientation of Chomsky's linguistic theorizing has formed a basis for subsequent neural-metaphysical speculations. For example, Steven Pinker writes: "Simply by making noises with our mouths, we can reliably cause new combinations of ideas to arise is each other's minds. The ability comes so naturally that we are apt to forget what a miracle it is."[158] If *all* that were emitted

---

[157] F. J. Crosson, "The Computer as Gadfly" in R. Cohen & M. Wartofsky (eds.), *Boston Studies in the Philosophy of Science, 1966-68* (Holland: D. Reidel, 1969), p. 229.

[158] Steven Pinker, *The Language Instinct* (London: Penguin, 1995), p. 15. We might call this the 'miracle gap' which is an artifact of the form in which materialists present their problems. The

from our mouths were 'noises', we should certainly confront something of a miracle in understanding how we speak and understand each other. Again, we are confronted with a familiar technique, that of portraying the relationship between 'input' and 'output' in terms that are calculated to exaggerate the 'discrepancy' between them, thus licensing the claim that a complex machinery is required to carry out all the necessary 'work' of turning impoverished inputs into enriched outputs. What emerges from our mouths when we speak are not 'noises' but words and utterances. Granted, these do have acoustic properties, but then we do not *detect* what is said by the words that we hear simply through such properties as might a computer equipped with a sonic sensor system: we *hear* words and utterances. The idea that such words and utterances as we hear evoke in our 'minds' combinations of 'ideas' traces back to John Locke, whose (in)famous version of the comprehension of speech went as follows:

"The chief end of language in communication being to be understood, words serve not well for that end, neither in civil nor philosophical discourse, when any word does not excite in the hearer the same idea which it stands for in the mind of the speaker... there comes, by constant use, to be such a connection between certain sounds and the ideas they stand for... the ideas they (words) stand for are their proper and immediate signification... "[159]

The notion that a word or sequence of words excites a corresponding 'idea' (or sequence of 'ideas') in the 'mind' of a recipient is redolent of what Roy Harris has aptly termed the 'telementational' conception of language.[160] Several issues present themselves. Firstly, since an idea is always an idea *of* or *about* something, or *that* something is the case, it must be expressed as such in some

---

spurious form of argumentation goes back at least to Quine, where the 'complex' output of our elaborate scientific understanding of the world contrasts with the 'bare' irradiations of our sensory surfaces that are supposedly the initial input. If, however, we keep in mind that the 'irradiation of our sensory surfaces' means nothing other than our capacities of sight, hearing, touch, taste, and smell, then there is no need to think that there is any disproportion between input and output.
[159] John Locke, *Essay Concerning Human Understanding* (ed. A. C. Fraser, 1894: republished in N.Y., 1959), Essay 111, ix, 4: ii, 6: ii, 1.
[160] Roy Harris, *The Language Machine* (London: Duckworth, 1987).

symbolic medium. Why not in words? But, if in words, then an infinite regress looms: if to understand what some word or utterance means is to entertain a corresponding idea, then it must follow that to understand *what* idea is expressed thereby requires yet a further 'idea' – but of or about what, and expressed in what expression(s)? Secondly, note again the use of the concept of a 'sound' here. Pinker is far too much impressed with Chomsky's claim that grammars unite mere 'sounds' with 'meanings'. Again, we reiterate a simple but important point: words have acoustic properties when uttered (and graphemic ones when written) but this does not entail that words, when uttered, are *simply* 'sounds'. If they were, and needed supplementation by their 'meanings' in order to be heard to be the words they comprise, where and when does such a supplementation actually occur? Consciously and simultaneously with hearing them? Hardly, because no-one is aware of continuously supplementing the words they hear – or the words they utter which they understand – with 'their meanings'! Unconsciously? Well, then, that would be of no use to a speaker-hearer who would be utterly unaware of whatever 'meaning' was being appended to the words he hears or speaks, and it is, moreover, not possible to clarify what could be meant by 'meanings' being 'appended' to anything as a feature of our mundane production and comprehension of what is said. Determined to pursue the Chomskian objective of revealing 'how the mind works' by revealing how language works, Pinker is drawn into a familiar nest of problems. There is the customary appeal to the postulate of a 'mental dictionary', somewhere housed in the mind/brain, which is said to specify the part-of-speech categories for the words included in it.[161] Following Chomsky's critique of Markov-chaining models of linguistic production, he asserts: "With a chaining device it's just one damn word after another, but with a phrase structure grammar the connectedness of words in the tree reflects the relatedness of ideas *in mentalese*."[162] But why 'mentalese' (whatever that might be)? Why not in English or any other natural language? Part

---

[161] Steven Pinker, *op. cit.*, p. 99.
[162] *Ibid.*, p. 101, emphasis added.

of the answer here depends upon the postulation of a Universal Grammar (or, more exactly, Universal Syntax). This postulate is defined by Cook and Newson in the following terms:

> "UG (Universal Grammar) is a theory of knowledge, not of behavior; its concern is with the internal structure of the human mind... UG theory holds that the speaker knows a set of principles that apply to all languages, and parameters that vary within clearly defined limits from one language to another. Acquiring language means learning how these principles apply to a particular language and which value is appropriate. Each principle or parameter of language that is proposed is a substantive claim about the mind of the speaker and about the nature of language acquisition."[163]

Nigel Love provides a useful example of a proposition of Universal Grammar – the 'subjacency' principle.[164] This principle asserts that a phrase cannot be shifted too far within a sentence, where 'too far' means 'beyond the limits of two bounding categories'. It is held to be universal, i.e., applicable to all natural languages. Both English and Italian (for example) exhibit subjacency, but they differ in respect of the way in which the choice of bounding category is fixed. Universal Grammar comprises sets of principles and parameters, the former universal, the latter differentially specifiable for particular natural languages. Another UG principle, 'structure-dependence', is discussed by Peter Hacker.[165] In transforming a simple declarative into an interrogative, it can appear that a simple linear rule is involved: shift the first occurring 'is' to the front of the sentence. Thus: 'The man is at home' becomes 'Is the man at home?' However, when confronted with a declarative with an embedded phrase such as: 'The man, who is happy, is at home', the appropriate transformation to construct a corresponding interrogative is given by a non-linear, 'structure-dependent', rule which states that the verb of the main clause of the sentence is the one to be moved to the front.

---

[163] Vivian J. Cook & Mark Newson, *Chomsky's Universal Grammar: An Introduction* (Oxford: Basil Blackwell 2nd edition, 1996), p. 2.

[164] Nigel Love, "Ideal Linguistics", *Language and Communication*, Vol. 8, No. 1, 1988.

[165] P. M. S. Hacker, "Chomsky's Problem", *Language and Communication*, Vol. 10, No. 2, 1990, pp. 145-46.

Thus, we do not get: 'Is the man, who happy, is at home?' but rather: 'Is the man, who is happy, at home?' In Chomsky's words: "... the child selects the rule R-Q [the structure-dependent one] at once, whereas the scientist must discover by an arduous process of inquiry and thought that R-Q is the operative rule... and that the principle of structure dependence is part of the structure of the language faculty."[166] Hacker notes that the depiction of what children are doing when they are learning to talk is quite remarkable. The child is construed as equipped from birth (in a manner left largely unspecified) with knowledge of the principles of sentence formation putatively 'underlying' all human languages, past and present! However, such 'knowledge' is completely disconnected from 'behavior' (see the quotation from Cook and Newson above). That is, *mirabile dictu*, the child 'knows' these universal principles and their parameters, but can neither state them nor answer questions about them and cannot recognize them when stated! He or she must then proceed to discover what values are correct for the various parameters associated with the various universal principles (e.g., if he/she is acquiring Italian, the parametric values associated with the subjacency principle will vary from those relevant to the acquisition of English). But children who are mastering compound interrogatives are not aspiring to write grammars, let alone putatively 'universal' ones, and when they produce a question of the form: 'Is the X, who is F, G?' they are *not* (ordinarily) deriving it from a declarative – such an operation is a specialized exercise unto itself, and one which certainly post-dates the capacity to utter a compound interrogative. Hacker poses the pointed question: "If he (the child) needs the R-Q rule to formulate the interrogative from the declarative, should he not need an R-D rule to formulate a declarative? From an interrogative? But speaking, asserting, asking questions, etc., are not computational processes of *any* kind."[167]

---

[166] Noam Chomsky, *Language and the Problems of Knowledge: The Managua Lectures* (Cambridge, MA: M.I.T. Press, 1988), p. 46.
[167] P. M. S. Hacker, *op. cit.*, p. 146.

The acquisition of one's native tongue is portrayed as a matter of grammatical analysis operating with syntactical concepts which the language-learner has not yet empirically mastered. Indeed, as we pointed out in our discussion of the 'projection problem', learning to talk is being mischaracterized in terms of the deployment of parts-of-speech categories which properly belong to the realms of orthography and textual analysis, both of which presuppose a considerable mastery of a language in the first place, and not of routine social interactions with parents, care-givers, siblings and others which actually play the crucial role in the actual development of his linguistic capability. If there is no empirical *evidence* whatsoever to support the substantive nativist thesis, the argument sometimes goes, this is because this thesis is not an empirical one in any conventional sense – it is a *theoretical* postulate. Nonetheless, this begs the question of what sort of a 'theory' of language acquisition can dispense so completely with evidentiary support? And, one must ask, what sort of empirical evidence could there *possibly* (logically) be for claims such as those above which purport to hive off attributions of highly abstract kinds of information (i.e., 'knowledge' of the putative UG principles and parameters) from any and all behavioral manifestations? That a child's compound question is well-formed will *tautologically conform* to the product of the R-Q rule, but not because the child has knowledge of and has *followed* such a rule. I may well take a route which is depicted on your map which I have never seen and know nothing about, but this scarcely licenses the claim that I have 'unconsciously' followed your map.

Roy Harris has referred to generativist linguistic theorizing as essentially 'scriptist' – i.e., overly preoccupied with analytical concepts and distinctions appropriate, perhaps, to the study of the written word but much less, if at all, to the spoken word.[168] This point can be brought out more fully by considering the claims made about the phenomenon of ambiguity. Chomsky's famous example-sentence, 'Flying planes can be dangerous', is asserted to be recognizably

---

[168] Roy Harris, *op. cit.*

ambiguous to all mature English speakers, since on one reading 'flying' can be an adjective, on another reading a present-continuous tensed verb. Its ambiguity is not something which has been explicitly taught to them, but is available to them, it is argued, as a result of their application of tacit grammatical principles of the sort which the syntactician analyses and formulates. However, when considering the role of such an expression *in speech*, it is clear that it would be embedded in a communicative context which would normally clarify the intended sense. The impression of a general ambiguity only arises if the sentence is considered in a context-free way – in other words, in a frame possible for the written word, but hardly for the spoken one. Simply staring at an aircraft and saying: 'Flying planes can be dangerous' might lead to puzzlement, but the same expression would have no ambiguous status if uttered during an especially strenuous course of airborne pilot instruction, or, conversely, if one has strayed too close to an aircraft runway in use for take-offs and landings. A more subtle example is provided by Lightfoot: 'John kept the car in the garage'. Here, the two different 'readings' can be brought out by the following alternative expansions: (1) 'John kept the car in the garage, but sold the one in the street' and (2) 'John kept the car in the garage, but left the bicycle on the porch'. In (1), 'in the garage' is an adjectival phrase, whilst in (2) it is an adverbial phrase modifying 'kept'. However, as Love[169] astutely points out, there is no reason to think that our language (or any other) contains one single, discrete, ambiguous item such as this in the first place, since in the actual spoken use the sentence would be embedded in wholly different communicative contexts. This point can be connected to the one quoted from Crosson earlier concerning the role of 'semantics' in fixing syntactical categories for the words in an expression: since ambiguity (and lack thereof) is context-dependent, again we see how syntactical parsing is itself contextually sensitive as an actual operation we can engage in. In the pursuit of a Universal Syntax, this point has been overlooked. The idealizations and abstractions required even to approach the

---

[169] Nigel Love, *op. cit.*, p. 84.

desiderata for such theorizing strip away what is actually essential to the very identification of the components which the principles are supposed to govern.

That Chomskian ideas about language have influenced cognitive neuroscientists is attested to by many of the things that Kosslyn and Koenig have to say about the neurophysiological bases of linguistic comprehension and production. "When one understands a sentence, one must compute a structure that organizes the words; the structure is apart from the words themselves", they assert.[170] This claim ignores the important conceptual point that *understanding* is not a performance-verb but an achievement-verb, hence not amenable to decomposition into any constituent processes (such as interpreting, analyzing, or, in this case, computing). It is true that, for certain sorts of sentences, comprehension might be the product of an analysis (as in, e.g., their example-sentence: 'Through rapid righting with his right hand he was able to right the capsized canoe'), but understanding is not analysis nor is it computation. We are told:

> "The sentence structure monitoring subsystem must check three kinds of information. First, it must monitor the *syntactic relations* among the words, checking that the emerging structure is grammatical... Second, it must monitor the *semantic relations* among the words. A 'colorless green idea' is unacceptable because the meanings of the words clash... Third, the sentence structure monitoring subsystem must register the *prosody*. The prosody is the 'melody' of the sentence, arising from variations in pitch, loudness, and phoneme duration... All three kinds of information are used together to determine the meaning of the sentence."[171]

These postulated brain functions exactly mirror the fundamental structure of Chomsky's reasoning. Leaving aside for the moment the fact that 'contextually-relevant particulars' – indeed *all* of the pragmatic dimension of

---

[170] Stephen M. Kosslyn & Olivier Koenig, *Wet Mind: The New Cognitive Neuroscience* (N.Y.: Free Press, 1995), p. 239.
[171] *Ibid.*, pp. 241-42.

linguistic usage – are oddly omitted from the depiction of the processes here stipulated to be at work, it is important to note that, for these neuroscientific theorists, the Broca and Wernicke areas are thought of as homuncular grammarians.

Let us examine in greater detail the vexed issue of 'compositionality' here. This is, as noted, a doctrine which asserts that the sense (meaning) of any sentence (utterance) is derived from the meanings of its constituent words and their syntactical arrangement. But clearly, this cannot be taken literally, since the sense that any sentence makes cannot be an additive function of lexical definitions of constituent words. Consider the word 'schedule'. Lexically, it can be defined (roughly) as 'time-table' or 'tabular statement', but this cannot account for its meaning in a phrase such as: 'on schedule'. This expression does *not* mean 'on time-table', even though it is true that the word 'time-table' has a high degree of substitutability in other expressions using 'schedule'. Consider, more extensively, the following sentences: 'Engagement was broken – Temperamental young man gassed himself'.[172] Given a narrow, compositionally-derived, reading of these expressions one might construe their sense in the following disparate ways: (1) that the engagement was for dinner, not for marriage: (2) that there was someone other than the young man who was engaged (not necessarily him): (3) that the engaged parties were engaged to others (and not necessarily to each other): (4) that the broken engagement was another's (and not necessarily the young man's): (5) that the gassing was an accident, not a suicide: (6) that because the young man gassed himself the engagement was broken and not the reverse, and (7) that the young man's gassing himself was a result of religious ecstasy or moral outrage and not a result of grief or disappointment over his broken engagement to be married. Mere lexical additivity not only can produce incoherence, it can generate counter-intuitive readings of simple sentences. *Of course*, in this example, our

---

[172] The following discussion draws heavily on Peter Eglin & Stephen Hester, "Category, Predicate and Task", *Semiotica*, Vol. 88, Nos. ¾, 1992.

natural understanding of the expressions yields the following: the engagement was for marriage – the suicidal young man was engaged to no-one else – the broken engagement was the young man's – the gassing was a suicide – the suicide by gassing was because of the broken engagement of the young man's – and that it occurred was because of the loss of his loved one. Lexical compositionality (alone) cannot be appealed to in elucidating the 'unity' of sense of the expressions as we can mundanely read/hear them.

Ryle once asserted: "Word meanings or concepts are not proposition components but propositional differences."[173] We take this to mean that the words which comprise sentences, although contributing to what they mean, are not specifiable in their syntactical nor semantic dimensions independently of what they are used to *say* in some specific context. As Palmer beautifully expresses this point:

> "To allocate an expression to a category is to give the rules which govern its use. To do so we are obliged to make linguistic expressions *when considered in the dimensions of sense and nonsense* the subjects of propositions. We are obliged, that is, to say that the linguistic expression 'Monday' is governed by rules which are broken in the sentence 'Monday sleeps peacefully' but which are not broken in the sentence 'Monday is the first working day of the week', whereas the linguistic expression 'My wife' is governed by rules which are broken in the sentence 'My wife is the first working day of the week' but which are not broken in the sentence 'My wife sleeps peacefully'. If we are trying to explain in this way why in each case we have a sentence which makes sense and a sentence which does not, then we are obliged to consider the expressions 'Monday' and 'My wife' as *independently* being governed by rules which we can then notice to be flouted when these expressions are conjoined by others."[174]

---

[173] Gilbert Ryle, "Letters and Syllables in Plato" (1960) in his *Collected Papers, Vol. 1* (London: Hutchinson, 1971), p. 61.
[174] Anthony Palmer, *Concept and Object: The Unity of the Proposition in Logic and Psychology* (London: Routledge, 1988), p. 70 (emphasis added).

However, and here is the thrust of Palmer's argument: "when we are considering linguistic expressions with a view to discovering which combinations of them make sense and which do not, this is precisely what we cannot do. To consider linguistic expressions with this aim in mind is to ask *what is said by means of them.*"[175] Divorced from such a consideration there is nothing to consider from the point of view of what makes sense and what does not. If we should ask for the meaning of a word in the context of a proposition or a sentence, "then there can be no such thing as the rules governing the use of an expression which will show that it is meaningful in some sentences and not in others."[176] As Ryle observed, what can be *expressed* in a language is not itself a feature of a language alone.[177] The combination, for example, Energy equals mass times the speed of light squared, which is composed entirely of familiar English words, is only comprehensible to someone who knows some physics, who knows, e.g., that light can have a speed, that 'squared' is a mathematical concept, and is a matter of multiplying a number by itself, etc. Knowing the standard meanings of words such as speed, light, mass and energy in English will not enable one to make sense of the expression without an understanding of the way the expression relates to the ideas and concerns of physics. Ryle was trying to remind us that the expression, Energy equals... , is part of physics, not part of the English language. This point must not be thought of as one specifically about specialized technical terminology, for Ryle's argument was that language is the stock of expressions that is used for saying things, but that what is said by using that stock is not itself part of language – Shakespeare's plays were indeed written in English, but they are not thereby a part of the English language.

Much of the syntactical fetishism in modern linguistics derives from the compositionality and generativity assumptions which, we have shown, are deeply

---

[175] *Ibid.*, emphasis added.

[176] *Ibid.*, p. 71.

[177] Gilbert Ryle, "Use, Usage and Meaning" as reprinted in G. H. R. Parkinson (ed.), *The Theory of Meaning* (Oxford: Oxford University Press, 1968).

problematic, and which owe a great deal to late 19th century attempts to construct a more comprehensive logic and to develop a logically ideal language. An even more basic assumption underlying the Chomsky-Pinker line of reasoning is this: the notion that there exists, prior to its variable linguistic 'clothing', a 'unity' to a *thought* (the fundamental concept in linguistic theory according to them both). Leaving aside the (very relevant) issue of the intentionality of 'thought' in the Brentano-Husserl sense (i.e., that a 'thought' is a relational notion – that there are only thoughts of, about, that, in, over, - up, etc.), the issue which we want to stress in this discussion is that first systematically elaborated by J. F. M. Hunter.[178] It strikes at the very heart of the myth of 'mentalese' and of the originating notion that linguistic expressions clothe our pre-existing, non-linguistic aethereal thoughts in acoustic or graphemic garb. Construing a linguistic 'system' such as is proposed by the Chomsky-Pinker line as a language-producing 'machine' underlying the production of our utterances, Hunter has this to say:

> "If whatever it is that what we say expresses were already in words, no machine would be necessary. We would only have to say out loud what we had said to ourselves, and for that the machine would not be necessary... The machine might still be necessary to explain how we arrive at what we want to say *to ourselves*, but this again would leave us with something pre-verbal as the input. One might avoid this consequence by supposing that our 'private thoughts and ideas' were always in some kind of crude language, and that the function of the machine was to render crudely expressed sentences into well-formed sentences. (That is, after all, the main function of the grammatical rules that we urge upon children and foreigners). But not only is there no evidence that this is so, there could be no better reason for supposing that crude expressions of what we want to say occur primitively than that refined ones do, or that we immediately understand ill-formed sentences, while having difficulty with those that are well-formed."[179]

---

[178] J. F. M. Hunter, "On How We Talk" in his *Essays after Wittgenstein* (Toronto: University of Toronto Press, 1973).
[179] *Ibid.*, p. 154.

Here note that not only must the input to the system or machinery which generates sentences/utterances be itself pre-verbal, it must nonetheless somehow be *content-laden*. That is, it must contain within itself "the entire content of what we end up saying".[180] *Imagery* is the closest phenomenon to something pre-verbal and yet still content-laden, to something having a sort of 'unity' unto itself which differs from the 'unity' of sense of a well-formed sentence. However, as Wittgenstein (and others) have argued on many occasions, no image in and of itself alone determines what it is an image *of*. Your image of an apple is consistent with your wanting one, believing that apples exist, depicting a variety of fruit, depicting a fruit which you happen to like although at this moment do not want to eat, etc. And one can say that one wants a large red apple without having either a 'mental' or a physical picture of one.[181] So, imagery will not perform that function of the content-laden, pre-linguistically-clothed phenomenon of the 'antecedent thought' or of the 'thing you want to put into words'. (And what form would 'energy equals mass times the speed of light squared' take in imagery?) There is no other remotely plausible candidate on offer, so the very foundation of the approach to language being advanced is seriously undermined. Note also that, if some candidate for the 'pre-verbal input' can have *intrinsic* sense, why can't the language we actually speak? How does assuming an 'inner understanding' as the basis for manifest understanding clarify what provides for understanding in either case?

Nothing in what is being argued here militates against the occasional utility and cogency of assigning words to syntactical categories for specific purposes. Nonetheless, it is clear that categories such as 'noun', 'verb' and 'adjective' are resistant to standardized formalization. That 'nouns' are kinds of words that conventionally designate 'things' or 'entities' is broadly true, but unhelpful in any generalizing application (nouns can designate abstractions,

---

[180] *Ibid.*
[181] *Ibid.*, p. 160.

among many exceptions to this 'rule of thumb' understanding). Listing a set of necessary and sufficient conditions for the 'noun-ness' of a word is a failing enterprise. Syntactical classifications do assist us in broadly guiding children and foreigners (and ourselves on occasion) in composing utterances which are normatively ordained to be 'well-formed', but the 'well' in 'well-formed' is (notoriously) a judgment call rather than predicated upon any sort of strict criterion garnering universal assent (as may a mathematical classification, for example). Chomsky's quasi-'algebraicization' of syntax is, thus, a contrivance requiring an enormous amount of idealization, stipulation and ad-hocery.

A deep sense of the apparent *complexities* involved in 'speaking intelligibly' has undoubtedly motivated much of the theorizing here discussed. An important distinction, however, needs to be kept in mind, and that is to take stock of the fact that 'speaking intelligibly' is not synonymous with 'speaking intelligently'. We may sometimes work something out carefully before we do it or say it, but we can also work something out *as* we do it or say it. The in-flight production of utterances should, therefore, pose no particular problem for which something antecedent needs to be postulated as a mechanism of guidance, so to speak. Moreover, the question: *Why* does one say what one says? cannot have a truly generic form as a question. On its occasions when it can be intelligibly posed, it can get some reason or purpose as a response, as can the cognate question: Why does what you say take the form that it does? It is a central part of our argument here to deny that simply locatable combinatorial tolerances of words and phrases (e.g., in English, the definite article must precede the noun in a noun phrase) can be extended into rules of sentence-formation. It is true that many sentences have a subject-copula-predicate organization, but equally true that very many do not. The multi-faceted nature of the *design* of what we say is irreducible to any generic specifications, and is not at all illuminated by alluding to hypothetical, antecedently-designing systems or mechanisms (in the mind or mind/brain).

The Chomsky-Pinker line on natural languages urges upon us the 'problem' of getting from 'sounds' emerging from mouths to the 'meanings' which utterances (can) have. This formulation animates the cognitive neuroscientific notion that speaking is essentially a physical process which derives its intelligibility from prior 'command' functions in the brain which allegedly endow utterances with an 'intended' meaning. However, although one may be sovereign as to what one says, one is *not* sovereign with respect to what one's utterances can mean. You can, in other words, say pretty much anything you like, i.e., mouth any combination of words that comes into your head, but you cannot *mean* (i.e., effectively express) whatever content you like by those arbitrarily thrown together words (in Humpty-Dumpty fashion), and no physical event or process in the brain can endow a string of words with an intention, semantic or otherwise. This is because 'intending to mean this rather than that' is exhibited only in the commitments which people display *qua* speakers, depending upon the public conventions and contexts of the language, and brains are not themselves speakers. Speakers do not move their lips and tongues *so as to produce* such-and-such sound-waves whenever they speak normally. Yet this odd attribution is exactly what those subscribing to the Chomsky-Pinker starting-point would have to endorse. It is sometimes true that a hearer may hear a speaker's words as (if they were only) sounds (if he does not know the language or that a speaker is, in fact, speaking rather than simply making noises), and one may on occasion hear a sound as (if it were) a word (as when the call of an owl is heard as 'who'). Such cases are utterly distinct from ordinary cases of speaking and hearing.

Chomsky has parlayed his grammatical analyses into the realm of psychology, and from here cognitive neuroscientists have attempted to identify neural mechanisms putatively involved in meaningful linguistic behavior. His idea that 'linguistic competence' may be strictly distinguished from 'linguistic performance' was a key point in Chomsky's explicitly (neo-)Cartesian mentalism (the 'competence' being the mentally stored abstract knowledge of the structure of a natural language), but he was initially very cautious about endorsing the idea that, e.g., his postulated transformation rules (*inter alia*, deletion and substitution operations) could be components of models of real-time mental processes (later: 'computations') facilitating speaking and understanding speech. Nonetheless, Roger Brown, one of the founders of the allied field of 'psycholinguistics', remarked that:

"... the psychological complexity of sentences, as measured by difficulty in remembering them or understanding them, is closely related to their grammatical (or 'derivational') complexity as defined in Chomsky's theory. Which seemed to mean that the theory of transformational grammar had 'psychological reality'."[182]

Further on, he elaborated upon this claim:

"A generative grammar is intended to represent the linguistic knowledge of the native speaker even though it does not represent the *manner* in which such knowledge is brought to bear in speaking and understanding. The native speaker's feeling for the way that a sentence cracks into a hierarchy of sub-wholes is represented by the phrase-structure rules and these also represent his feeling for such relations in a sentence as are called subject-predicate and verb-object. The native speaker's sense that large sets of sentences are related to one another in such a way that, for each members of one set, there is a specific counterpart in the other set is represented by transformation rules."[183]

Brown and many of his successors set about trying to specify the ways in which children master syntax understood in Chomskian terms, postulating mental operations based upon precisely those sequential-looking 're-write' and transformation rules enunciated by Chomsky himself. Nonetheless, just as Chomsky has occasionally disparaged too close an adherence to the 'computer model of the mind' whilst still invoking 'computational' processes as a feature of language, his actual relationship to much psycholinguistic work has been

---

[182] Roger Brown, *Psycholinguistics* (N.Y.: Free Press, 1970), p. 155.
[183] *Ibid.*, p. 160.

somewhat ambivalent. Although claiming for himself the mantel of 'cognitive psychologist' as well as linguist, Chomsky has not explicitly endorsed any model of competence-application procedures to the best of our knowledge. Indeed, Brown himself commented:

> "Noam Chomsky was there [Yale University, May of 1956, at a conference – JC & WS] and I heard about transformational grammar for the first time. Following Chomsky's talk there was an exchange that went something like this:
>
> Brown: 'It sounds to me as if a transformational grammar might be what children learn when they learn their first language'
> Chomsky: Oh, do you think so?'"[184]

In recent years, Chomsky has sought flatly to deny that children *learn*[185] any language at all: rather, their 'innate language organ' or module 'matures' in relation to varying environmental conditions. Whatever the changes have been in Chomsky's own theorizing, it is clear that, from Brown through to Fodor, Pinker, and Kosslyn and Koenig, the idea that our human linguistic capacity is a matter of psychological states and processes (thence, 'ultimately', states and processes of the hybrid 'mind/brain') has become the foundation of what we regard as spurious neuroscientific speculations. In our efforts in this book to expose the deep conceptual problems which beset cognitive neuroscience and its philosophical devotees, we have attempted to demonstrate to how large an extent are these enterprises, essentially, baseless. Their 'problems' are so misconceived, their empirical substance extremely thin, and their theories so question-begging that we cannot take them seriously as a promising 'new wave' of scientific research in the bio-behavioral sciences.

---

[184] Roger Brown, *op. cit.*, p. 17.
[185] For some discussion of Chomsky's (and others') very narrow conception of 'learning', see our discussion of the 'projection problem'.

CONCLUSION

We have done everything that we can to demystify the mind/brain notation and to show that it is the emptiest gesture, ineffective as a means of evading the serious, long-standing and persistent difficulties which afflict materialism (including its mentalist forms) at the very roots, and worthless as a contribution to understanding those issues. It would be a serious misreading of our arguments to try to identify our alternative position on the relationship between mind and brain whilst we have been attempting to show that, although there are innumerable problems for neuroscientific investigations of the brain, it is almost impossible to pin down what it is that, supposedly, we do not understand about 'the mind'. We have tried to point out as well that the confusions which attend the understanding of the mind do not embody genuinely empirical problems, and that the difficulties attendant upon them are not, nor will they be, eased by reference to the results of science.

It is clear that the issues we have been reviewing will not be settled by a proper scholarly reading of the up-to-date neuroscientific literature, for the reason that the questions involved are not asked and answered in the investigations there being conducted into the structure and functioning of brains. The issues involved do not form the research questions that serious investigators into the brain are attempting to solve. They are questions which ask not what such studies tell us about the brain, but, and rather, what is it, by virtue of telling us about the brain, that such studies can tell us about the mind. It is an interesting paradox about the mind/brain hybrid that its incorporation into the discourse does not simply put an end to the philosophy of mind since, after all, if the mind and the brain are one and the same, then we can and surely must just leave it to the brain scientists to get on with their work, await the results, and then we shall see from those results everything that there is to know about the mind. Their reports on the brain will *ipso facto* be reports on the mind. Another paradox is that the eliminativist impulse does not strike down the notational convention itself: in its terms, mind/brain is a pleonasm, and 'mind' is surely the element that should be dispensed with.

In fact, then, the mind/brain notation itself gives the game away. The puzzle is not to understand the mechanics of the brain but (a) to understand what we could possibly be saying when we say that the mind and the brain are one and the same thing? This asks (b) with respect to the brain sciences: how do their findings speak to an understanding of the mind? These questions indicate the presence of a self-refuting conception: the results of brain research are not, as they stand, as purely scientific findings, *ipso facto* findings about the mind. To be counted as such they will have to be converted from the discipline-specific technicalities that constitute them as *bona fide* findings into expressions that can be understood to speak of 'the mind'. We have been promised, however, that paying attention to the results of brain science will help us to understand the nature of the mind only to find that in order to be able to pay appropriate attention to the work of scientists we will need better to understand the nature of the mind. The actual work of the scientific investigators immediately takes a back seat and the philosopher steps forward – which recognizes, too, that whilst you might be able to take the philosophy out of brain science, you cannot always take the philosopher out of the natural scientist. It cannot be, after all, that the neuroscientist, *qua* neuroscientist, can speak about 'the mind', save by way of speaking about the brain. With respect to the mind/brain combination, this ought to be enough, but it is not and cannot be, but not because of any deficiency in the scientist's understanding of the phenomena he or she investigates. It cannot be because the neuroscientist's science does not tell him or her how these results speak of the mind (unless one accepts a more rigorous and stringent implication of the mind/brain hybrid, which is that neuroscientific results, raw and freestanding, pure and unvarnished, say all that there is to say). The basic problem of the relationship between mind and brain will only be eased when someone answers the question: *how* do the neuroscientific results speak of the mind? Which throws us back to the question, what is it to speak of the mind, what are we saying when we use sentences deploying the mentalistic vocabulary of so-called 'folk psychology'? Materialists abort this question by understanding it to ask: what is it to speak of the mind scientifically? However, this question takes us further away from the results of neuroscience and requires a view of what it is to speak scientifically. What could it be to speak scientifically of the mind such that the results of brain researches could tell us all we need to know about the mind? But, regressively, this requires clarity about the nature of the mind as a precondition of understanding what it is to determine how it could – if it can – be subsumed within the topical domain of one or more sciences. This is why the scientific results cannot affect the arguments involved here, since these do not pertain to what those results themselves amount to, what properties, features and behaviors of the brain they report, but raise instead a question of classic philosophical form: what are we to say about those results, what further are we to say about them with respect to how, showing what they do about the brain, they also say specific things about the mind?

The materialist can be absolutely certain that talk of the mind either speaks of the brain or it speaks of nothing. This follows from the fundamental conviction that science tells us what there is, and that science tells us that there are only material things. Talk of the mind, if it is not to be entirely vacuous, must be talk of some material entity. There is no other candidate for the material entity other than the brain, and so folk psychology must either speak (somehow) of the brain, or of nothing. However, the fundamental conviction does not resolve the problem, for investigations of the brain itself will not tell us whether talk of the mind does speak of an entity, for clarity on that point depends upon an understanding of how we speak when we speak of 'the mind'. Do we speak in such a way that what we say will turn out to have spoken about the brain, or is the way in which we speak of the mind a matter of speaking of nothing? And how are we to decide that? It would seem that which is called for is a careful examination of how we do speak, of how the concept of mind (and related concepts) function(s) in the language – but this is exactly what is disdained by materialists who think that arguments about the form of explanation will settle the issue, and who otherwise beg the question by holding out expectations of, and occasionally attempting explanations of, neuroscientific inquiries. Any such interpretations require considerable scruple in the redescription of the brain science necessary to give them cogency, with respect both to (i) the way in which the science is 'popularized' to render its strictly technical relevancies into something that the neuroscientifically untrained philosopher can understand as comprising a finding about 'the mind' and (ii) the way in which such non-technical renderings are aligned with the ways in which the concept of mind works. In other words, what is required is some sort of alignment with the ways in which the language speaks of those aspects of 'the mind' that correspond to the mentalistically interpreted topic of the specific neuroscientific research in question.

The power which the materialists find in their deduction of mind/brain unification relies upon an arbitrarily restricted definition of entities, for human beings are excluded from that category, precluding an understanding of the argument that what 'the mind' speaks of is the lives of human beings – save to understand this as a form of behaviorism. For them, human beings are not entities in their own right, but are only composites of two other entities, body and mind (or brain). There seems no sound materialist reason why materialists should effectively exclude human beings from the universe save from the fact that it would nullify their inference. After all, the body and brain that materialism topicalises in debates about mind are, perhaps tacitly, but invariably, those of human beings – we are not discussing cats or pigeons in these cases. If human beings are allowed into the ontology, then the question as to what is being spoken of when 'the mind' is invoked allows the above-mentioned possibility: that it may speak of human beings, perfectly respectable material entities. In such a case, talk of the mind may no more talk of the brain than talk about John's BMW talks only of its engine, even though, of course, John's BMW does have, and is powered by, that engine. There is no advantage, however, to insisting that because the BMW in question consists in an engine and a chassis that the car is not itself an entity in its own right. There is much more to be said about John's BMW than can be formulated by restricting discourse to what can be said about its engine and its chassis, and there is also little point in trying to reformulate what can be said about the BMW as an indirect way of talking about its engine. Here is a simple way of revaluing Ryle's *Concept of Mind* which voids the stereotype of behaviorism: it is to insist that the concept of mind speaks not of the movements of bodies but of the doings, capacities and characteristics of human beings.

These remarks reaffirm our continuing theme, that the issues between materialists and others are always about the way in which language works, as we have latterly been insisting that efforts to direct our attention to the (possible, rather more than actual) achievements of brain science simply pose the problem: what are we to say when confronted with those results? The challenge here is not to investigate phenomena or to gather data, but to choose the right words to render the significance those results (may) have with respect to our understanding of 'the mind'. To finalize these deliberations, we will make this point once more, this time with respect to the idea that persons, and possibly some animals, are properly attributed a 'theory of mind'.

Intentional States and the 'Theory of Mind' Theory

As always, there is the possibility that the idea of a 'theory of mind' is a new name for something that is already familiar. It is clear that, for example, people are able to do such things as anticipate another's actions or see things from another person's point of view. If someone wants to call a rather ill defined range of capacities such as these a 'theory of mind' we can at least understand what they are saying and see no reason to object to the use of such an expression. Close observation of some animals makes us more sensitive to their capacities and it may be noted that these animals are able to anticipate (some of) the reactions of their keepers/trainers. The question might then be raised: should we say that they, too, possess a theory of mind? If adult human beings are the exemplars of possession of a 'full blown' theory of mind, then the question that results is one of degree: do apes have a sufficient number and variety of relevant capacities or do they not? Similar questions might be asked about children, for 'theory of mind' is something that they progressively acquire: at what age do they develop the theory of mind, is there any orderly progression to the sequencing of the capacities they acquire, etc.? The question about both apes and children is to be answered by continuing relationships with apes, by making more and perhaps closer observations of their relations with us humans and with each other, perhaps creating test situations to see how they react, and so on. We do not need to, nor would there be any value in, investigating the brains of apes in search of physiological markers constituent of this theory as a means of establishing whether they do or do not have a theory of mind. After all, the nature of their transactions with us and their performances in the tests will be necessary for us to decide whether there would be anything for the physiologist to look for. In other words, unless we are confident that apes do possess a theory of mind, i.e., are responsive to us in certain relatively complex ways, then there is nothing physiological to be found.

However, we do not need the notion of 'theory of mind' to pose the questions about apes and children, for we can ask the same questions without any mention of a theory of mind at all. Adoption of this form of expression is an optional matter, and so long as it understood thus, there can be no objection to it – if you want to call this range of abilities a 'theory of mind' feel free to do so, though no obvious advantages attach to the locution. Nonetheless, the expression 'theory of mind' is apt to be loaded with additional, unnecessary and, in our judgment, counter-productive assumptions. To do justice to the way that the notion 'theory of mind' is understood among those who recommend it, we have to recognize its affiliation with the usual repertoire of neo-Cartesian suppositions. The term 'theory' is a residual of the cogito: each of us is certain, from our own experience, of our possession of a mind, but our relationship to others in this respect is asymmetrical – they cannot be certain that we have a mind, and we cannot be certain that they do. Hence, the possibility that anyone else has a mind becomes an irreducibly inferential matter. The question which the 'theory of mind' does raise is one that requires the fixing of a boundary to a category – how many of what sorts of abilities will be judged enough to justify the ascription of 'a theory of mind'?

The danger with the mentalist branch of modern materialism is that it encourages misplaced intellectualist conceptions. Chomsky again deserves recognition for inspiring this unfortunate tendency through his efforts to treat the acquisition of the rules of language as though it must either be an intellectual exercise in general theory construction or it must be a matter of hard wiring. For an intellectualist, our treatment of the 'theory of mind' theory would be faulted for not treating the word 'theory' seriously enough. Intellectualists would argue that more is involved in attributing a 'theory of mind' than noting the respects in which the conduct of small children or adult apes resembles that of adult humans and arguing that it is within our discretion to decide when such resemblances license the attribution of a 'theory of mind'. For the intellectualist, the expression 'theory of mind' betokens the possession of an actual theory, the construction and operation of "abstract and unobservable postulates used to explain and predict observable human behavior".[186]

---

[186] J. W. Astington, "What is theoretical about the child's development of mind?" in P. Carruthers & P. Smith (eds.), *Theories of Theories of Mind* (Cambridge: Cambridge University Press, 1996), p. 185.

Many of our arguments have focused upon the ways in which the forms of language are misunderstood by materialists, but we have not systematically argued that one of the reasons why their theorizing falls so far short of its objectives is that they pay no attention to the role of language in human life. This is perhaps an unfortunate result of setting up disciplinary demarcations which make psychology the study of individuals and, under the post-behaviorist dispensation, of the mental life of individuals. This means that the interest in language is confined to either (a) its role as a medium of mental processing or (b) an understanding of the putatively mental mechanisms which operate in the composition of grammatical linguistic strings. Sociology is no less engaged in setting up definitions of its disciplinary provenance, but our emphasis on the primacy of languages' social existence is not offered in the interest of disciplinary imperialism (not least because sociology is almost equally neglectful of this important point). The issue was addressed very pertinently many years ago by Alfred Louch who pointed out that whilst it may be the case that, in the natural sciences, theoretical schemes enhance our understanding of phenomena, in the social and human 'sciences' it is more commonly the case that we already understand things that facilitate our grasp on what the theories could possibly be saying.[187] Thus, we suggest that the theories which are supposed to enable us to understand language better are only apparently viable if they ignore the extent to which the language itself does the work for them, as, with respect to the theory of a 'theory of mind', it is the presupposition of a fine grained language which is necessary in order for such theorizing ever to gain a foothold.

There is an instrumentalist view of language, that it was developed to serve a particular purpose or function, which is widely espoused today. In this respect, the 'theory of mind' conception can be seen to embrace a speculative theory about the origin of language (or, certainly, of our 'mentalistic' vocabulary).

---

[187] A. R. Louch, *Explanation and Human Action* (Cybereditions, 2000: originally published in 1966).

If not asking, why do we have language at all, it is at least a matter of asking: why do we have the kind of language that we do with its 'mentalistic' vocabulary? The answer given is: because it is useful. How is it useful? Well, it enables us to predict and control the behavior of others. Presumably, then, cats cannot predict and control each other? The reply would be: the human level of prediction and control of our behavior is more effective, sophisticated and fine grained than cats are capable of. Is this not because our human lives are built out of the use of language? The root idea, then, of the 'theory of mind' theory is that language is developed to formulate a theory that will enable us to predict and control other people's behavior. In short, language is developed so as to state a set of deductively integrated general propositions – but doesn't it seem more likely that language enables us to predict and control people's behavior because we share the language? Intellectualists leave human life, as it is actually lived, out of the picture, depicting the prediction and control features of our existence as a matter of implementing the postulates of a general theory. But the obvious truth of the claim that 'language is useful in the prediction and control of other people's behavior' is surely an outcome of the equally obvious truth that our lives are organized in and through language, and not testimony to the notion that language provides a theoretical means of representing patterns which human behavior already possesses. Two lines of possible critical development open up here: (a) is it not the case that prediction and control are made possible substantially because language is so awesomely and intricately involved in the regulation of our behavior? And (b) how does one manage, without an 'intentional' or 'mentalistic' vocabulary, to begin to identify the regularities which are to be the basis for the generic postulations of the theory of mind?

To elaborate: (a) the capacity to predict and control each other's behavior is surely made easier by, for example, being able to schedule activities, but scheduling facilities are constructions that depend upon possession of a language: they do not accomplish their prediction and control functions by bringing people's activities within the range of some psychological generalities but rather by enabling people to make their activities 'predictable' to one another because they bind people to certain actions at certain times and places. Making an appointment is a way of 'predicting' that one will be available to do something at a given time and place, but is more centrally a matter of giving other people the entitlement to depend upon this. When one makes an appointment one does not so much make a prediction about tomorrow as one gives an undertaking.

According to the 'theory of mind' theory, the ascription of mental states is necessarily *theoretical* because these mental states are 'not directly observable' and their attributions 'can be used to make predictions about the behavior of others'. Vital to such an argument is the supposition that the attribution of a mental state is a matter of attributing an *inner* state which is a causal condition of some behavior. This poses the problem: how can we escape from the circle in which the content of the postulated inner mental state is simply the content of the observed behavior? We know that we can attribute different mental states to a single individual, so that we can say that someone is angry and that someone is depressed. What difference is there between these two mental states, construed materialistically? No one who attributes anger or depression to another person has any idea about what the material properties of such mental states might be, and therefore no idea about what their material *differences* might be. All that anyone knows is in what the differences between anger and depression consist, in the sense that we know how to distinguish them in terms of conduct. Also, the way in which these states can play an explanatory role is very variable.

Are we being asked to pretend that each child individually invents a theory of mind for him or herself? Or are we being invited to accept a phylogeny-repeats-ontogeny metaphor according to which the child's position vis-à-vis others is a reproduction of a primal human condition? That is, are we to imagine human beings as not much more than mere brutes who had no relations except co-presence? In such a scenario, such beings are available to each other only observationally: one brute can observe another from a distance but has no language in which to formulate what it can observe about those others. If we are to have the mentalistic language that we have, then a brute must have begun to observe regular patterns in the behavior of other brutes and begun to postulate generalities which would subsume those generalities as deductive outcomes from such generalities. The envisaged primordial state represents a transition that all human beings must make, from one in which the behavior of other creatures is sheerly unintelligible to one in which it is predictable, therefore identifiable. However, the primordial condition is not one in which human beings actually live (if, indeed, it is more than a caricature), one in which they only observe other creatures, for the initial problem has been solved: a language has been created. The nature of the language is to be understood as having been shaped by the primordial requirement to come up with some explanatory theory for the behavior of other creatures. That is, the language is being understood as if it embodies a solution to the problem of constituting an explanatory theory on the grounds that, at some point in human history, this problem must have been solved. The explanatory theory being postulated has taken the form of a vocabulary which names mental states.

First of all, the child's theorizing is not imagined as a genuine condition in which the child is confronted with other human beings and must come up with some theory that will make their behavior predictable – we wait with extreme interest to see what this theory is. On the contrary, the child's theorizing is imagined as a matter of converging on the existing solution, of coming to acquire the same theory of mind that everyone else already has, so that tests of the children's theory of mind are constructed precisely to discern how far they have mastered the standard vocabulary, the extent to which their mastery of that vocabulary progressively, not instantly, conforms to the standard pattern of usage. Thus, our test of whether the child has acquired the theory of mind seeks to determine whether the child does say the same (sort of) things that the rest of us say in such-and-such a situation.

As mentioned earlier, the language is being construed as possessing the form it does because it is 'a solution' to the primordial problem, and thus embodies the constituents of a theory of mind, namely expressions which postulate/identify an array of 'mental states'. Therefore, there is no need for the child to independently replicate the solution, for it can simply take it over from the rest of us and can do so simply by learning the language. The root issue is not about any 'psychological processes' of learning, but is about the form of expressions in the language. We have already questioned whether expressions comprising a 'folk psychology' are theoretical terms. The primary justification for thinking that they are is that they are speculative: the mental states ascribed are 'not observable'. Thus, the ascription of such states is taken to be a postulation: they have only a theoretical existence, there being no evidence for their actual existence. However, this use of 'theoretical' is rapidly absorbed to the sense of 'constituents of a system of proposition', or theory, which system is itself unobservable. Hence, the vocabulary of the theory of mind is understood as postulating external relations between the concepts in the language, as though it were a merely contingent connection that a person who was in a state of anger threw the crockery around the room.

We argue that the capacity to construct anything like plausible connections for a 'theory of mind' must make surreptitious use of the fact that these concepts have internal relations. They involve spelling out, in distorted form, what is built into the very vocabulary itself. The state of being hungry is a state of wanting something to eat, and that someone is in this state explains why he seeks food, but we do not need some generality such as that 'persons who are hungry tend to seek food' in order to connect the two since the claim amounts to the tautology that people who want something to eat want something to eat. The explanation of why they are eating is because they wanted something to eat. Rather than setting out empirical hypotheses, these pseudo-propositional structures are tracing around the linkages within the language. This is why the focal question is about the form of the linguistic expressions, in particular whether what is required is only the mastery of rules and the criteria of application for the identification of 'mental states' or whether their form involves an irreducibly inferential element. Again, though, there are two very different kinds of questions: one asks about whether attributions of mental states can ever be correct – i.e., are there really any states corresponding to the observed behavior – but the other asks about whether attributions of mental states can ever be definitive. Suppose that we all attribute irritation to X, are we not going beyond the evidence in doing so? No matter how X is behaving, his conduct does not clinch the fact that he is, for sure, angry. We can all observe him kicking the cat, throwing the crockery around, spitting on the other, all the while yelling about how goddamn angry he is, but we need to recognize that we are only seeing all the *signs* of anger, and we cannot be certain that we have read the signs aright, can we? J. L. Austin rightly observed that the loaf itself is not included amongst all the signs of bread.

The inspiration for thinking that there is a major problem here is the legacy of Cartesian skepticism, although Descartes did advise that one not try this out at home. We can be certain that X is doing all of the things that enable us to attribute anger to him, but perhaps he is pretending. That possibility invites the idea of postulating inner states for it permits a discrepancy between how someone seems to be and how he actually is. This difference can only be one between 'the inner' and 'the outer'. Outwardly, the person is angry, but whether X is indeed angry depends upon whether there is an inner state matching with the outward appearance. Surely, the argument goes, it is the inner state which is decisive in the attribution: if X is behaving in this angry manner without being angry inside, then X is not angry, X is just play acting, pretending, or something of that sort. The idea gains plausibility from imagining how it is with each of us personally. Imagine yourself promising someone that you will return his book tomorrow, doing so in a persuasive and assuring way, all along thinking to yourself: Dream on, sucker! That you have not really promised depends solely upon the inner withholding of a real commitment to do what you said you would do. However, before buying into this picture of the relations between the inner and the outer, think not of the situation of pretending because, as Austin said, pretending is parasitic upon authentic cases: think, rather, of a case of sincerely promising. You say to the person: I really will bring the book back tomorrow, I promise. You are inwardly accompanying this with the thought: '.. and I really am sincere on this occasion in making such a promise.' Do we actually make 'inner' endorsements of our promises? And why would we need to? Do we not know whether our words are sincere or not? Do we need something other than the words to tell ourselves if they are? No 'inner' counterpart of the 'outer' behavior occurs in such a case: the sincerity of one's words does not depend upon any identifiable inner accompaniment. Conduct an investigation to answer the question: how can you know that you can tell that you are sincere when you sincerely promise someone to do something!

Dennett again: we treat people as if they possess intentional states because it works. If people do not have intentional states then why do they act as if they do? What astonishing fortuity enables the coincidence of the pattern of our intentional attributions and their performances? The only thing that can assure this is a match between the internal content of the intentional states and the patterns of use of our folk-psychological vocabulary to demarcate segments of an individual's observed behavior (in our resolutely non-behaviorist sense of this word). Since X's arm waving, yelling and proclamations are as they are, we say that X is in a rage. If, in so doing, we are saying that X is in a rage because this whole pattern of behavior is made into rage by the prior/accompanying existence of an inner state of rage, then we must accept that the only notion we have of what such a state consists in, or what its content is, is one which has exactly the same content as the conduct we observe: it is a state which produces waving arms, aggressive assertion, raised voices, etc. The discrimination between one mental state and another requires – and can only consist in – a specification of the different situations and behaviors with respect to which we would apply the state-identifying label. Thus, the same conditions of attribution apply for the classification of observable behavior and the attribution of a mental state: consequently, the attribution of the former does not depend for its instrumental efficacy upon the attribution of any corresponding mental state, so again the question arises as to why one would think that identifying a certain pattern of behavior is the same thing as treating people as if they possessed a corresponding mental state. Such reasoning really does require an oscillation between using 'mental state' in the vernacular and using the expression in a neo-Cartesian manner. One can say that X is in a disturbed mental state and be reporting that he is agitated, crying, making rapid mood switches and so forth, and this is, for all intents and purposes, a correct report of X's mental state if he is indeed agitated, crying, etc. Having such an attribution in one's hands, one can then apply the neo-Cartesian construal of a mental state: a mental state is something other than observed behavior, therefore the attribution of the mental state to X cannot be a successful one because it makes claims about that which is unobservable, viz., the inner, extra-behavioral condition of X's mind. But what is claimed about that mental state other than is claimed in the description of X's behavior? Are we to suppose that some additional claim is appended, if not stated, namely that X is not pretending? So X is agitated, volatile and not pretending to be these things (there being no inner accompaniment of deceptive intent, etc.), but again there is no additional content – i.e., that X is agitated, volatile and not pretending can be elaborated in equally behavioral and situational terms – X has not been previously made up to look tearful, has not been previously rehearsing things to say and ways of creating an impression of volatility, and has no skills sufficient to put on such a convincing performance, and so on. If this line of argument is right, then it turns out that rather than the determination of the content of the observable behavior being made on the basis of theoretical attributions of inner, mental states, the actual procedure upon which the 'theory of mind' arguments are constructed is one in which our means of identifying patterns of observable behavior provides the model for the content of those supposed theoretical attributions. Thus, someone's angry behavior is caused by their being in a state of anger, occupancy of which state is a precondition for their behavior being that of someone who is angry. It cannot be otherwise, for we have to know what kind of behavior would be explained by what inner state. There are other motivations for the postulation of the inner state. The inner state is said to be the proximate cause of someone's behavior, for it is the representational and causal features of that inner state which combine to connect the individual's angry reaction with a prior occurrence that the anger is directed toward (anger being commonly if not always Brentano-intentional). Yet the same consideration applies: unless we can recognize something as an anger-provoking occurrence, we have no content for the representational mediations of the inner state. It is only if something is the kind of thing that could provoke anger (in this individual, at least) that it can be causally connected (albeit in a mediated way) to the ensuing behavior which it explains. When it comes to explaining why someone gets angry in response to some occurrence, the explanation can be given by way of the characteristics of the occurrence and the appropriateness of the response in a *direct* connection and without any need for a detour through the interior.

Insofar as children can be said to have a theory of mind, it is because they have learned that theory from others, have been socialized into it. However, their socialization process is not primarily a matter of constructing theoretical hypotheses but of picking up the rules of the language. Strictly construed as a system of theoretical hypotheses, the theory of mind could find no purchase in observable behavior to endow it with predictive power, would have no means of identifying the occurrences constituting an *explanans/explanandum* pair in any individual instance, let alone recognizing regular connections that could be subsumed under a generality. What is required of a 'theory of mind' in the innocuous sense is already built into the language, and so it is that the acquisition of the constituent concepts comes along with the learning of the language, though not as a particular phase or specific aspect of learning the language. Think of trying to teach a small child that other people have visual experiences, that they see things. The availability of shared visual experience is built into and presupposed by the whole range of transactions involved in the relationship between adult and child – indeed, mutual visual accessibility to a large extent comprises the relationship between adult and child, but nowhere is the child taught, nor does the child need to figure out, that vision is a reciprocal matter, and the capacity to use one's visual powers to identify, recognize and describe the things that populate one's visual field comes along with the learning of much more of the language. For us, then, the learning of the language involves much more than the acquisition of grammar, much more than the language in the restrictedly linguistic sense, for learning the language involves learning what can be said in the language, involves learning how to talk as a participant in social life and as a part of specific kinds of activities. 'Can you see?' asked of a small child is not usually a question as to whether it is sighted, but is likely to be related to the availability of an appropriate visual experience. If one takes a child to an adult game, an art gallery, a theatrical event, then the question makes sense as a query about the availability of an uninterrupted view of the field of play, the art work, or the events on stage. To understand and to answer that question the child has to learn about spectatorial participation in sporting and cultural activities.

We are prepared to say both (i) that the child learns a 'theory of mind' in the strictly innocuous sense, and (ii) that learning a language is not something that children *do*. The notion of learning a (first) language is, with respect to children, much more akin to an achievement expression than it is to an activity descriptor. Learning a language is not a specific activity on the part of children, separable from learning participation in activities: Margaret's grandson is being taught to say 'sorry', and to that extent can be said to be learning the language, but he is being taught to say 'sorry' as a matter of apology, which is involved in trying to get him to inhibit his inclinations to bite and hit out. He is learning sociability, not learning 'the language'.

Our arguments do not make any bid for the priority of sociology over psychology on the grounds that sociology makes us aware of language as part of culture in a way that psychology assiduously overlooks. Turning to sociology would not offer a better understanding than psychology can provide. Our intention has been to emphasize that it is the determination to force a single form of explanation upon whole categories of phenomena (minds, societies) that causes the trouble to begin with. All of the problems we have dealt with here arise because of the conflict between the ideal of explanation which motivates ambitions to construct a scientific psychology and the forms of explanation which are built into the grammar of the language that is in use amongst those whom psychologists would study, the same language upon which psychologists massively depend to do their theorizing and make their studies at the same time as they disavow its adequacy for their purposes. The whole idea of mentalism and of a theory of mind involves the notion that scientific and commonplace language conflict in respect of the formulation of rival hypotheses, but, we have argued at length, the conflict is a result of the projection of the image of the hypothesis onto connections which are, in the ordinary use of the language, rule-given. The final consequence is that the issues really are all about language, about whether all expressions using the 'mental' vocabulary have an irreducibly inferential element, have a form which combines an observational report (properly stated only in a strictly behaviorist manner) with an hypothetical element that speculates about some corresponding inner state. The idea is that the inferential component cannot be eliminated from our natural language (since the brain is not amenable to observation, although the development of brain science might change all this). Our point is that the idea that there is an inescapably inferential aspect is not a product of the form of the utterances in question but results from understanding those utterances from a skeptic's point of view. From such a standpoint, the observational and inferential elements refer to two entirely segregated elements, an observable exterior and an inaccessible interior. This picture of language does not originate with any development of science, nor with any of its needs, but with philosophy's artificial construction, the other minds problem.

As we remarked at the very outset, it is words like 'in' and 'part of' that cause trouble, just as much as words such as 'mind', 'body', 'thought' and 'consciousness'. The way we use the term 'mental' to indicate the character of certain phenomena encourages and rapidly yields to the temptation to employ it in a locational manner, in a spatial sense. Consider a pain in the arm. A pain is a sensation, and sensations, being matters of feeling, are to be conceived as mental phenomena. So conceived, it can then seem that a pain is in two locations simultaneously – it is both in the arm and in the mind. If the mind is in the head, then the pain in the arm is also the pain in the head, which awkwardness leads some to attempt to relocate the pain in the arm – the pain is not really in the arm, for the pain cannot be in two places at once, thus it is in the mind (in the head) and not in the arm at all. The 'in' involved in the identification of the pain in the arm as being 'in the mind' is not a locational /spatial term, but one of inclusiveness: the proposal is to count pains in the arm, leg, ear and all other bodily locations in the category of events that are deemed 'mental' and that also include thoughts, visual experiences etc., and includes them because they have an 'experienced' aspect. The pain caused by indigestion is a mental event because it is felt by the subject, but the digestive process is not a mental process because the subject is unaware of it. It is in this trend of thought that we relatively recently find attempts to modify the materialist/cognitivist conceptions by introducing the idea of an 'extended mind', the 'extension' being from 'in here' to 'out there', a matter of construing some features of the 'external world' as 'part of' the mind.

Extended Mind.

The interest that such a maneuver provokes should not be in the intriguing possibilities of a solution it might offer, but in regard to the necessity driving the adoption of such a desperate move, one which is presented as an improved modification of the materialist/cognitivist viewpoint but which, in fact, retreats from the fundamental suppositions that define the whole approach. Conceiving the connection between experience and its objects locationally requires us to ask whether color, for example, is (really) 'out there' or 'in here', giving rise to a controversy between 'color realists' and 'color subjectivists'. The latter locate colors 'in our minds' whilst the former 'put them back out there in the world' amongst real 'primary' things like size, shape and motion. Combine the locational conception with two perennial empiricist preoccupations, the requirement of a foundational certainty together with the idea of the immediacy of personal experience, and one can then see the appeal of 'the extended mind' as overcoming problems resulting from the attempt to give a spatial construal of 'mind' – the mind is no longer remote from the objects of visual perception but reaches out to them, being in immediate contact with their properties. From our viewpoint, one can equally well understand the idea of the extended mind as more revealing of the difficulties with the initial terms of the problem, and as recognizing that there is something fundamentally flawed with the locational treatment of 'mind', attempting to put that right by introducing yet additional meanings of 'inner' and 'outer' into an environment already involving various and confused uses of such expressions. We have recently had occasion to argue against the idea that a line in a James Taylor song, 'I've gone to Carolina in my mind', is a locational expression – it says that someone has imagined being somewhere else than they are, and implies no suggestion that anyone has actually been anywhere or that anything has happened in a particular place, the mind[188].

---

[188] Wes Sharrock & Jeff Coulter, "ToM: A Critical Commentary", *Theory and Psychology*, Vol. 14, no. 5, 2004, pp. 597-98.

Combine the idea of the mind as (having a) location with a distinction at least akin to that between 'primary' and 'secondary' qualities in philosophy, and we have the position that Wes's Beemer is 'out there' in the world, whilst the red painted color is 'in here' (in the mind), which contrast immediately occasions the wonder as to why 'the mind' does not notice the fifty-foot gap between the Beemer's bonnet and its red color? As we say, multiple uses of 'out there' and 'in here' are in play, and only erratically coordinated with each other, such that the sense of 'in here' and 'out there' will sometimes have the sense of 'on the subjective side of the veil of appearances' and 'on the other side of the veil of appearances' whilst, at other, or even at the same, times conveying the quite mundane sense of 'over here in the living room' or 'out there by the curb'.

An almost inevitable consequence of following through the line of thought lightly sketched is the asking of the question: 'Where does the mind stop and the rest of the world begin?' This question, we are told by Clark and Chalmers, "invites two standard replies. Some accept the demarcations of skin and skull, and say that what is outside the body is outside the mind. Others are impressed by arguments suggesting that the meaning of our words 'just ain't in the head', and hold that this externalism about meaning carries over into an externalism about mind. We propose to pursue a third position. We advocate a very different sort of externalism: an active externalism, based on the active role of the environment in driving cognitive processes."[189] The idea of externalism involved in the argument that 'meaning ain't in the head' is unsuitably expressed insofar as it solicits the inclination to think that one is using expressions locationally, supposing that meaning is 'out there' rather than 'in here'. Since 'out there' and 'in here' are twinned in their unsuitability for expressing the issues, we cannot be any keener on externalism than we are on the cognitivism it replies to. The 'externalist' argument is really an argument about the nature of reference, and is often cast in terms of 'Twin Earth' arguments. These are meant to illustrate the idea that people

---

[189] Andy Clark & David J. Chalmers, "The Extended Mind", *Analysis*, Vol. 58, 1998, pp. 10-23.

using what is ostensibly the same word in different environments may be using the word with different meanings even though there is no distinguishable difference in their meaning-intentions. We are invited to imagine a twin to our present Earth where, for example, the chemical constitution of some natural phenomenon varies, but since the two Earths are unknown to each other their respective speakers are unaware of this difference. 'Meaning' is understood as 'reference' in these arguments, and so one development of the line is the following: 'Water' is a word both sets of speakers (here and on Twin Earth) have in common, and the substance which fills the seas of their respective planets is identical in all respects save its chemical composition, so that the speakers on both planets intend to refer to the same properties, those of a colorless, tasteless liquid (etc.). Since the speakers are unaware of the chemical difference, the question arises: does the reference of water remain constant across the two cases? Clearly, this is meant not to depend upon what 'is in the minds' of the speakers, but to depend upon the facts about the chemical composition of water. Although the speakers' intended references are the same on each Earth, they are nonetheless referring to two different substances: the water on our Earth has a different chemical composition to the water on Twin Earth, so they are not the same substances. Perforce, what the speakers are – could possibly be – referring to is determined not by their intentions but by the objective conditions to which they make reference, by the chemical differences between the two kinds of 'water'.

In these cases, 'in the mind' is not really a spatial locution but more a way of noting that a speaker's intentions are not definitive in fixing the reference of expressions they use. The trouble with Twin Earth arguments is that they beg the question, which is: are we to use the chemical constitution of a substance as a criterion of identity? Does the Twin Earth example present us with a case in which the same substance can have two different chemical compositions (for, after all, in every other respect they are the same substance)? Or are we to use chemical constitution as the criterion of identity, such that we now need to talk about 'water 1' and 'water 2'? Perhaps all of this highlights a tendency on the part of many philosophers to confuse the idea that speakers' intentions fix what they intend to refer to with a certain word, with the fact that it is not speakers' intentions but the language that fixes the meanings of the words they use to make reference – the meaning is 'in the language' and not 'in the mind' of the individual speaker. It is not, after all, the chemical constitution of water that fixes similarity or difference of reference, but the grammatical role of chemical constitution in the given case. The ostensible necessity of a notion like an 'extended mind' could be recognized as a retreat from the dichotomization of 'inner' and 'outer' and from the conception of cognitive processes, but it is offered as a continuation of these ideas, though it is, we would suggest, rather inconsistent with them.

The use of 'extended' is surely to signify the 'extension of a scheme of classification', that is, we are to find ways in which we can include cases that previously did not fall under it, although the confused attempt is made to project this novel enumeration in terms of a spatial employment: we are moving a set of boundaries 'outside', from 'within the skin' to 'outside the skin'. The proposal for 'an extended mind' is one which advances an essentially innocuous suggestion, that the use of various intellectual and mnemonic aides, such as filing cabinets, diaries, computers and so on, might be counted as being involved in our 'cognitive processes'. This may well be an allowable linguistic recommendation, but it is hard to see how it adds much to calling them intellectual and mnemonic aides in the first place. It is, nonetheless, only a very thin metaphor – a diary does not operate in terms of any processes, let alone a memory process, but is a substitute for having to remember: we do not have to remember what is entered in our diary, and looking up our appointments frees us from the necessity to remember them. Similarly, talking about a filing cabinet as fulfilling a memory function is not to be understood as suggesting that memories, rather than records, are what are stored in their drawers. The 'extension' of the cognitive conception of the mind is an analogical extension only. The proposal surely cannot fit too well with a cognitivist conception, for, in that framework it is the 'inner cognitive processes' that are required to make sense of the use of filing cabinets, computers and the rest, and the 'extension' is not a necessary step to achieve the same effect. Further, allowing the extension would allow the damn to break – the canonical division is not between the body and what is outside of it, but between 'the mind' and 'the brain', and the (rest of the) body is just as much 'outside' the brain and its representations as is the filing cabinet, so there seems no reason why 'the body' should not be included within the extended mind. After all, it is one's fingers that are used in service of cognitive processes such as typing into the computer, rifling through the filing cabinet, etc., so are these also not part of the cognitive processes?

In the case of both the theory of a 'theory of mind' and the proposal for an 'extended mind' we have allowed that there is an understanding of these in which they are acceptable but wholly inconsequential, for they involve merely a re-classification of certain commonly known occurrences which adds nothing to their comprehension and which invites serious misconstruals, even by those who advance them. We now turn to our final theme, a brief concluding discussion of the role of biology in the understanding of human cognition.

It will have been noticed that the substance of neuroscience has scarcely entered our discussions of the topics we have covered in this book, but this should not leave the impression that we are in some sort of denial about the biological nature of human beings. Several times we have made reference to the very influential but entirely dubious miasma of philosophical arguments that enwraps Noam Chomsky's linguistics. These arguments have been used for disciplinary reallocation, to assign the study of grammar – for this is all that Chomsky's schemes consist in – first to psychology, and then to a branch of biology. Chomsky's arguments for this latter subsumption owe nothing to his studies of language, for these merely record the forms of grammar, but are entirely dependent upon platitudes: the acquisition of language comes naturally to human beings as it does not to other animals such as cows; the acquisition of language is developmentally phased; it is at a certain point in their maturation that children become capable of acquiring language. These facts are certainly well known to all parents and probably to everyone else, but this does not mean that the analytical understanding of language thereby becomes a province of the biological sciences, any more than driving does because it is only at a certain level of growth that children become capable of controlling an automobile. It certainly does not follow that skepticism of Chomsky's many (speculative) claims puts one in denial of a connection between human biology and language acquisition. We stressed that Chomsky's grounds for reallocating grammar to biology are platitudes, and his opponents need be no less aware of these commonplaces than Chomsky is. Clearly, there is a connection between human biology and language acquisition, which is why we are surprised and disappointed if children do not naturally begin to evince linguistic competences by a relatively early age and also why we do not go down to the beehive to see if we can teach the bees Serbo-Croatian. The issue which distances people like us from Chomsky and his followers has to do with the question: what *kind* of connection is there between human biology and language? Chomsky's speculation is that there is a very specific form of connection between language and brain physiology, but this speculation does not derive from studies of brain physiology but from a string of inferences that there must be such a specific connection if Chomsky's philosophical doctrines about language and its acquisition are correct. But that is a very big 'if', and the analysis of language – actually, of syntax – need not be interrupted or postponed awaiting the results of neurobiological investigations and proceeds without concern for any such results. Refusal to be drawn down Chomsky's garden path (an expression much elaborated by Rudolf Botha) does not lead to denying that human physiology is indeed distinctive with respect to language acquisition, only skepticism that language has the character that Chomsky assigns to it and thus must or even does have the *kind* of dependence on neural structures that Chomsky imagines. The extent to which neurophysiological explorations can be involved in postulating an innate 'mentalese' (to use Fodor's terminology for the inbuilt 'language of thought') hinges entirely on the validity of Chomsky's philosophical arguments, not the other way around. It is only to be expected that the study of human physiology will eventually yield a much better understanding of just what it is about human biology that enables human beings to learn language, but there is no reason to think that this understanding will explain to us why the languages that human beings have are the languages that they are. That human beings have a certain capacity is certainly to be understood in terms of their biology, but why that capacity is realized in one way or another is a matter that has to do with the conditions of human lives. The kinds of lives that human beings lead have to do with their biological capacities, of course, but the ways of life that people possess arise out of the contingencies of their practical, social existence, and, with the broad parameters of human capacities, abilities, dispositions and the like as givens, are to be understood in terms that have nothing *specific* to do with that biology.

Our opponents have a rather peculiar idea of human biology. For them, a human being is pretty much just a brain with a body attached, whereas our approach insists that human biology involves an organism, and one capable of very complex ways of life. The idea that understanding human conduct involves focusing entirely upon the brain seems wholly misguided, overlooking the elementary point that the human organism is participant in assorted ways of life, and that an individual human being's conduct will need to be understood in terms of, relative to, those ways of life. One cannot identify those ways of life by studying the brain, but only by considering the public ways in which people behave (in our resolutely non-behaviorist sense of 'behave'). Just as with Chomsky's linguistics, the attempt to determine what an understanding of the brain can contribute to our understanding of human conduct depends upon a prior possession of a proper grasp of what that conduct is, of how it features in the lives of persons, and we have been insistent throughout that our opponents assiduously disregard this requirement. Our main platform has been, then, that our (philosophical) opponents are busy trying to encourage brain researchers to undertake projects that will attempt the explanation of illusory phenomena.

BIBLIOGRAPHY

Astington, J. W., What is theoretical about the child's development of mind? In P. Carruthers & P. Smith (eds.), *Theories of Theories of Mind*; Cambridge University Press, Cambridge, 1996.

Bennett, Max & Hacker, P. M. S., *Philosophical Foundations of Neuroscience*; Blackwell Publishing, Oxford, 2003.

Blakemore, Colin & Greenfield, Susan (eds.), *Mindwaves: Thoughts on Intelligence, Identity and Consciousness*; Basil Blackwell, Oxford, 1987.

Brown, Roger, *Psycholinguistics;* Free Press, N. Y., 1970.

Bunge, Mario, Emergence and the mind, *Neuroscience*, Vol. 2, 1977.

_____. *The Mind-Body Problem*, Pergamon, Oxford, 1980.

Carlson, N. R., *Physiology of Behavior*; Allyn & Bacon, Boston, 1981.

Cavell, Stanley, Must we mean what we say? In Colin Lyas (ed.), *Philosophy and Linguistics*; Macmillan, St. Martin's Press, London, 1971.

Chomsky, Noam, *Syntactic Structures*; Mouton, The Hague, 1957.

_____. *Language and the Problems of Knowledge: The Managua Lectures*; M. I. T. Press, Cambridge, Mass., 1988.

Churchland, Patricia, *Neurophilosophy: Toward a Unified Science of the Mind/Brain*; Bradford Books, M. I. T. Press, Cambridge, Mass., 1989.

Churchland, Paul, *Scientific Realism and the Plasticity of Mind*; Cambridge University Press, N. Y., 1979.

_____. *Matter and Consciousness*; M. I. T. Press, Cambridge, Mass., 1984.

_____. The continuity of philosophy and the sciences, *Mind and Language*, Vol. 1, Spring 1986.

_____. Cognitive neurobiology: a computational hypothesis for laminar cortex, *Biology and Philosophy*, Vol. 1, No. 1, 1986.

Churchland, Paul & Churchland, Patricia, Conceptual analysis and Neuropsychology: John Marshall and Jennifer Gurd, In Robert N. McCauley (ed.), *The Churchlands and their Critics*; Basil Blackwell, Oxford, 1996.

Clark, Andy & Chalmers, David J., The extended mind, *Analysis*, Vol. 58, 1998.

Cook, John, Human Beings, In Peter Winch (ed.), *Studies in the Philosophy of Wittgenstein*; Routledge & Kegan Paul, London, 1969.

_____. The fate of ordinary language philosophy, *Philosophical Investigations*, Vol. 3, No. 2, 1980.

Cook, Vivian & Newson, Mark, *Chomsky's Universal Grammar: An Introduction* [2nd Edition]; Basil Blackwell, Oxford, 1996.

Cottrell, A., Sniffing the camembert: on the conceivability of zombies, *Journal of Consciousness Studies*, Vol. 6, 1999.

Coulter, Jeff, The informed neuron: issues in the use of information theory in the behavioral sciences, *Minds and Machines*, Vol. 5, No. 4, 1995.

_____. Neural Cartesianism: Comments on the epistemology of the cognitive sciences, In David M. Johnson & Christina E. Erneling (eds.), *The Future of the Cognitive Revolution*; Oxford University Press, Oxford, 1997.

Creese, Ian & Snyder, Solomon H., Biochemical investigation, In John C. Shershow (ed.), *Schizophrenia: Science and Practice*; Harvard University Press, Cambridge, Mass., 1978.

Crick, Francis, *The Astonishing Hypothesis: The Scientific Search for the Soul*; Charles Scribner's Sons, N. Y., 1994.

Crosson, F. J., The computer as gadfly, In Robert Cohen & Marx Wartofsky (eds.), *Boston Studies in the Philosophy of Science*; 1966-68, D. Reidel, Holland, 1969.

Deecke, L., Scheid P., & Kornhuber, H. H., *Experimental Brain Research*, Vol. 7, 1969.

Dennett, Daniel C., The unimagined preposterousness of zombies, *Journal of Consciousness Studies*, Vol. 2, 1995.

Dilman, Ilham, *Quine on Ontology, Necessity, and Experience: A Philosophical Critique*; State University of New York Press, Albany, 1984.

Drestske, Fred I., *Knowledge and the Flow of Information*; M. I. T. Press, Bradford Books, Cambridge, Mass., 1981.

Dreyfus, Hubert, *What Computers Still Can't Do: A Critique of Artificial Reason*; M. I. T. Press, Cambridge, Mass., 1993.

Eccles, Sir John, Brain and free will, In Gordon G. Globus, Grover Maxwell & Irwin Sarodnik (eds.), *Consciousness and the Brain*; Plenum Press, N. Y., 1976.

_____..Brain and mind, two or one? In Colin Blakemore & Susan Greenfield (eds.), *Mindwaves: Thoughts on Intelligence, Identity and Consciousness*; Basil Blackwell, Oxford, 1987.

Eccles, John C. & Popper, Karl R., *The Self and Its Brain* [Part 2]; Springer International, N. Y., 1977.

Eglin, Peter & Hester, Stephen, Category, predicate and task, *Semiotica*, Vol. 88, 1992.

Feinberg, Joel, Action and responsibility, In Alan R. White (ed.), *The Philosophy of Action*; Oxford University Press, Oxford, 1968.

Fischbach, Gerald D., Mind and Brain, *Scientific American*, Vol. 267, No. 3, September 1992.

Flanagan, O. & Polger, T., Zombies and the function of consciousness, *Journal of Consciousness Studies*, Vol. 2, 1995.

Fodor, Jerry A., *Psychological Explanation*; Random House, London, 1968.

_____. *The Language of Thought*; Thomas Y. Crowell, N. Y., 1975.

_____. Methodological solipsism considered as a research strategy in cognitive psychology, In John Haugeland (ed.), *Mind Design*; M. I. T. Press, Cambridge, Mass., 1981.

Franks, J., Toward understanding understanding, In Walter B. Weimer & David S. Palermo (eds.), *Cognition and the Symbolic Processes*; Lawrence Erlbaum Associates, Hillsdale, N. J., 1974.

Ghez, Claude, Voluntary movement, In Eric R. Kandel, James H. Schwartz & Thomas M. Jessell (eds.), *Principles of Neural Science* (3rd Edition); Prentice-Hall International, Englewood Cliffs, N. J., 1991.

Gibson, James J., *The Ecological Approach to Visual Perception*; Houghton Mifflin, Boston, 1979.

Gouras, Peter, Color vision, In E. Kandel et al. (eds.), *Principles of Neural Science* [3rd Edition]; Prentice-Hall International, Englewood Cliffs, N. J., 1991.

Gregory, Frederick, *Scientific Materialism in Nineteenth Century Germany*; D. Reidel, Boston, 1977.

Gunderson, Keith, Philosophy and computer simulation, In Oscar C. Wood & George Pitcher (eds.), *Ryle*; Macmillan, London, 1971.

Hacker, P. M. S., *Appearance and Reality*; Basil Blackwell, N. Y., 1987.

_____. Chomsky's Problem, *Language and Communication*, Vol. 10, No. 2, 1990.

_____. *Wittgenstein: Meaning and Mind (Vol. 3 of an Analytical Commentary on the 'Philosophical Investigations')*; Basil Blackwell, Oxford, 1990.

_____. *Wittgenstein: Mind and Will (Vol. 4 of an Analytical Commentary on the 'Philosophical Investigations')*; Basil Blackwell, Oxford, 1996.

Harris, Roy, *The Language Machine*; Duckworth, London, 1987.

Hodges, Andrew, *Alan Turing: The Enigma*; Simon & Schuster, Touchstone Book, N. Y., 1984.

Hunter, J. F. M., 'Forms of life' in Wittgenstein's *Philosophical Investigations*, In E. D. Klemke (ed.), *Essays on Wittgenstein*; University of Illinois Press, Urbana, 1971.

_____. *Essays after Wittgenstein*; University of Toronto Press, Toronto, 1973.

Hyman, John, *The Imitation of Nature*; Basil Blackwell, Oxford, 1989.

_____. (ed.), *Investigating Psychology*; Routledge, London & Boston, 1991.

Johnson-Laird, Philip, How could consciousness arise from the computations of the brain? In Colin Blakemore & Susan Greenfield (eds.), *Mindwaves*; Basil Blackwell, Oxford, 1987.

Julien, Robert M., *A Primer of Drug Action*; W. H. Freeman & Company, N. Y., 1995.

Kandel, Eric et al. (eds.), *Principles of Neural Science* [3rd Edition]; Prentice-Hall International, Englewood Cliffs, N. J., 1991.

Katz, J. J., *Language and Other Abstract Objects*; Rowman & Littlefield, Totowa, N. J., 1981.

Kenny, A. J. P., *The Legacy of Wittgenstein*; Basil Blackwell, Oxford, 1984.

Kirk, Robert, Zombies versus materialists, *Proceedings of the Aristotelian Society* [supplementary volume], Vol. 48, 1974.

_____. Why there couldn't be zombies, *Proceedings of the Aristotelian Society*, Vol. 73, 1999.

Kornhuber, H. H., Cerebral cortex, cerebellum and basal ganglia: an introduction to their motor functions, In F. O. Schmitt & F. G. Worden (eds.), *The Neurosciences Third Study Program*; M. I. T. Press, Cambridge, Mass., 1974.

Kosslyn, Stephen & Koenig, Olivier, *Wet Mind: The New Cognitive Neuroscience*; Free Press, N. Y., 1995.

Libet, Benjamin, Unconscious cerebral initiative and the role of conscious will in voluntary action, *The Behavioral and Brain Sciences*, Vol. 8, 1985.

Livingston, Paul M., *Philosophical History and the Problem of Consciousness*; Cambridge University Press, Cambridge, England, 2004.

Locke, John, *Essay Concerning Human Understanding*; ed. A. C. Fraser, 1894: republished in New York, 1959.

Louch, Alfred, *Explanation and Human Action*; Cybereditions, 2000: originally published in 1966.

Love, Nigel, Ideal Linguistics, *Language and Communication*, Vol. 8, No. 1, 1988.

Lynch, Michael, Pictures of nothing? Visual construals in social theory, *Sociological Theory*, Vol. 9, No. 1, 1991.

Malcolm, Norman, Rejoinder to Mr. Sosa, In C. V. Borst (ed.), *The Mind/Brain Identity Theory*; Macmillan, N. Y., 1970.

_____. The myth of cognitive processes and structures, In Theodore Mischel (ed.), *Cognitive Development and Epistemology*; Doubleday, N. Y., 1971.

_____. *Memory and Mind*; Cornell University Press, N. Y., 1977.

_____. *Nothing is Hidden: Wittgenstein's Criticism of his Early Thought*; Basil Blackwell, Oxford, 1986.

Marr, David, *Vision: A Computational Investigation into the Human Representation and Processing of Visual Information*; Freeman, San Francisco, 1982.

Marx, Karl, *Capital*, Vol. 1; Foreign Languages Publishing House, Moscow, 1954.

McCorduck, Pamela, Artificial Intelligence: An Apercu, *Daedalus*, Winter 1988, re-issued in the *Proceedings of the American Academy of Arts and Sciences*, Vol. 117, No. 1, 1989.

McHugh, Paul & Slavney, Phillip R., *The Perspectives of Psychiatry*; Johns Hopkins University Press, Baltimore, 1986.

McLellan, David, *The Young Hegelians and Karl Marx*; Macmillan, London, 1969.

Mehring, Franz, *Karl Marx*; University of Michigan Press, Ann Arbor, 1962.

Mesulam, M. M., Schizophrenia and the brain, *New England Journal of Medicine*, Vol. 322, No. 12, 1990.

Miller, G. A., Galanter, E. & Pribram, K. H., *Plans and the Structure of Behavior*; Holt, Rinehart & Winston, N. Y., 1960.

Monk, Ray, *Ludwig Wittgenstein: The Duty of Genius*; Penguin, Harmondsworth, 1990.

Moore, G. P., Mathematical techniques for studying information processing by the central nervous system, In H. M. Pinsker & W. D. Willis (eds.), *Information Processing in the Nervous System*; Raven Press, N. Y., 1980.

Newell, Alan & Simon, H. A., *Human Problem Solving*; Prentice-Hall, N. J., 1972.

Palmer, Anthony, *Concept and Object: The Unity of the Proposition in Logic and Psychology*; Routledge, London, 1988.

Pinker, Steven, *The Language Instinct*; Penguin, London, 1995.

_____. *How the Mind Works*; W. W. Norton, N. Y., 1997.

Polanyi, Michael, *Personal Knowledge*; University of Chicago Press, Illinois, 1958.

Putnam, Hilary, Reductionism and the nature of psychology, In John Haugeland (ed.), *Mind Design*; Bradford Books, Vermont, 1981.

_____. *Representation and Reality*; M. I. T. Press, Cambridge, Mass. 1988.

Rorty, Richard, *Philosophy and the Mirror of Nature*; Princeton University Press, Princeton, 1979.

Ryle, Gilbert, *The Concept of Mind*; Penguin University Books, Harmondsworth, Middlesex, England, 1973: originally Hutchinson, 1949.

_____. *Dilemmas*; Cambridge University Press, Cambridge, England, 1954/1987.

_____. Use, usage and meaning, In G. H. R. Parkinson (ed.), *The Theory of Meaning*; Oxford University Press, Oxford, 1968.

_____. Letters and syllables in Plato, In Gilbert Ryle, *Collected Papers, Vol. 1*; Hutchinson, London, 1971.

_____. Mowgli in Babel, In Konstantin Kolenda (ed.), *On Thinking*; Rowman & Littlefield, N. J., 1979.

Shanker, Stuart G., Wittgenstein versus Turing on the nature of Church's Thesis, ` *Notre Dame Journal of Formal Logic*, Vol. 23, No. 4, 1987.

_____. Review of 'Mindwaves', *Human Studies*, Vol. 13, October 1990.

_____. Wittgenstein versus James and Russell on the nature of willing, In J. V. Canfield & S. G. Shanker (eds.), *Wittgenstein's Intentions*; Garland Publishing Inc., N. Y., 1993.

Shannon, Claude & Weaver, Warren, *The Mathematical Theory of Communication*; University of Illinois Press, Illinois, 1949.

Sharrock, Wes & Button, Graham, Do the right thing! Rule finitism, rule skepticism and rule following, *Human Studies*, Vol. 22, 1999.

Sharrock, Wes & Coulter, Jeff, On what we can see, *Theory and Psychology*, Vol. 8, No. 2, 1998.

_____. ToM: A critical commentary, *Theory and Psychology*, Vol. 14, No. 5, 2004.

Shear, Jonathan, *Explaining Consciousness: The 'Hard Problem'*; M. I. T. Press, Cambridge, Mass., 1997.

Shershow, John C., *Schizophrenia: Science and Practice*; Harvard University Press, Cambridge, Mass., 1978.

Sprague, Elmer, *Persons and their Minds: A Philosophical Investigation*; Westview Press, Boulder, Colorado, 1999.

Strawson, P. F., *Individuals*; Methuen, London, 1959.

Thomas, N. J. T., Zombie killer, In S. R. Hameroff et al. (eds.), *Toward a Science of Consciousness II: The Second Tucson Discussions and Debates*; M. I. T. Press, Cambridge, Mass., 1998.

Thorp, John, *Free Will: A Defense Against Neurophysiological Determinism*; Routledge & Kegan Paul, London, 1980.

Tye, Michael, *Ten Problems of Consciousness: A Representational Theory of the Phenomenal World*; M. I. T. Press, Cambridge, Mass., 1996.

Velmans, Max, *Understanding Consciousness*; Routledge, Philadelphia, 2000.

Wartofsky, Marx, *Feuerbach*; Cambridge University Press, Cambridge, 1977.

Wittgenstein, Ludwig, *The Blue and Brown Books*; Harper & Row, N. Y., 1965.

_____. *Zettel* [G. E. M. Anscombe & G. H. von Wright, eds.: trans. G. E. M. Anscombe]; Basil Blackwell, Oxford, 1967.

_____. *Philosophical Investigations* [trans. G. E. M. Anscombe]; Macmillan, N. Y., 1968.

_____. *On Certainty* [G. E. M. Anscombe & G. H. von Wright, eds.]; Basil Blackwell, Oxford, 1969.

_____. *Lectures on the Foundations of Mathematics*; University of Chicago Press, Chicago, 1976.

_____. *Remarks on the Philosophy of Psychology, Vol. 1* [G. E. M. Anscombe & G. H. von Wright, eds.: trans. G. E. M. Anscombe]; Basil Blackwell, Oxford and University of Chicago Press, Chicago, 1980.

INDEX